The WorldWideWeb Handbook

A guide for users, authors, and publishers

Peter Flynn

The WorldWideWeb Handbook

A guide for users, authors, and publishers

Peter Flynn

INTERNATIONAL THOMSON COMPUTER PRESS

I(T)P An International Thomson Publishing Company

London • Bonn • Boston • Johannesburg • Madrid • Melbourne • Mexico City • New York • Paris
Singapore • Tokyo • Toronto • Albany, NY • Belmont, CA • Cincinati, OH • Detroit, MI

The WorldWideWeb Handbook

Copyright © 1995 International Thomson Computer Press

I⬦P A division of International Thomson Publishing Inc.
The ITP logo is a trademark under licence

British Library Cataloguing-in-Publication Data
A catalogue record for this book is available from the British Library

Library of Congress Cataloguing-in-Publication Data
A catalogue record for this book is available from the Library of Congress

First printed 1995

Printed in the UK by Clays Limited, St Ives plc

ISBN 1–85032–205–8

International Thomson Computer Press   International Thomson Computer Press
Berkshire House   20 Park Plaza
High Holborn   14th Floor
London WC1V 7AA   Boston MA 02116
UK   USA

Imprints of International Thomson Publishing

Table of Contents

Foreword

Early in the development of the WorldWideWeb, writing any paper document would prompt teasing, a wondering why paper was necessary any more. At the same time, there were never enough paper documents. The reply, 'It's all on the Web!' is all very well but it doesn't yet give most people something to take down to the beach or onto the plane. At least, lest anyone imagine that the Web came from an urge for a paperless world or the idea of doing away with books, I can write a forward to a book to show my continued support for the medium.

The defense of those of us who claimed never to have time to produce paper documents was that paper is always out of date: and so it is. Of course the Web is always out of date too, so it's just a matter of timescale. By writing this book, Peter has taken on the task of describing something which is changing rapidly.

I first met Peter in a European Academic and Research Network (RARE) working group, and learned he was engaged in a project to put all Ireland's medieval manuscripts online in SGML. He was clearly equipped with two of the basic ingredients of the Web, and so it was not surprising that he got involved fairly early on.

There are many aspects of the Web which seem to change day by day, some which change occasionally, and others which have been expected to change for many years but never have. Perhaps the area which changes most often is the language used to exchange documents, HyperText Markup Language, or HTML. Changes to HTML allow more power of expression for online documents, and all sorts of fancy features, but they don't change the basic philosophy and way of working of the Web. Changes to network protocols happen less frequently, and are often invisible to the user, but allow the introduction of greater power in the future. Meanwhile, a change I had hoped for, to an interactive Web, is still, at the time of writing, waiting to happen.

As a foreword provides one with a little space to say something at a slight angle to the main run of the book, perhaps this is worth dwelling on a moment.

The Web was conceived as a way for people and machines to communicate using shared knowledge. As machines make dull peers, its rôle is principally human communication through shared knowledge. The idea is that when people communicate in any way, they are building a common set of concepts, facts and feelings. If people communicate by building a shared hypertext, this becomes explicit.

The original WorldWideWeb program was a hypertext editor which allowed links to be made as easily as followed (with the click of a mouse), hiding all the mess of HTML and URLs. For example, when reading a document, one could with a key combination create a new hypertext node linked to the selected text in the old document, and start typing in a comment, question, or clarification. Similarly, one could browse to some related resource on the Web, hit a key, then go back to the document in question and make a link: 'Hey, this has already been solved by Joe'.

When used in a team, this becomes a way of remembering why you did things in a particular way, of keeping the argument attached to the results. It leaves a legacy of a consistent common view of the world which you can give to a new member to get up to speed. At least, this was the original idea. The history from that point on has been of the development of browsers—that is, Web clients which didn't allow editing—and therefore of information on the Web which has been painstakingly produced by some dedicated individual or group for consumption for the wide world. The editors which are now coming out have therefore been billed as (and designed as) easier publishing tools, rather than group hypertext tools.

In a web which is world wide, the 'few write, many read' model does make a lot of sense, for while we might be very interested in the inner workings of a few groups, notably those of which we are members, for the bulk of the rest of the information we tend to be more interested in quality of content and production. The high quality is only achieved by the use of the bottleneck of a production person or team. However, it is not the bulk of the information which consumes our attention: it is our work of the moment. We can make good use of all the excellent published material if we can weave references into our own hypertext jottings. If there is a continuum of hypertext from my note pad, though the diaries and letters and notes of my family and my groups, into the world of selected edited and published material, then we have a world in which the regular person has been re-enabled as a writer, a thinker and a linker, rather than just a clicker.

The difference in the Web is that a web to which one can contribute, even in a private way, seems friendlier than a read-only web which emulates more a million TV channels.

That is one difference between the Web as it is described in this book and the Web which we might see in the future. There are many other big changes to come, and I think Peter will have pointed to some of them. However the essence of global hypertext which is the Web will not change much while you read this book. So welcome to the Web, welcome to this book, and have fun.

Tim Berners-Lee

Cambridge, Massachusetts 1995

Preface

When Tim Berners-Lee started working on a networked hypertext information system at CERN (Switzerland) in 1989, he had little idea of the effect it would have on the networking community worldwide.

I first saw the system when Tim demonstrated it to the members of one of RARE's working groups (of which we were both members): RARE is the association of European research networks, so we had a room full of computer network gurus, and I still don't think any of us really appreciated the full potential of what we were seeing.

It took the upsurge in Internet connectivity in 1992 to bring home the fact that here was a system which anyone could use, not just the academic community, and which exploited exactly those features of networking which many people had been recommending for years: global coverage, open-standard protocols, simple connections, and an interface which didn't need a computing background.

Quite a lot of people disliked the idea, too. One senior administrator in a European university made it clear to me that he thought all this computer networking was just a gimmick to allow operators to chat to their friends, and that it was a fad which would soon pass. And more than a few computer services people were aghast at the idea that users would be able to roam the network so freely, browsing and downloading information in an unrestricted and unstructured way.

They had a good point, one which I try to address in this book: the Internet *is* still largely unstructured, an amorphous Sargasso Sea of information through which all but the hardiest navigator needs the tools of the trade to steer. Compass, chronometer, map, and sextant may have been replaced by electronic mail, Telnet, FTP, and Usenet News many years ago: but we now also have the hypertext link, the file-archive database and the image-mapped graphic. Even the WorldWideWeb needs competent pilots to chart the waters for the users, whether they are supertankers, coastal freighters, passenger ferries, weekend family sailboats, or surfboards.

The work of Tim and his crew was rapidly added to by other developers, producing versions of client and server software for almost every kind of computer and operating system. Marc Andreessen's *Mosaic* and its progeny are probably the best-known, but there are many others described in these pages. Tim, Marc, and many others are now involved in further research or commercial development which will bring the Web to even more people.

Development is never complete, least of all in software projects. There are changes in style and needs, changes in expectations and in standards and protocols: sometimes they all arrive at once, and the Web is no different in this respect to any other computing system. As I write this, there are arguments being waged with religious intensity over new proposals, divergent standards, the use of committees and the needs of business.

But this is preferable to stagnation, and is one of the strengths of the WorldWideWeb: everyone can participate, and if this book helps you to do the same, then I know you'll enjoy it.

Cork, May 1995

Acknowledgments

The ethos of the Internet is one of cooperation, and I could not have written this book without the cooperative effort and spirit of many kind people all over the world.

In particular I need to thank the members of the IETF Working Group on HTML: so many that I must excuse myself for not mentioning them all individually (their names appear at the back of the HTML 2.0 specification which will make up the RFC). Their discussion and analysis has been vital and I hope they will forgive any technical slips which have crept in (I know they'll point them out!). Among them I must, however, thank specially Dan Connolly, Dave Raggett, Eric Sink, and Eric Schieler, Tim Berners-Lee (of course), Bill Perry, Terry Allen, Lou Montulli and Marc Andreessen for their rapid replies to my questions (and on several occasions, their forgiveness when I put my foot in my mouth).

Outside the Working Group, I owe a debt of gratitude to Mary Axford, Internet Librarian at Georgia Tech, whose electronic clippings enabled me to keep up with developments; Ang Gilham of the Arts Faculty Computer Unit at Glasgow University, whose Unix expertise solved many technical problems; Thomas Boutell for his invaluable work in maintaining the FAQ in such a lucid manner; the many contributors who read and used my original guide to HTML, which was the starting-point for this book; Larry Press at ISI for trying some of it out on his students; and all the inhabitants of IRC channels, Usenet newsgroups, and assorted mailing lists who encouraged me to persevere, even though it was past 3 a.m. I am also indebted to Nelson Beebe of the University of Utah, to Pierre Mackay at Washington University, and to Tom Rokicki at Stanford for their help with font files at the last minute.

I am grateful to the many companies and individuals who lent me software, hardware, and support, particularly Yuri Rubinsky and Donald Teed of SoftQuad, whose *Author/Editor* program did sterling service; Richard Stallman and Lennart Staflin for *Emacs* and `psgml` respectively; Paul Hourican of PFH Computers, whose loan of a modem at a critical point kept me online in the deep of night; Ken Fitzgerald-Smith and Paul Duggan, Mac gurus *extraordinaires*, who resuscitated an antique SE and were always on hand to answer questions about Apples; Christa Keil of INS and Hannes Deeken of Omnilink for their help at the WWW Conference; and Chris Biber of Microstar Inc., whose *Near&Far* system let me view HTML from a new standpoint.

And of course my wife and family, whose forbearance when I disappeared into my study each evening knew no bounds.

Roadmap

This book is in three parts: *How to get started*, *How to make WorldWideWeb files*, and *Running a service*.

Part One starts with a short introduction to the WorldWideWeb. Chapters 2 to 4 are for beginners in networking and contain a guide to connecting to the network and using the facilities of the Internet that are needed for the WorldWideWeb. The fifth chapter builds on this by introducing Web software itself: how to get it, how to install it, and how to run it. The last chapter in this part gives some more technical details of how the Web works, as a preparation for Part Two.

The second part is a complete tutorial on how to create your own Web files. Chapters 7 through 10 cover all of the HyperText Markup Language (HTML 2.0) starting with the simplest constructions and progressing to fill-in forms, graphics, image maps, tables, and mathematics, and Chapter 11 discusses some of the ways of maintaining control over the appearance of your files.

The last part shows how to run a service of your own, using the knowledge gained in Parts One and Two to install a server and organize the information you provide with it (Chapter 12) and create dynamic information using scripts (Chapter 13). The remaining chapters (14–18) cover some unresolved issues of security and authentication, privacy, copyright, and intellectual property.

The appendices contain suggestions about text conversion; the proposals for HTML3; some pointers to useful reference sites containing repositories or details of commercial, technical, and other information about the Web; and a reference list of country codes and language codes.

Technical note

The following typographical conventions have been used:

- Typewriter type is used for the names of commands, computers, directories, files, HTML elements, and URLs, e.g.

```
ls -l
ftp.ncsa.uiuc.edu
/pub/sgml/ISOLat1
tcpman.exe
<head>
http://www.ucc.ie/cgi-bin/archie
```

and for computer output such as terminal listings, e.g.

```
<html>
<head>
<title>Personal data</title>
</head>
```

Where long names (especially URLs) are broken across two lines, breaks occur at punctuation only, so any hyphen which may occur at the breakpoint *is* a part of the name: extra hyphens are not introduced, e.g. `http://www.abc.org/sales-info/current-products/price-lists/plastic-widgets.html`

● Examples of HTML fragments as they might be displayed in a text-only browser are shown with a dark shaded background:

```
                              Example of text-mode HTML display


             TEXT-MODE BROWSER DISPLAY


   This uses fixed-width (typewiter) type.
```

Examples for graphics-mode browsers are shown with a light background:

Document title: Example of graphics-mode HTML display

Graphics-mode browser display

This uses variable-width (printers') type.

● Bold typewriter type indicates input that the user keys in, where this is not otherwise obvious:

```
login: jdoe
```

● Slanted typewriter type means that the user should substitute a meaningful value for the mnemonic used:

```
mpegplay  filename.mpg
```

● Bold text type is used for the first significant occurrence and explanation of key **technical terms**: these also appear in the index, and are repeated if they reoccur in another context.
● Bold italic type is used for the names of functions in programs, especially browsers, where these are represented as generic terms (they are also indexed).

- *Italic type* is used for the names of programs and other products which are indexed.
- Specific keyboard keys are shown in keycap form: ⌧, distinguished by the rounded corners from graphical system on-screen button items, which are shown as [File]
- As is conventional in computing examples, parts of commands which are optional are given in [square brackets].

Since I started writing this book, a lot of people have asked me if I was using HTML for it. The answer is no: although it might just be possible to write a book using HTML3, the requirements of large-scale technical writing are best met by more specialised DTDs.

I used the DocBook DTD from O'Reilly/Davenport, fairly heavily modified to allow more flexibility in the part/chapter structure, and to let me embed parsed HTML into the `<screen>` and `<display>` elements, so that I knew the examples would be valid. For editing I used SoftQuad's *Author/Editor* and GNU *Emacs* with `psgml-mode`.

The file was printed using *TEX* with Karl Berry's *Eplain* macros, plus some of my own to handle the structural output from *SGML2TEX*, which I used to convert the file for printing. Illustrations were taken from the screen with *xgrab* and a variety of PC and Mac screen-grabbers, and embedded as Encapsulated *PostScript* files. Fonts came from the Monotype CD-ROM, and final output was generated at 1200 dpi by Tom Rokicki's *dvips* and supplied on disk to the printer.

Any merits this approach may have are due entirely to the expertise of the relevant authors: the mistakes are all mine.

Part One

How to get started

- O Introduction and quick-start
- O Description of the WorldWideWeb
- O Getting used to the Internet
- O How to use a WorldWideWeb browser
- O How the Web works

Chapter 1

Introduction

○   Where it all began

○   The size of the Internet

○   Quick-start for existing Internet users

○   What to do if you're not yet connected

'Begin at the beginning, go on to the end, and then stop,' Alice was told. The beginning, in the case of the **WorldWideWeb**, is 1989–90, in Switzerland, at the European Laboratory for Particle Physics (better known as CERN after its former title, the *Centre Européenne pour la Recherche Nucléaire*), where Tim Berners-Lee developed the first Web servers and clients.

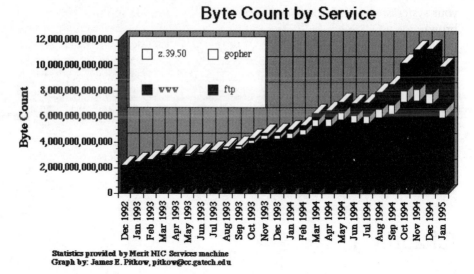

Figure 1.1   Growth in FTP, Gopher, WorldWideWeb, and WAIS traffic, 1994 (NSFnet backbone, USA)
Produced by James Pitkow, Georgia Institute of Technology

The end is as yet nowhere in sight: I downloaded the statistics for network traffic (Figure 1.1) from which it is clear that while none of the three most popular networked information services (WorldWideWeb, Gopher, and WAIS) comes anywhere near file transfer (FTP) in terms of raw volume, the rate of growth in Web traffic has far outstripped the other two combined, even allowing for the fact that both Gopher and WAIS information can be retrieved using Web browsers. As of January 1995, Web traffic is the second largest mover of data on the NSFnet backbone (although only a part of the Internet, a very substantial part).

Quick-start for existing Internet users

If you are already using a full Internet connection, getting started using the Web is very straightforward: all you need is a **browser** (sometimes referred to as a Web client or HTML client). You can buy one or download several from the network and try them out: there is a brief review of the most common ones on pp. 74–92.

Because you already have your networking software loaded and functioning, there is little to do in the way of configuration apart from telling the browser some routine stuff like your email address and the name of your Usenet News server. This is usually done by editing a configuration file, but some browsers ask you the relevant questions when you install them, or provide an *Options* or *Preferences* function for the purpose. You may need to check the details with your systems administrator or Internet Service Provider. If you pick a graphical browser, you will need the 'helper' applications, which are the utility programs to handle graphics, sound, and video, but these can also be downloaded, usually from the same place you got the browser from (some browsers include these programs in the package). You may already have them, as many helper applications are popular public-domain packages (Table 1.1). You put the names of these in the configuration file as well, so the browser knows where to find them: see the example in Figure 5.17 on p. 93. You can add others such as *GhostView* emulation using *GhostScript* for displaying *PostScript* files, or *xdvi* for T$_E$X output. If you have a computer equipped for multimedia, you may have suitable applications already.

Table 1.1   Some 'Helper' applications needed by graphical browsers

There are many more: these are some of the most popular ones that are easily available

Operating system	Graphics	Sound	Video
Unix/VMS with X Windows	xv	xaudio	mpegplay, Xanim
MS-Windows	lview	wplany	mpegplay, mplayer
Apple Mac	JPEGview	SoundMachine	MPEGview

If you're not connected yet

If you don't yet have an Internet connection, the details and a short introduction are in Chapter 3. If you're connecting a domestic or small business computer over the phone, you'll need a **modem**, some communications software, and an account with an Internet Service Provider (**ISP**, p. 22). If you're going for a faster and more permanent connection, you'll need a private circuit or ISDN line from your telecommunications company to connect you to your ISP. Your ISP may offer to handle the installation of this kind of line as part of their service.

If you're going to become an information provider, you'll need the permanent connection, plus some editing software (and graphics software if you intend to illustrate your 'pages'). To avoid the expense of a permanent connection, many ISPs now offer space on their machines to run a Web service for their customers: you provide the files of information, they provide the hardware.

Mary Morris of Finesse Liveware maintains the WWW Service Providers list. If you have no connection yet, but have a friend or colleague connected to the network, you could ask them to get a copy for you, which is available in the `inet-marketing` archives (FTP to `ftp.einet.net` and look in the `pub/INET-MARKETING` directory for the file `www-svc-providers`). They can also retrieve a copy by sending the command `get INET-MARKETING www-svc-providers` to `listproc@einet.net`. If they have a Web browser, they could get a copy of the list maintained by the NCSA at `http://union.ncsa.uiuc.edu/www/leasing.shtml` or search the one provided by Network-USA at `http://www.netusa.net/ISP`.

Chapter 2

WorldWideWhat?

- O Description of the Web
- O What is Hypertext?
- O Graphics and hypermedia

Web. The term was coined in 1990 [Berners-Lee 1990] to describe an information system project for the high-energy physics community which has ended up spanning the planet like a giant spider's web, with threads linking knowledge and information from all over, available to everyone. To get some idea of the scale of it, in the spring of 1995 there were estimated to be well over 12,000 computers able to provide information to Web users [Gray 1995]; the number of computers on the Internet has been placed at between 2,000,000 [Treloar 1994] (many of these are large multi-user systems) and 4,852,000 [Lottor 1995] (January) and is growing exponentially (that is, the rate of increase is itself still increasing): an estimated 13.5 million people can now use interactive Internet services [Treese 1995]. The current version of the *Internet Index*, maintained by Win Treese, which gives details of the size and growth of the network, can be retrieved at `http://www.openmarket.com/info/internet-index/current.html`.

There have been many other information systems, but rarely one which has caught people's imagination like the WorldWideWeb. Its attraction seems to be a combination of factors, not just simplicity, coverage, or compatibility. Yes, it's simple: in most cases there are no commands, you just point your mouse or use your arrow keys and go click. Yes, its coverage is wide: it gives access to a greater range of topics from more sources than any other single information system on the Internet. And yes, it's compatible: you can get a **browser**, one of the programs that let you retrieve information, for almost any computing system, and the files that are used are readable by all systems. The two key factors, however, are the Web's hypertext and multimedia capability.

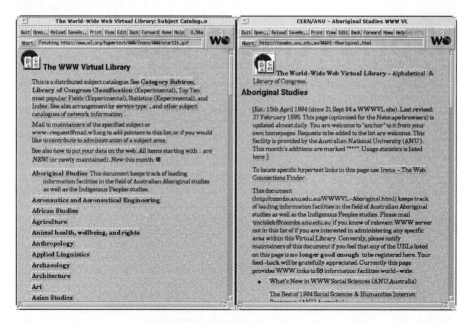

Figure 2.1   Hypertext in the WorldWideWeb
Two screenshots of the Arena browser showing (left) a page from CERN's topic index (note the highlighted link to 'Aboriginal Studies'); and (right) the screen which results from clicking on that phrase

Hypertext is (loosely speaking) a concept which allows you to follow a train of thought rather than a single argument. The term was coined by Theodore Nelson in the 1965 to describe his *Xanadu* concept of the whole of human knowledge stored in a single browseable form. Although a substantial amount of work has been done in the field, the idea of linked items of information only came to a wider public with the implementation of *HyperCard* on the Apple Mac. Its most common instantiation nowadays uses the ability of a computer to link two separately-stored pieces of information so that you can jump from one to the other without having to pass though a lot of other information on the way. Unlike linear information, where to get from A to Z you have to read your way there via B, C, D, etc., hypertext is non-linear, letting you move at will from one item to another. Hypertext is not new: in fact the concept is not unlike a well-equipped library, where you can instantly look up the right book for any reference you come across. Hypertext on computers is not new either, but using it across a worldwide public network is a significant advance.

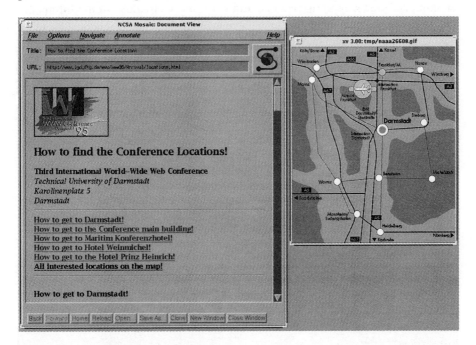

Figure 2.2   Graphics in the WorldWideWeb

Figure 2.1 shows what an example might look like on your screen, before and after clicking on the highlighted link which says 'Aboriginal Studies'. The left-hand ('before') window came from Switzerland; the right-hand ('after') window came from Australia, but you don't have to be aware of that; all you need to know is that you can click on a highlight to follow that particular thread of discussion.

Multimedia is the use of text, sound, and pictures to convey information more effectively than any one of them alone. Again it is not new, but the application of it on the Internet in a form which was tightly integrated with hypertext gave the Web an impetus which was lacking in other information systems, no matter how efficient or well-designed they might be. It was the release of the *Mosaic* program which brought the Web to public attention by making a fairly consistent point-and-shoot interface available for *MS-Windows*, Apple Mac, and Unix with full graphical integration in this way. Figure 2.2 shows a page with embedded ('inlined') images as well as an external graphic (one which appears in another window). Graphics can be used for simple embellishment as well as to provide illustrations to the text such as photographs or diagrams.

I can't make these pages speak or show a movie, but Figure 2.3 shows a page of information which does: it contains links to sound and video files. The percentage of Web users who are equipped to view movies is not known, and the time-delay in downloading them is substantial, but faster communications and the growth of 'multimedia' are likely to make audio and video more attractive in the future.

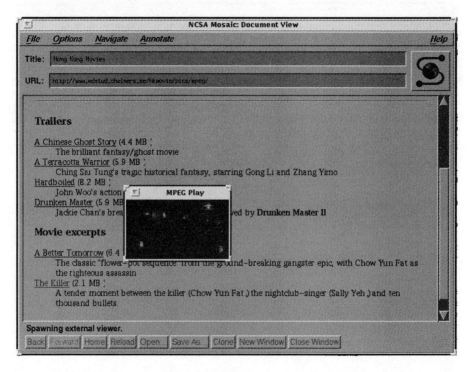

Figure 2.3   Multimedia in the WorldWideWeb
A page from the Hong Kong movie database, showing a film clip linked from an information page

Commercial and business use of the Internet has given the Web a further boost, as companies discover that what was originally a research network can just as easily put them in touch with suppliers and customers, and provide a new marketplace for them to display their goods and services to a wider audience. It's new: there are still a lot of things to sort out, like security and privacy, copyright, and intellectual property, and these are discussed in Part Three.

The Web is still young, and its ultimate direction cannot be predicted with accuracy. There is a vast amount of information already available, and it is clear from mailing lists and Usenet newsgroups that a lot of people plan to use it even more. Political and commercial decisions affecting the Internet may impact the way it develops, but it has already established a model for the future of information access which seems likely to remain with us for a considerable time.

Chapter 3

For beginners

○   **What you need to know**

○   **How to get connected to the Internet**

○   **Internet services**

○   **Hardware and software**

This chapter is a summary of how to get your computer connected to the Internet. It is not intended as a replacement for the much more comprehensive books on the network as a whole, but as a set of guidelines or pointers to get the new user online and using the WorldWideWeb. It therefore omits some of the fine detail of telecommunications, and deals only with the mainstream ways of doing things. It doesn't presuppose any foreknowledge or experience of the Internet, but it does assume four things which are fairly essential:

- you have a computer (or access to one) and are familiar with using it;
- you know how to create, save, delete, rename, move, and copy files and folders (directories);
- you know how to run a program (either by clicking on an icon or by typing its filename);
- you know how to use a text editor or wordprocessor for producing plain unformatted text.

If you haven't done some of these things before, you may want to look them up in your manuals, or get someone who knows your kind of computer and software to show you. They're pretty straightforward, and they form the fundamental building-blocks for working with the Web files you will encounter in Parts Two and Three.

For Part Three, you will need to know a little more about downloading and installing software. The mechanics of retrieval are explained in Part One, but if you are working on anything bigger than a PC or Mac (for example, Unix or VMS), you may need to have some experience in using system software and utilities, and you may need privileged ('root' or 'system') access to the machine for some functions like installing a server.

If you've already got all your software installed, and know how to dial your service provider's machine (or you're in an office and your computer is already connected), you can go to p. 35.

Getting connected to the Internet

This is where you start if your computer is not yet connected to the outside world. We'll look at the kind of computer you need, what the Internet is and what services it provides, how much it costs, where you go to get connected, and what methods of connection you can use.

What kind of computer can I use?

The WorldWideWeb was designed to be as universal as possible, so almost any reasonably modern computer will do: IBM-style PC, Apple Macintosh, Unix workstation, Atari, Amiga, BBC micro, but even a plain old terminal (a keyboard and screen without any processing capability) can be used if you have a connection to someone else's Internet computer. The essential thing is that it must have the capability to communicate with the outside world in one of two ways:

Serial communications

A serial communications socket (known variously as a serial port, RS-232C port, phone port, modem port or comms port) is standard equipment on the back of all modern desktop computers. It lets you connect over the phone (or over simple 'twisted-pair' wiring in an office) to another computer. The kind of socket varies, so see your manual and the illustrations in Figure 3.1 to identify it.

Figure 3.1   Varieties of serial port
25–pin D-connector; 9–pin D-connector; 8–pin DIN connector

Network card

A network card or adapter goes inside your computer and is plugged into to a wall outlet which connects you directly to the Internet. A network card allows more complex transmissions and higher speeds.

One or other of these is essential if you want to use the Internet. A dial-up serial port connection is temporary: you're connected through the phone system only as and when you want to use the network: when you hang up, you're no longer connected. If you want to become an information provider, you need to have a permanent connection using a network card and a separate data line. If you're not sure if your computer or terminal fits this bill, it's probably best to ask your Internet Service Provider (ISP) or a local expert. Other hardware and software requirements are dealt with on p. 23 and p. 27 respectively.

What is the Internet?

The **Internet** is the world's biggest computer network, made up of lots of smaller networks all using the same networking software (programs), so that they can cooperate in the way they transmit and receive information and provide and use services. It grew out of the old ARPAnet (the US Department of Defense's Advanced Research Projects Agency network, originally connecting military research establishments with academic research institutes), but it is now a collection of independent cooperative networks, connecting millions of commercial, governmental, research, academic organizations, public bodies, and private individuals worldwide.

From being the preserve of academics, scientists, and the military, the Internet has developed into a general-purpose tool which anyone can use. A computer **network** on its own simply provides the means of communication: it's the services which are available which make the Internet what it is: a combination of office, library, club, and playroom: the modern equivalent of the Roman Forum, town hall, village green, business park, shopping mall, college, and kitchen rolled into one.

What makes a network of computers all function together is that they all talk the same language to each other, no matter what languages they speak individually. In the case of the Internet, it's an established collection of **protocols** (agreed ways of working) called Transmission Control Protocol/Internetworking Protocol, or **TCP/IP** for short.

What can you do with the Internet?

You will find people from all walks of life and all countries doing business, conducting research, pursuing hobbies, or just having fun, but the basic idea is that the network is a way to exchange information. Like the postal service or the telephone service, it can connect people individually; and like the radio, cinema, or TV, it can connect providers of information with consumers of information. Like a library, you can use it to go and find information, and like a notice-board, you can use it to publicize information. Like all of these, you can use it to make your information available to others. Looked at this way, there are four groups of activities:

1   exchange information with other people on a one-to-one basis;
2   exchange information within and between groups of people;
3   find and retrieve stuff from collections of information;
4   provide information or services for other people to use.

Some of these are business or work activities: you can buy and sell goods, services, or just information itself: you can conduct negotiations, arrange and hold meetings, write reports and publish the results. Given the right equipment you could even run machines and do physical manufacturing remotely, although that is not yet practicable on a production scale.

Some of it is for research or keeping up-to-date, like reading a newspaper, book, magazine or journal, or discussing matters with colleagues, friends, or partners, either for business or personal purposes. When something new is invented or discovered, it's likely that the news will break first on the Internet.

And some of it is for recreation: hobbies, sports, and other pastimes, even social or political activism. The Internet is international, multicultural, and as diverse as human nature can make it (which means there is also an etiquette to dealing with other people's cultures and beliefs. . . see pp. 268–272).

Services on the Internet

To do all this takes a variety of different services, just as the phone, TV, and newspapers are different services. Some of them you may already have heard of: electronic mail, file transfer (FTP) and Telnet are the three traditional ones. There's also the Usenet News bulletin-board system, and there are other networked information services in addition to the WorldWideWeb: Gopher and WAIS (Wide Area Information Server) are two examples.

Electronic mail

Email is the transmission of messages between individuals or within groups, and is probably the most frequently demanded of all network services. It is not unique to the Internet: **email** works uniformly across all the world's interconnected networks although the *de facto* standard is of Internet origin. Most messages are text, but mailing systems are becoming more common which can embed other objects such as images, sound, programs, or data in the message.

File transfer

The Internet File Transfer Protocol (**FTP**) is the commonest method of transferring files from one computer to another: millions of megabytes of data are moved in this way each year. Apart from private file transfer between individuals, the majority of this is the transfer of scientific and research data, and the anonymous retrieval of files from the public archives held on thousands of machines worldwide. We will look in more detail at examples of how to do this on pp. 52–68.

Telnet

Telnet is a program to let you login to another computer on the Internet and work on it as if it was your local computer. Normally, you need authorization to do this, in the form of an account with a valid username and password on the remote machine, although many public services do exist to which you can login without the need for a password, and we shall be mentioning some of them later. The commonest uses of Telnet are probably when you are away from your home base (for example, using a friend's or colleague's terminal to let you login to your own machine to read email) and for searching public databases, especially library systems.

Usenet News

News is a worldwide bulletin-board system, divided into thousands of topics called newsgroups. Like email, it is not specific to the Internet, as it is accessible from all kinds of other networks. Messages are 'posted' in the newsgroups, where you can read them and respond to them: the messages are all public, unlike email where messages are aimed directly at an individual or group of individuals. The topics are hierarchically divided, the top-level divisions being `biz` (business), comp (computing), soc (social), alt (alternatives), rec (recreation) and sci (scientific). Subsidiary topic levels are named by separating the subtopic with a period (e.g. comp.infosystems, rec.soccer or biz.jobs.offered), and there can be many further subdivisions. News is probably the most widely-accessed information system, and the Web has its own section, in the newsgroups comp.infosystems.www.* (there's a full list in Appendix C).

If you don't get or can't get a 'newsfeed', it's possible to get messages into the Usenet News system via email. Send your message to *newsgroup*@psw.bull.com or *newsgroup*@cs.utexas.edu (replacing *newsgroup* with the name of the news-group but using hyphens between the elements, rather than periods, e.g. comp-infosystems-www-users@cs.utexas.edu). This doesn't provide a means to get all the other messages *from* the group, only to allow you to send messages *to* the group, so you would need to include a request for replies by email.

Archie

FTP is fine for retrieving files, but if you don't know where to go to find them, you need help. Archie is a database of files that are available for anonymous FTP, and you can use the *Archie* program to search the database and find where the file you want is located.

Gopher

The Internet **Gopher** is a directory-based information system. Directories are presented as menus, making it very easy to navigate up and down. Each menu entry can be a file, a subdirectory, a searchable index, or a link to Telnet for connecting to another information service. Gopher offers excellent search capabilities using tools like *Veronica* (Very Easy Rodent-Oriented Net-wide Index of Computerized Archives!) or *JugHead*. You can download and run the Gopher program separately, but access is also available through Web browsers.

WAIS

The Wide Area Information Server is a sophisticated indexed-retrieval system which lets you search multiple collections of data archived from the Internet at many sites around the planet. Queries can be phrased in fairly plain English, making it very simple to use. As with Gopher, separate WAIS interfaces are available, but you can also get at it using Web software.

There are more details of the individual services in many of the books available which cover them as part of the Internet in general. I recommend in particular Ed Krol's *The Whole Internet User's Guide and Catalog* [Krol 1994], and Daniel Dern's *The Internet Guide for New Users* [Dern 1994], both of which give an excellent general introduction to the network. There is also the Electronic Frontier Foundation's *Guide to the Internet* [Gaffin 1993] which is available by anonymous FTP from ftp.eff.org in the directory pub/Net_info/EFF_Net_Guide.

How much does it cost?

In the 1990s, faster telecommunications, cheaper computers and better software all mean that the Internet is no longer just for big companies, research institutes, and universities, but for anyone who has a computer and wants to make use of the information available. What you pay depends on the level of service you want and the speed and reliability of your connection.

It also depends on the nature of your telecommunications carrier's attitude to doing business. In the USA, with competition between carriers and traditionally low rates and ease of access, getting onto the Internet is cheap. In the UK a similar position holds since partial deregulation. But in many other countries, where the telecomms carrier was (or is still) the Post Office, telecomms development risks being strangled by three pairs of hands: governmental monopolies which move at a snail's pace; the antiquated ideas of some senior people who still think in terms of mechanical or manual telephone exchanges; and the puzzlement of some of their accountants, who have not grasped the simple economics of supply and demand, and cannot understand why charging for installation is counter-productive. However, the position is changing, and customer pressure should ultimately win out.

In general, there are three broad levels to costing:

1   Basic dial-up services with an Internet Service Provider (ISP) can be very cheap: a sign-up fee of perhaps $25-50 plus a fixed-rate charge per month of $10-20 is possible, or its equivalent in other countries, but the service may be restricted to text-based software (even if you are accessing the service through a graphical interface on your own machine) and provide only indirect access to the Internet (you do your networking on your provider's machine, not your own). An account with a public FreeNet, if there's one in your area, costs nothing except a local telephone call each time you use it. Ask at your town hall, library or college campus, or read the ads in computing or network magazines, even your local newspaper.
2   More sophisticated dial-up services need additional software and faster communications equipment, but give you direct access to the Internet from your own computer. This can also make use of the phone line more efficient by allowing you to do several tasks at once. Dial-up direct access is usually charged for by usage, starting at around $10 an hour.
3   Permanent network connection at an individual or corporate level requires a special line, and the cost can range between the hundreds and the thousands of dollars per month, but offers much faster speeds, and the ability for organizations to connect many users simultaneously.

In the case of the first two, you also pay the cost of the phone call. With a permanent connection you usually pay a fixed rate per month or year no matter how much or how little you use it.

Packaged solutions

Complete 'get you started' packages are also available which in most cases let you install the software, plug in your modem and go straight online.

Spry, Inc.'s *Internet-in-a-Box* is for *MS-Windows* and includes *AIR Mosaic Express* as well as news, mail, Gopher and file transfer applications. They offer immediate access using *SprintLink* as well as discount offers with other participating service providers.

The *Warp* version of *OS/2* from IBM comes with a bonus pack which includes self-installing dial-up access to the *IBM Internet Connection* and a copy of their *WebExplorer* browser (but you can use other browsers as well or instead).

NetManage produce the *Chameleon* package of many TCP/IP applications for *MS-Windows*, *Windows NT* and *X Windows*. A sampler version for *MS-Windows* can be downloaded as a self-extracting archive (`sampler.exe`) from many FTP servers. Details of contents and licensing are at `http://www.netmanage.com`.

Intercon makes *TCP/Connect II* for the Mac, which provides the dial-up interface necessary to make the connection with *MacTCP* as well as a range of Internet tools. Further information is available at `http://www.intercon.com/pi/tcp-connect-mac.html`.

InterMind Corporation and Cyberspace Development, Inc. (makers of the *TIA* TCP/IP connectivity program) supply the *EnCompass* Internet application installer and toolbar. This is free to individual users of *TIA*, and host licenses are available for providers. It was developed as a solution to the problem of automatically configuring an *MS-Windows* machine with SLIP software.

EnCompass can be downloaded by FTP from `marketplace.com` and prompts you to enter your login name and choose your service provider and nearest phone number from a drop-down list. It then automatically installs and configures *Trumpet Winsock*, *Netscape*, and email, news, FTP, Gopher, Archie, IRC, and Telnet clients (all public domain or shareware).

Some ISPs provide their own tailored kits to new and existing customers. For beginners this can be a more convenient (although usually more expensive) route into the Internet than taking a plain SLIP or PPP connection and downloading the free or shareware versions of the popular software and installing them yourself.

Method of connection

The way in which you use the network depends on your method of connection. As we have just seen, there are three main ways of connecting: 1) simple dial-up (indirect access), 2) direct-access dial-up, and 3) permanent connection. The kind of connection determines whether you can become a Web information provider or not: to do so requires a permanent connection, not a dial-up one.

Indirect dial-up access (terminal connection)

Your computer acts simply as a terminal, and you run Internet programs on the computer you connect to (which belongs to your service provider) rather than on your own machine. This means you don't have to get involved in installing or maintaining Web software on your own machine, but you are normally limited to a text-based interface (but see below).

Direct-access dial-up (temporary full networking connection)

If you have a full network connection via dial-up (SLIP or PPP: see p. 29), your computer becomes an integral part of the Internet in its own right for the duration of your call, and you will be able to install and use graphical Web software directly from your own machine.

Permanent full connection

With a full network connection on a permanent (leased) line, you can also run Web software to become an information provider (a server). This is not possible on dial-up lines, as when you disconnect the world will no longer be able to access your server.

There is in fact a fourth class: indirect connection on a permanent basis, as for example in an organization where people use simple terminals permanently connected to a central Internet computer. This is equivalent to indirect dial-up access without the dial-up.

The difference as far as Web browsers are concerned used to be that with an indirect dial-up connection, you could not run graphical programs such as *Mosaic*: your interaction with the network had to use character-based ones like *Lynx* instead. This is now changing: there are at least two products you can buy which let your indirect terminal connection mimic a direct one and run graphical software, although you need at least a 14.4Kb/s connection (Panel 3.1) to make sensible use of this. We will look at details of how to do this on pp. 29–30.

With an indirect connection, files that you retrieve from the network end up on your provider's machine first, and you must download them with a further step to get them onto your own computer (p. 38). With a full network connection, either permanent or dial-up, you can use all the facilities of the network, and downloading or uploading is performed directly to and from your own disk.

If you want to run a Web service and you can't afford the permanent connection or don't want to get involved in running a server of your own, there are many ISPs who will sell you time and space on their own server. They provide full access to the rest of the Internet for people to use your service: you provide the files and maintain them on their machine. For the smaller organization this can be a very cost-effective way of getting a presence on the network, as the ISP can register the server in your name, so that as far as the rest of the world is concerned, it looks like your own machine on a permanent connection.

How to find an Internet Service Provider (ISP)

There are Internet Service Providers springing up in almost every major city in the world, and in many other places round the planet. Some of the least well-provided nations are among the most forward-looking and dynamic in pursuing Internet connectivity, while it is not unusual to read mail messages and Usenet postings from isolated would-be users in some areas of Europe, the Americas, the Pacific Rim, and the Antipodes complaining that they cannot find a local provider.

The first place to ask is among other users: if you know other people using the Internet in your locality, ask them where they connect to. Computer clubs and computer stores often have lists of local suppliers, and computing and networking magazines have advertisements from many of the large nation-wide providers as well as more local ones.

As with many network-related matters, the best place to look is on the network itself, but that is a Catch-22 situation if you don't already have some form of access. I mentioned at the beginning Mary Morris's list of providers in North America and some other places, and the Usenet newsgroups `alt.internet.access. wanted` and `alt.internet.services` are for the discussion and identification of service providers. If you have no access at all yet, it is a good idea to ask colleagues, friends, or neighbors who do have access if they can download some of the relevant discussions or recommendations for you.

If you are choosing an Internet Service Provider, you should call several of them, if there is a choice in your area, and compare their rates and levels of service by asking them the following questions:

- What speeds can I connect up at?
- Is any special computer setup needed?
- Is the charge flat-rate or based on usage?
- What is charged for? Storage? Transmission?
- What method(s) of connection do you offer?
- Are there any third-party charges (e.g. Tymnet, Telenet)?
- Can you supply all the software?
- Can I change method later without penalty?
- Do you provide telephone support?

And of course, most importantly, ask if they provide a Web browser or whether you have to download one yourself. Choosing between competing suppliers can be difficult: in many circumstances you may need to rely on the recommendations of others who have first-hand experience. The large providers of what used to be non-networked email and discussion-list services such as CompuServe, Inc., Prodigy, or CIX (CompuLink) have now brought their services online to the Internet: while they have a great deal of experience in providing their traditional services, they need to be compared carefully on the range of specific services you want, especially the Web, of course: Prodigy now provides users with its own browser.

When you open an account with an ISP, you will be given a **username** (sometimes called an access code or login ID) and a **password**. These two go hand in hand: you can (and should) tell anyone your username because it usually forms part of your email address, but you should *never* tell anyone your password (to do so is like giving them the keys to your house). Don't write it down either, and if you change it, don't use passwords which are easy for others to guess (avoid proper names, stick to non-dictionary words, use mixed upper- and lower-case letters and digits or punctuation if possible).

Hardware: the boxes and wires

If you are getting a permanent network connection, the installation will most likely be done for you by a networking specialist from your ISP or from within your organization, so you probably won't need to do much of it by yourself. If you are having to make such a connection on your own (maybe *you* are the specialist!), there is a short explanation at the end of this section, but the deeper technical aspects of permanent connection are outside the scope of this book.

If your organization already has a permanent Internet connection, and you simply want to attach your computer to it, see p. 27. For both of the other methods of connection (direct and indirect dial-up), the only hardware you need is a phone and a **modem**.

Connecting over the phone

You can connect to the Internet from almost anywhere which has a phone line (it is even possible to use a cellular phone). Apart from the phone, you need a modem, a modem cable and a regular phone cord. You also need a communications program, which we'll look at on p. 28.

Figure 3.2   Varieties of phone plug required for global travel
Photograph courtesy of Impactron Ltd

Modems

A regular voice-grade phone line can't handle computer codes by itself, so a modem turns the codes into high-pitched tones which *can* go down the line. At the other end (your ISP's computer), another modem turns the tones back into codes again (a technique called *mod*ulation and *dem*odulation, hence the term 'modem'). When you go to buy one, there are three things to check (apart from price, of course):

Speed

Buy the fastest you can afford, in line with the speeds your ISP operates at. The slowest practicable speed for text-only work is 2400 baud (240 characters per second), but it is pretty tedious although such modems are cheap ($20–30). Speeds go up in steps: 2400, 4800 and 9600 baud, and then in Kb/s: 13.2, 14.4, 28.8 and 56 (see Panel 3.1). Older IBM-style PCs had a serial communications chip (called a **UART**) with a maximum speed of 9600 baud: some ISPs require you to use the newer 16550 UART which runs faster. If this is the case, older PCs may need to be upgraded.

Compatibility

The *de facto* standard for a computer to control a modem is called the Hayes command set, after the company who established it. All common communications software for small computers can use the Hayes commands, so check that your modem supports it.

Compression and error correction

There are several methods built into some modems for speeding data transfer and correcting errors when they are connected to similarly-equipped modems. The Microcom Networking Protocol (MNP) is one of the most common, so if your ISP supports this, you can take advantage of it with such a modem.

Many ISPs offer modems to new users at close to cost price: a good 14.4Kb/s modem costs around $150–200. Physically, you can choose between an internal modem, which goes inside your computer, and an external modem, which sits on the desk beside it. Either will do, but if you have a laptop or notebook computer, it's more convenient to have an internal one, to avoid carrying the extra box, or you can use a subminiature modem on a PCMCIA card which slots in the side of many portables.

Panel 3.1   Communications Jargon

The speed of a modem is the rate at which the modem transmits and receives data, and is measured in **bits** (binary digits) per second, referred to as a **baud**, after Baudot, the inventor of the old Telex code. Eight bits make up one **character** (or **byte**), but there are usually two extra bits transmitted to help with synchronization, making ten, so you get 2400 baud=240 characters per second (cp/s). Faster speeds are measured in thousands of bits per second (Kb/s), so a rate of 9600 baud is the same as 9.6Kb/s or 960 cp/s, equivalent to just under half a standard screenful of solid text.

These codes are transmitted one by one down a single pair of wires (serially, hence the term 'serial'), as distinct from transmitting all eight signals simultaneously down eight parallel wires (which is how most PCs do their printing).

As the most basic set of characters (ASCII: see Table 6.1) only actually needs seven bits, many communications systems simply don't bother about the eighth bit. Equally significant is the way in which modems signal to each other that they are free to send or receive more data, in order to control the flow. Two control characters called XON and XOFF are sometimes used in programs for this (called 'software flow-control'), but the more common standard in eight-bit communications is to use two pins on the modem called RTS and CTS (Request-To-Send and Clear-To-Send: 'hardware flow-control').

Cables

An external modem needs a **serial cable** to go to your computer's serial port, so it has to end in the right kind of plug to fit the socket on the back of your computer (Figure 3.1). Your modem may come with a cable for this: if not, make sure you buy the right one, or get your supplier to make one up. Internal modems don't need this kind of cable, they connect straight into the computer. Both internal and external modems also need a standard phone cord to go to the phone outlet on your wall, but this is supplied with most modems.

If you are traveling with a laptop computer, you may need to have several different cables. In North America and many other countries, the standard phone plug is an RJ–11. In Britain, the standard is the BT phone plug, which is slightly different, but travelers can buy adapters in most good computer stores in the UK, or snip off the RJ–11 from one end of another cable and install a BT plug (but you have to swap the outer two wires for the inner two in doing so). Other countries may have their own plug styles (Figure 3.2), and if you plan on a lot of travel, you can buy adapter kits such as the one provided by Impactron.

Connecting from an office

How you get onto the network from an office will depend on what level of connection your organization offers. This may range from no connection at all (in which case you'll have to make your own by phone) through indirect connection (where you connect to another computer elsewhere to get through to the network) to direct connection.

If your organization is not yet connected to the Internet

You will have to make your connection by phone to a local service provider. This works exactly the same way as connecting from anywhere else by phone, except that not all office telephone systems can handle a call to a computer properly (the computer signals can confuse some phone systems) so you may need a separate external direct phone line rather than one which goes through your switchboard.

If your organization has a direct connection to the Internet but offers only indirect connection at the office level

This lets you connect in the same way as for indirect phone connections, but without the phone and modem. This is the way in which ordinary computer terminals were connected in the days before desktop computers (it's still known in the jargon as a 'dumb terminal' or 'glass teletype' connection), but it's still very common where full network connections have not yet been established to all offices. Your computer connects to some other (usually faster or bigger) computer elsewhere in the organization, which is where the direct connection to the Internet is. In this case you don't need a modem, and the communications cable runs directly from the computer's serial port to a wall outlet.

If your organization offers direct connection to the Internet

You should be able to get connected by asking your organization's computing or network services. As with all permanent connections, you need a network outlet (wallbox) and cable, but these are usually different from their serial counterparts, as they use different wiring and plugs.

You also need a network card installed in your computer. This operates at much higher speeds and in a quite different way to a serial port: the prevailing standard is called Ethernet, but many local-area networks (LANs) designed for office use now have the ability to connect to the Internet by using their server computer as a gateway (Microsoft's *Windows for Workgroups* and Novell Corporation's *Netware* do this). In these cases the users' individual computers remain connected to the LAN as before, but the server computer gets connected to the Internet: you should ask your LAN supplier and your ISP to cooperate in making your connection for you. If you have a Unix or VMS workstation, it probably has Ethernet capability built in already, so you won't need a separate card or adapter.

Before you start plugging into the network, you need to talk to whoever administers your organization's connection to the Internet, and obtain an **IP address** and **hostname** for your computer from them (p. 30). In return, they will need the **Ethernet address** of your machine (either engraved on the network card or on the box it came in).

Your organization will have a **domain name**, which is the network name by which they are known on the Internet, like `acme.org`, and your machine's hostname will be tacked onto the front of this, separated by a period, to form your full name (like `www.acme.org`).

Connecting more than one computer to the Internet in an organization with a permanent connection requires a data switch or router to handle the multiple simultaneous transmissions, as well as the cabling from it to each computer. It also needs someone to take responsibility for maintaining the installation and managing the **namespace** (the allocation of names to additional computers within your domain). In general, these are specialist tasks, and should not be undertaken unless you have the relevant training. Many computer companies, consultancies, and networking suppliers offer facilities management services, however, where they take over the management and maintenance of your connections on a regular contract basis.

Software: the programs

Whichever method of connection you use, you will need programs to communicate with the network. In the case of an indirect connection over the phone, the software needed is minimal. For a full connection, dial-up or permanent, you need different programs, but there are many packages available.

Software for indirect connections

The only software needed for an indirect connection is a communications program, which turns your desktop computer into a terminal. It translates the codes received from the modem or serial port into characters which it can display on your screen, and sends back the keystrokes you type as codes for transmission. Most modems come with a free communications program (varying from the excellent to the disastrous), and you can download dozens of others once you get connected, but the Internet Service Provider you choose should be able to recommend suitable software if you haven't already got it.

For the PC, a simple terminal program like *ProComm* (for DOS) from Datastorm Technologies, Inc. or Microsoft's *Windows Terminal* (which comes with *MS-Windows*) will get you started. On the Apple Mac, common packages are Alverson Software's *Zterm* and Abelbeck Software's *VersaTerm*.

Software for direct connections

For a direct connection, you need two levels of software: one handles the communications between you and the computer you connect to, and the other controls the flow of data according to TCP/IP. There is a wide choice of packages, especially for the PC. Some combine both functions in one package, such as Peter Tattam's *Trumpet Winsock*.

When you dial up to a direct Internet provider's computer, the connection is initially made in the same way as for an indirect connection, using a communications program to login in the same way. Once the link is established, the second level of network software turns the link from a plain serial connection into one that can handle the Internet Protocol (IP).

A permanent connection is by its nature already connected, and needs no dial-up, and the software to handle the communications comes with the network card.

A full Internet connection of any kind encloses all the data you transmit and receive in **packets**. These packets contain the address of the computer on the network that they are aimed at, as well as the address of the computer that sent them, so they can be put onto the network much in the same way that a postal packet can be mailed with a destination and a return address. This mechanism is fundamental to the way in which the Internet operates, as it allows packets to be routed to their destination by intervening machines without you having to be aware in advance of the exact route they will take: you just send data and it arrives. On a permanent connection this is handled for you by the network card and software which comes with it: for a direct connection by dial-up, it has to be done with one of two packages, SLIP or PPP.

SLIP and PPP

There is a choice of two ways of doing this for a direct dial-up connection: SLIP (Serial Line Internetworking Protocol) and PPP (Point-to-Point Protocol). In most cases, your ISP has made this choice for you, and will supply you with the relevant programs to make the connection. Most TCP/IP software that you buy comes with the ability to handle SLIP or PPP built in, but you can also download public-domain versions. PPP has the reputation of being a little faster and more robust than SLIP, but either will do the job adequately. Both in effect replace the need for a network card in your computer, which would be needed for a permanent connection: your link still won't be as fast as using such a card, but the advantage is that you only need dial-up access, rather than a leased line.

SLIP and PPP connections only work if your ISP has installed matching SLIP or PPP software on your account: such accounts cost more to use than plain terminal (indirect access) dial-up accounts because of the much greater volume of traffic you can put through them. Typically, SLIP and PPP accounts are charged by the hour rather than as a flat rate per month.

Your provider will allocate you an IP address, and you get to choose a network name to go with it (p. 30). Whoever installs the software will also need the IP addresses of the relevant servers (p. 32) so that your computer can find its way around the network properly.

Faking it (1): emulating a SLIP connection using software on the host

If you have an indirect dial-up account on a Unix computer, it is possible to emulate a SLIP connection and get the equivalent of a full network connection by using *TIA* (*The Internet Adapter*) from Cyberspace Development, Inc. This is a program (called `tia`) which you download and install in your account. You can test it free for 14 days, after which you can buy the license to continue using it for $25 (single user). The program is available for Unix only, but a VMS version is under development.

You use regular SLIP software on your own machine, just as for a real SLIP connection. You dial up and make your connection in the normal way with your communications program, then login and run the `tia` program. This switches you from indirect to direct access: the only difference is that you do not have a separate IP address for your computer—your account continues to use the IP address of the machine to which you are connected.

The speed is slightly slower than a real SLIP or PPP account, but the advantages are significant: using a 14.4Kb/s modem (or faster) you can run graphical Web software as well as have simultaneous access to Telnet and FTP over a dial-up line from your desktop computer without the expense of a SLIP account (at the time of writing, *TIA* does not work with PPP).

The only communications requirement is that you *must* have a full eight-bit connection using a hardware flow-control (Panel 3.1 on p. 25). Most dial-up systems offer this, but some corporate and campus networks do not.

You do need to check with your ISP that this approach is acceptable. If they also supply full SLIP access, they may not be very happy about you getting the equivalent access while only paying for an indirect dial-up account!

To get *TIA*, download the program itself from `marketplace.com` in the `tia` directory, making sure you pick the right version for your system, and then send an empty mail message to `tia-single@marketplace.com` (single user) or `tia-host@marketplace.com` (for the corporate host version). This returns you an email form which you fill in and send back, and you then get a reply containing a test license code valid for 14 days. Extract the license details into a file called `.tia` in your login directory and then follow the instructions which you will receive in a separate message. Installation of your own IP software is unaffected: you do it just as if you had a full SLIP account, including the eight-bit hardware flow-control connection. There is good email support from Cyberspace Development, Inc.

Faking it (2): running graphical software over an indirect connection

Another way of getting graphical access to the Web from an indirect dial-up account is to run a program called *SlipKnot* in *MS-Windows*. This can communicate with a character browser like *Lynx* or *WWW* running on a Unix dial-up account, and use it to retrieve the Web files you want, then download them using *Xmodem* (p. 38) for display in its own graphical browser. Although this is significantly slower than direct access, it is a good introduction to graphical use of the Web for users who are not in a position to establish a full direct connection or use *TIA*. It is unclear whether or not this approach finds favor with ISPs: if in doubt, ask. *SlipKnot* comes from Peter Brooks (MicroMind), and you can download the software from `ftp.netcom.com` in the directory `/pub/pbrooks/slipknot`.

SlipKnot also requires an eight-bit hardware flow-control connection. It takes a little while to set up so that it can login by itself, check *Lynx* or *WWW*, upload and download the programs it uses, and generally establish itself, but once running it is convenient way to get Web access if you don't need simultaneous terminal jobs, FTP sessions, or other Internet facilities.

Names and addresses

Every machine with a direct connection to the Internet (permanent or temporary) has to have a network address, called an IP address. This is in the form of four numbers separated by periods. If you have a permanent connection, or have taken out a SLIP or PPP account, you will have been allocated an IP address which your service provider will tell you. In addition to this, there is your hostname, which is the alphabetic name of your computer. Usually you get to pick this, so you can choose anything you want provided no-one else has it with the same provider. Pick something you can live with, as this name will become part and parcel of your email address and network identity. Your full network name is made up of your hostname plus the domain name of your provider, so if you decide on `fozzybear` and your provider is, say, `abfab.org`, then your machine becomes `fozzybear.abfab.org`, and if your username is `piglet` then your email address will be `piglet@fozzybear.abfab.org`. Not all providers let you pick the name, so you may be allocated something more administrative like `slip9927.abfab.org`.

When installing your IP software, you need the IP address you have been allocated, and the IP addresses of your 'gateway' and 'nameserver' machines: your ISP will tell you these. If you are going to be doing email or News direct from your desktop machine, you will need to know the names of your mail gateway and your News server as well. If you're doing SLIP with TIA, you don't need your own IP address: it uses the address of the machine you connect to (p. 32), but you still need the addresses of the gateway and nameserver.

Making the connection

Whichever method of connection you pick, you have to set up a few things first: there's no way to avoid this, but you only have to do it once. When it's done, you can dial your ISP's computer and make the connection. Finally, you can login (notify the computer who you are) and you're off!

Setting it up

There will be a setup screen or menu in your communications program which lets you select or type in these values and store them permanently.

The phone number to dial

You get this from your service provider. Your communications program will have a menu item which lets you store this number so you don't have to type it in every time.

The dial command

This tells the modem to use either pulse (rotary) or tone dialing. It probably comes set for tone dialing, but if your phone system uses pulse dialing, set this value to ATDP instead of ATDT.

The transmission speed

Try 9600 or 14,400 to start with unless you have been told otherwise by your provider.

The kind of parity check to use

N (for None) is usually good.

The number of bits per character

This is usually eight.

The number of stop-bits

This is usually one.

This is the most common setup, but check with your ISP. The last four are described as '9600,N,8,1', for example, for obvious reasons, and you often see online services quoting four settings like this. If your provider uses some other settings you will need to change them accordingly: some services use E,7,1 instead.

The last task is setting up the modem. Unfortunately, each make and model is different, so I can't tell you how yours works, but the easiest route is to try it as it comes. The manual will explain what you can change if it doesn't work, but the best expert in these cases is your ISP. The most significant change you may need to make is if you are going to use SLIP/PPP or one of the emulations described on pp. 29–30: the modem must use a method of stopping and starting the flow of data called 'Data Terminal Ready' (DTR) and *not* the method called XON/XOFF. If this needs changing, you do it by flipping one of the tiny switches inside or on the back of your modem: see your modem manual for details.

Installing IP software

If you are going to be running a full network connection, or using SLIP or PPP (or the *TIA* emulator), you need to install your IP addresses. There will be at least three of these: the first will be your own IP address, which is the numeric equivalent of your hostname; the second will be the address of your gateway to the outside world, normally the IP address of your ISP's gateway machine; and the third will be the address of your Domain Name Server, which is the machine which will convert between name and numeric forms of an IP address. You will need to check with your supplier for a fourth: the value of the 'netmask' (usually either 255.255.0.0 or 255.255.255.0).

These numbers need to be entered into the configuration of your IP software. In the case of *MacTCP* or the *Trumpet Winsock* and similar products, you type them

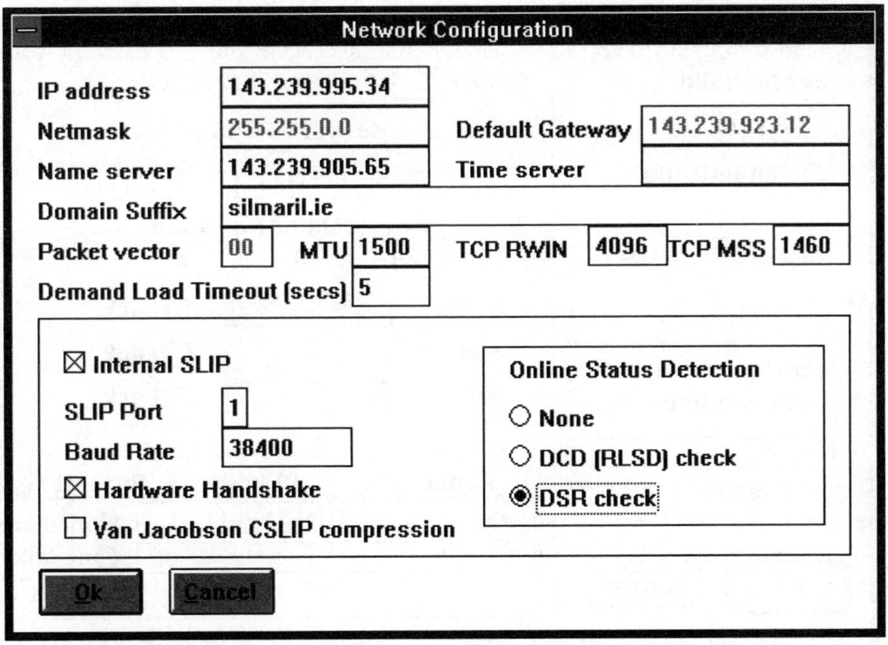

Figure 3.3   Installing IP addresses in the *Trumpet Winsock* `tcpman` configuration

into the relevant dialog boxes of the ***Setup*** function (see Figure 3.3 for an example of the *Trumpet Winsock* setup using the `tcpman` (TCP Manager) program, and Figure 3.4 for the *MacTCP* setup). For DOS IP software such as FTP Software, Inc.'s, you edit the numbers into a configuration file. Some ISPs don't allocate you a fixed IP address for SLIP connections, as their server will allocate you a number at random from a 'free pool' each time you connect. In this case, you have to enter the IP address allocated anew each time into the relevant box in the setup screen, after having logged in.

If you want to access other IP services apart from the Web (such as email or Usenet News), you will need the addresses of your provider's mail gateway and news server. These are known by the names of their respective protocols, SMTP (Simple Mail Transfer Protocol) and NNTP (Network News Transfer Protocol), and they too will have their slot in the configuration or setup screen.

On an Apple Mac, you need the *MacTCP* package (available from your supplier) which provides the IP facility. To make a dial-up connection you also need software which provides a terminal screen to make your initial connection, such as *MacSLIP*, *InterSLIP* or *VersaTerm* SLIP.

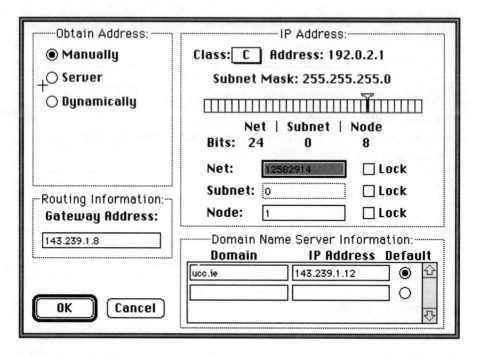

Figure 3.4   Installing IP addresses in *MacTCP*

Dialing a service

Now you can dial: your communications program will have a ***Dial*** function (menu item or command) which makes it do the dialing for you. If everything is set up correctly, the modem will dial the number, and you may hear it beep the tones or click the pulses while it dials. The number will ring out, answer, and then the modems will whistle at each other while they establish the connection. When they finish (2–3 seconds), you should get the keyword CONNECT on your screen, followed by the speed and some echo of the settings. My local connection echoes the settings and the dial command as well:

```
ATQ0V1E1S0=0
OK
ATDT274315
CONNECT 14400/ARQ/V32/LAPM/V42BIS
```

If you are using a more sophisticated interface than just a plain communications program, you may not hear the modem doing its work, or see any of the process actually happening on the screen until you are connected. Some software also allows you to specify in advance your username (access code or ID) and password, so you don't have to type them by hand every time. In this case, these would have to be entered in the setup along with the other settings. If you use this function to store your username and password, remember that it will allow anyone who uses it to connect to your account without them having personally to know the password, which may be a security risk.

What can go wrong?

The number might be busy. If the number you dialed is engaged in another call from another user, and there are no spare lines, your only hope is to call back later. Most communications programs have an ***Auto-redial*** function, which will recognize the busy tone, hang up, wait for a short while, and then try again. If you regularly have problems with a busy line, you might want to change your service provider.

If it rings and never answers, you may have typed in the wrong number, or your provider has a technical problem on that line and it's out of use.

If it answers but fails to connect, then you've got a bigger problem. You can fiddle with the settings if you understand something of modem communications, but it's often quicker to hang up and call your service provider for help. There should be a ***Hang up*** function among the menu items or commands, but if you can't find it, type three plus signs, wait for the response OK, and then type **ATH0** (that's a zero, not a capital O) and press the Enter or Return key. Service providers are well used to dealing with recalcitrant modems and unusual manufacturer's settings: it's not possible here to go through all the diagnostic procedures necessary to do this yourself. Once it is set up correctly, you should never have to change it unless you decide to change your provider or method of connecting.

Starting and finishing work

Once your computer is connected, you may have to press the Enter key a few times to wake up the machine you connected to. If the system you are connecting to has a front-end like a terminal server (a corporate or campus DECnet is a common example), you will get an initial message and a prompt such as **Local>** and you have to type a command like **connect *machinename*** in order to get into the system. Either way, you should then get some kind of identification message and a prompt inviting you to log in.

Logging in and logging out

You need to identify yourself to the computer so that it knows you are authorized to use it and can keep a log of your usage. This process is known as logging in.

When you get the login prompt, it will ask for your username first: you type it in and press the [Enter] or [Return] key. It will then ask for your password: type this in carefully, as it does not usually show up on the screen (for security, in case anyone is looking over your shoulder) and press the [Enter] or [Return] key again.

```
CONNECT 14400
SVR1a 23-Dec-1994 04-22-15.46 IST
You are connected to subnet 20
NETWORK# con 27
SVR1a connecting to system 27, please wait...
#27 fornix.wes.ie LINUX 1.03
login: pflynn
password: abc123
This is FORNIX, one of the WES computers
It is 4.23am on Friday, 23rd December 1994
You have 15 new mail messages
fornix% tia
```

Figure 3.5   Example of logging in to a computer

If you typed correctly, you will now be logged in and ready to start work. If you made a mistake (for example, you mis-typed or forgot your password), you will usually be allowed to try again, but you may have to press the [Enter] or [Return] key first. After a fixed number of tries (usually three) if you still don't get it right, the system may disconnect your call and you'll have to dial again, having first checked to see that your username and password are correct.

There will usually be some kind of welcome message, and information from the system or the operators about any changes. If you have new email, there will be a message saying so. Most systems will detect what type of terminal or terminal emulation you are using. If the system does not recognize your terminal, you will have to tell it, with a command like set term=type where *type* is the right code for your terminal type. Your service provider will tell you which code is correct for the software you are using, but the commonest is VT100, so try that first if there's any problem.

When you have finished work, you need to logout. This signals to the computer that you have done for now. Different computers use different ways of doing this, but it is usually a command like bye, log, logout, logoff, quit, done, finish, stop or exit (followed by pressing the [Enter] or [Return] key) or a key like [Ctrl][D]. This terminates processing and you can hang up the phone line: your communications program will have a *Hang up* function or menu item to to this: if not, type three plus signs, wait until OK appears on the screen, then type ATH0 (that's a zero, not a capital O) and press the [Enter] or [Return] key.

Running SLIP or PPP

If you have a SLIP or PPP connection, you log in as normal, then use your software's **Start SLIP** or **Start PPP** function to switch from plain serial communications into SLIP or PPP. The exact command or menu item you use depends on the package you have installed: for example, the *Trumpet Winsock* `tcpman` program for *MS-Windows* asks you to press the <kbd>Esc</kbd> key.

If you are using *TIA*, you type the `tia` command before using the **Connect SLIP** function to switch to SLIP operation. To log out from *TIA* use, you turn off your SLIP software and type five <kbd>Ctrl</kbd><kbd>C</kbd>s, then logout as normal.

Many communications programs (and the communications program part of some TCP/IP software, like the *Trumpet Winsock*) have the ability to run 'scripts', which are short programs to automate the login and logout process, including switching to SLIP or PPP, so you don't have to do it manually each time.

SlipKnot manages the process by itself, with an automated setup to get file transfer working between your service provider's computer and your own, and it lets you write a control file to specify how SlipKnot is to react to the things that appear on the screen during login so that it knows how and when to transmit your username and password.

Doing your work

How you do your work depends on the method of connection you use.

Indirect connection

An indirect connection usually means you type commands such as `mail` to use electronic mail, `news` to use the Usenet News bulletin-board system, or `lynx` or `www` to run a character browser for the WorldWideWeb. These would all be programs which run on your provider's machine: you should get documentation on how to use them from your provider when you open an account. Normally you can only run one such program at a time (but see 'Emacs' on p. 124). Some more advanced systems present you with a menu of things you can do, so that you just pick them by number rather than type commands. A few service providers actually use Lynx, one of the Web browser programs, to provide the interface for dial-up users, which is very convenient.

Direct connection with a graphical interface

Using a direct connection via SLIP or PPP (or *TIA* or *SlipKnot*) with a graphical interface, you run programs on your own computer by using the mouse to click on them in the usual way. You can run many different programs simultaneously, depending on your computer's capabilities and connection speed, and they can be a mixture of local programs (like your wordprocessor) and networking programs (like Web software or other Internet tools).

Direct connection without a graphical interface

If you are using a direct connection but not a graphical interface, you run Internet software on your own computer by typing commands, but usually only one program can be active at a time.

In the case of the Web software that we will be looking at in the remainder of this book, there is a wide choice of programs. These are discussed in more detail in Chapter 5.

Downloading files on an indirect connection

If you are using a remote computer on an indirect connection by dial-up with terminal software, any files you download from the Internet (by FTP, for example) will end up on your disk area on the supplier's machine. To get them down onto your own desktop requires an additional step.

Most terminal software includes the ability to download files, using built-in versions of several file-transfer protocols. There are lots of these, but the most common are probably the varieties of *Kermit, Xmodem, Ymodem,* and *Zmodem*. The idea is that you run the same program on your provider's machine as on your desktop one, and the two programs talk to each other and negotiate the file transfer between them. You instruct the remote machine to get ready to send or receive a file (as appropriate) and then tell your desktop machine to do the opposite, so that one machine sends and the other receives.

Unfortunately, there are far too many different communications programs in use for it to be possible to document them all here. One simple example, though, is downloading a file from a Unix computer to a PC running *ProComm*, a popular terminal program. Using *Xmodem*, one of the downloading methods available, you would typically type `sx filename` (for 'Send Xmodem') to tell the Unix machine to send that file, then press `PgDn` (for 'Download') on the PC, pick option `1` for *Xmodem* and type the name you want to give the file when it arrives (this lets you rename the file if you need to). The two computers then synchronize themselves and transmit the file from the Unix machine to the PC. To do the reverse, you would use the command `rx filename` and press `PgUp`: this would set the remote computer to receive a file and make the PC send it.

The concept is the same in all terminal programs although the exact keystrokes or menu item names will differ. In a windowing system you can preset the protocol you most often use, so that you just have to click on the **Download** or **Upload** function after typing the command to the remote machine.

Getting Web documents if you only have email

If you only have an email connection, with no direct access to the Internet, you can retrieve individual Web documents by electronic mail. Surprisingly, some quite large commercial 'online' service providers were until recently still operating an email-only service, although they are now making full connections. If you are in this position, you need to know the Uniform Resource Locator (URL) of the document you want (pp. 95–103). A **URL** is the address of a file in the WorldWideWeb, like an extended filename. For example, the Web project description page has the URL http://www.w3.org/hypertext/WWW/TheProject.html

URLs of new, popular, or interesting sites are frequently mentioned in email messages and in Usenet newsgroup postings as well as in computing and networking magazines. When you know the URL you want, there are two Web-by-email services you can choose from.

Agora

To get help on using *Agora*, send an email message to agora@mail.w3.org saying just

WWW

To retrieve a file, send an email message to the same address with a single line containing the keyword **send** followed by the URL in full, for example:

SEND http://www.w3.org/hypertext/WWW/TheProject.html

Files are returned in displayable form with a list of the links at the bottom, so you can retrieve further files. You can get the HTML source file for a URL by using the keyword **source** instead of **send**.

Webmail

To get help on using Webmail, send an email message to webmail@www.ucc.ie saying just

help

To retrieve a file, send an email message to the same address with a single line containing the keyword **go** followed by the URL in full, for example:

GO http://www.w3.org/hypertext/WWW/TheProject.html

Files are returned to you in two forms: the original HTML file, and a formatted copy. Because the formatted version might contain non-printable characters or characters which are not valid in some email systems (like accents), it is encoded using the *UUencode* program, so you'll need a copy of *UUdecode* to decode it. The **uuencode** and **uudecode** programs are available free for most computer systems: ask your provider if you cannot locate a copy and see p. 67 for how to use it.

If you use the keyword **get** instead of **go**, the formatted copy is omitted and only the HTML version sent to you.

Note that you cannot retrieve files from FTP archives using *Webmail*, nor graphical images, sounds, or video clips, only text files. Don't include any other text in messages to the mail servers, especially not an automated signature block (a **.sig** file).

The CERN Email server

Mail to the old address (**listproc0@www.w3.org**) is now forwarded to the new service, *Agora* (above).

Chapter 4

Getting used to the Internet

○ Email and addressing

○ Usenet news

○ Telnet and FTP

○ Archie: files

○ Finding your way around

Because this book is about the WorldWideWeb, this chapter deals only with Internet facilities which are directly related to the Web. There are many other facilities which are not specifically Web-oriented, and you will find these amply documented in the large number of general-purpose books on the Internet, especially the two by Krol and Dern which were mentioned earlier (p. 18). The major applications such as email, Telnet, and FTP were briefly described in pp. 17–18 , and the examples here are intended to give you an introduction to how to use them, so that you are aware of how they work, even if you do not plan on using them in their raw form in your work on the Web.

The majority of the examples are drawn from Unix computers, which are more common on the Internet than any others in the rôle of hosts. Although the growth of direct access from PCs, Macs, and other desktop machines means that fewer users need raw command-line access to Unix, it remains the *de facto* standard for illustrating the principles of Internet usage.

Electronic mail: communicating with other users

There are dozens of different email programs, but they all offer the same basic service: sending messages to other users of the network. The differences lie in the way you use them, and are often based on their original programmer's view of how email 'ought' to work. For normal everyday sending and receiving mail, however, the differences are very slight, so it's not particularly important which one you use.

Before you start sending email, though, you need to know the address of the person you want to send it to. An Internet email address is made up of your username and your computer's full name, separated by an 'at' sign (@), so it looks like these:

```
jane@sales.widgets.com
brutha@cs.unseenu.edu
president@whitehouse.gov
bailey@beetle.army.mil
john@research.acme.co.uk
zazie@dansle.metro.fr
emil@drei.zwillinge.de
pflynn@danann.hea.ie
```

(Only two of those are valid, by the way). Notice that your computer's own name is followed by the name of the organization or company to which it is connected, and then by the name of the country or subnetwork where it is located. In each case this additional addressing information is separated by a period. There is a list of country codes in Table D.3.

Some systems require the username to be a special set of characters rather than your real name, such as `cbts8001`, `jzr39qk`, or `li40163`. In these cases you

Panel 4.1 International addressing for email

Most of the examples of addresses are fairly self-explanatory, if rather terse: the Internet standard of **username@computername** is very common. The final part of the address (after the last dot) is the most significant, as it indicates the sender's country (or a subnetwork of the USA).

In the case of countries outside the USA, they are all international standard (ISO 3166) two-letter country codes (see Table D.3 for a full list). You can see France, Germany, and Ireland in the examples on p. 42. The use of **.uk** is an exception for historical reasons: the ISO 3166 code for the UK is actually **.gb**, which is used by email systems like X.400.

Within the USA, the first four examples in p. 42 show commercial, educational, governmental, and military networks, and there are others like **.org** and **.net** which are used worldwide as well, as shown in Table D.3, p. 321. There are also fifty of the two-letter state codes which have to be followed with **.us** (making California **.ca.us** so it doesn't get confused with Canada, which is just **.ca**).

The only time email addresses get more complicated is when you have to send messages to someone on another network outside the Internet. In this case, you need to know the address of the computer which acts as a gateway between the two networks. The technique is to replace the **@** sign with a percent-sign (**%**) in their address, add the name of their network after a period, and add the name of the gateway computer to the end, separated with a new **@** sign. A common example is email to users on BITNET: you can send mail to a BITNET user whose address is **JOESOAP@BSAFGD** via the gateway at **bitnic.educom.edu** by addressing it as **joesoap%bsafgd.bitnet@bitnic. educom.edu**. The gateway machine strips off its own address, identifies the other network, and replaces the percent sign with an **@** sign and forwards the message.

can usually request an 'alias' to be set up, like **peter**, **paul**, or **mary**. This then works as the first part of your email address, so that other users find it easier to remember (you still have to login with the original username, though).

In most cases, people will tell you their email address in paper or phone communication before you start to use email, or you can call them the first time and ask (put yours on your business card and letterhead too). Unfortunately there is still no single authoritative worldwide directory of email addresses, although there are many places you can look, and these are explained in more detail on pp. 69–71.

Armed with an address, you can now run your email program, either by clicking on the icon or by typing the name of the program. On most computers used for indirect access, the command **mail** will work, but if you are using a Unix computer, you may have to type the explicit name of a mail program like **elm** or **pine**. Because email is so frequently used, it is worth trying out several programs, if you have a choice, and finding one you are comfortable with. On PCs and Macs there is a big choice of mail programs, but avoid those which are based on local or office networks unless they have been specially installed for use with the Internet.

I can't give the exact commands for every mail system in use, as there are too many of them. Graphical mailers use menus in the regular manner: so do some character-based systems. Other character-based mailers used on indirect connections use either typed commands or single keystrokes. In each subsection I will give the name of the function (which is usually the name of the item in the menus of a graphical mail program) plus common forms of the typed command and keystroke, but these may not match exactly the commands or keystrokes in your mail program. You should read the documentation for your own mail program as it will certainly provide many other facilities not listed here, and may use different menus, commands, or keystrokes.

Sending email

To write and send a message, use the ***Compose new message*** function or type a command like **send** or a keystroke like ⌊m⌋ (for 'mail', beware of ⌊s⌋ which often stands for 'save' instead). You will be asked for two or three items of information:

1   the email address of the recipient (usually on a line labeled **To:**)
2   The subject of the message (usually on a line labeled **Subj:**)
3   You may be asked for the addresses of people to send additional copies to (on a line labeled **CC:**)

In each case you type in the information required and press the ⌊Return⌋ or ⌊Enter⌋ key or click on the ⌊OK⌋ button.

The mailer then lets you enter text so you can type your message. Here comes the only major problem for the new user: to do the text requires knowing how to use the editor that the mailer uses. In many cases it is a simple text editor, and if it's in a windowing system, it's probably fairly obvious how to use it. If it's a plain text editor you're familiar with, though, the emergency instructions in Panel 4.2 may help you get unwedged.

When you have finished typing the message, use the ***Send*** function to send the message. If the editor has taken over the whole screen while you type the text, use the editor's ***Exit*** to leave the editor: this causes the mailer to send the message (you may be prompted to save the file first: answer *Yes*). Some systems also offer you a get-out at this stage just in case you've changed your mind and decided you really don't want to send it after all, or have forgotten something and want to go back and edit the text again, or make changes to the addresses or subject.

To avoid having to remember all the addresses of people you correspond with, most systems let you create a private list of aliases (like nicknames), so that you just have to type the alias instead of the full address, and the mailer will look up and use the full address for you. How you do this is very system-dependent, so

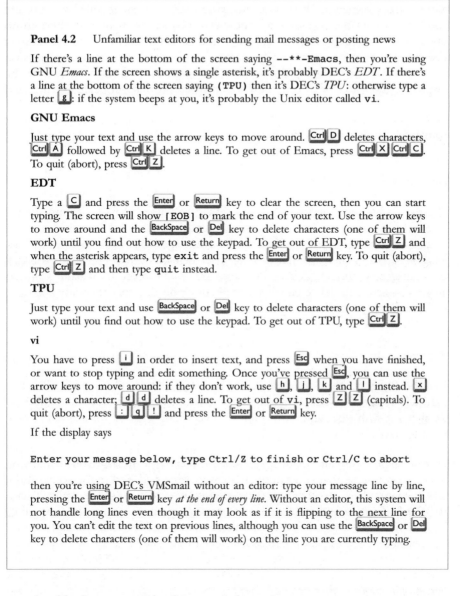

Panel 4.2   Unfamiliar text editors for sending mail messages or posting news

If there's a line at the bottom of the screen saying `--**-Emacs`, then you're using GNU *Emacs*. If the screen shows a single asterisk, it's probably DEC's *EDT*. If there's a line at the bottom of the screen saying (`TPU`) then it's DEC's *TPU*: otherwise type a letter g : if the system beeps at you, it's probably the Unix editor called *vi*.

GNU Emacs

Just type your text and use the arrow keys to move around. Ctrl D deletes characters, Ctrl A followed by Ctrl K deletes a line. To get out of Emacs, press Ctrl X Ctrl C . To quit (abort), press Ctrl Z .

EDT

Type a C and press the Enter or Return key to clear the screen, then you can start typing. The screen will show [EOB] to mark the end of your text. Use the arrow keys to move around and the BackSpace or Del key to delete characters (one of them will work) until you find out how to use the keypad. To get out of EDT, type Ctrl Z and when the asterisk appears, type `exit` and press the Enter or Return key. To quit (abort), type Ctrl Z and then type `quit` instead.

TPU

Just type your text and use BackSpace or Del key to delete characters (one of them will work) until you find out how to use the keypad. To get out of TPU, type Ctrl Z .

vi

You have to press i in order to insert text, and press Esc when you have finished, or want to stop typing and edit something. Once you've pressed Esc , you can use the arrow keys to move around: if they don't work, use h , j , k and l instead. x deletes a character; d d deletes a line. To get out of *vi*, press Z Z (capitals). To quit (abort), press : q ! and press the Enter or Return key.

If the display says

```
Enter your message below, type Ctrl/Z to finish or Ctrl/C to abort
```

then you're using DEC's VMSmail without an editor: type your message line by line, pressing the Enter or Return key *at the end of every line*. Without an editor, this system will not handle long lines even though it may look as if it is flipping to the next line for you. You can't edit the text on previous lines, although you can use the BackSpace or Del key to delete characters (one of them will work) on the line you are currently typing.

you should ask your provider for more information.

Dealing with incoming mail

When new mail arrives for you, it gets stored by the computer until you start your mail program. If new mail has arrived since you last logged in, you will see a message saying so the next time you log in. Some systems will beep if mail arrives while you are logged in. When you start your mail program, it will also tell you if you have got new messages to read, and will display a list of them with the address or name of the sender, with the subject and date. From the list of new messages, you can select the one you want to read first, either with the mouse, or by using the arrow keys, or by typing the number of the message. Some systems start by displaying the whole of the first new waiting message without being asked.

Once you've read a message, you can either delete it, reply to it, forward it to someone else or save it for future reference.

Deleting mail

Use the *Delete* function (type `del` or press ⌨️d). Most mailers don't immediately delete the message, but just mark the message as deleted and wait until you exit from the mail program, before erasing all the messages you marked as deleted. This lets you recover a message that you may have deleted by accident. Once you exit the mail system, though, deleted messages are gone forever. It's usually regarded as good practice to delete email you really don't need, rather than stockpiling it and using up a lot of disk space.

Replying to mail

Use the *Reply* function (type `reply` or press ⌨️r). The mail program will auto-matically re-use the sender's address as the recipient, and re-use the subject by prefixing it with `Re:`, and from then on everything goes as for sending a new message (see above).

Some mail programs automatically include the text of the message you are replying to, in the editor, so that you can see what was being said, and re-use some of the text in your reply. With other programs you may have to request this explicitly with the *Reply/Include* function (sometimes `reply/extract` or press the capital ⌨️R key). While it is useful to have the text there to read and edit, don't include it if it's not relevant: it only makes the message longer than need be.

Forwarding mail to other people

Use the *Forward* function (type `forward` or press ⌨️f). The mail program will ask you for the address of the recipient, and re-use the subject by prefixing it with `Re:`.

You may be asked if you want to edit the text before you forward it: answer Yes or No as appropriate. If you say No, then the message just gets sent as-is. If you say Yes, then from then on everything goes as for replying to a message (see above). Some systems don't ask: you have to request explicitly that you want to edit the message by using the ***Forward/Edit*** function (type `forward/edit` or press capital F).

Saving mail for future reference

Use the ***Save*** function (type `save` or `file`, or press s). The program will ask you where you want the message saved or filed: most systems let you create folders or directories in which you can store messages by category. Type the name of the folder you want to message stored in.

Recalling old messages

If you have saved messages that you want to refer to again, use the ***Change folder*** function (type `folder` or `dir` (for 'directory') or press c (for 'change') or o (for 'open'), followed by the name of the folder where you stored the messages you are interested in. A list of messages should be displayed and you can pick the one you want to re-read.

Mailing lists

Person-to-person messaging is not the only use of email. There are thousandsof topic-oriented discussion groups based on lists of email addresses to which individuals can subscribe. Once your address is added to a list, you receive a copy of each message that other subscribers post to the list, and any messages you send to the list get redistributed to the other subscribers in the same way. ('Subscription' is purely a technical term for adding an address to the list: there is no direct per-subscription cost involved for being on a mailing list, although if you pay your service provider according to the volume of mail you receive, your total bill will increase if you subscribe to mailing lists.)

Mailing lists have two addresses: one administrative one where you send requests for subscription, and the other for the discussion messages themselves. *It is very important to keep this distinction in mind*, as a lot of time can be wasted by sending requests for subscription to the address of the discussion itself: all that achieves is the rebroadcasting of your request to all readers.

LISTSERV mailing lists

The best-known mailing list service is operated by a program called *LISTSERV*, which runs on many large mainframes on the BITNET network, but they are all accessible to the Internet as well. All the *LISTSERV* programs communicate with each other behind the scenes (a technique known as 'peering'), so you can send subscription requests to any of them and it will be forwarded automatically to the right one. You can get a list of all the mailing lists by sending a 1-line mail message saying `list global` to any *LISTSERV* (your service provider can tell you your nearest one, or you can use `listserv@bitnic.educom.edu`). This gives the names and addresses of the lists, a short description of the topic of each, and the address of the specific `listserv` server which handles subscriptions for each of them. You can also query the list interactively using your Web browser by pointing it at `http://www.clark.net/pub/listserv/listserv.html` (see p. 99 for how to do this). For example, to subscribe to the SGML discussion whose address is `sgml-l@uicvm.uiuc.edu` you send a 1-line message to `listserv@uicvm.uiuc.edu` saying

```
subscribe sgml-l Jill Doe
```

(substituting your own forename and surname). You will get back an acknowledgement and a file of details about how to unsubscribe, how to temporarily turn off the flow of messages when you go away, and other administrative commands. Once you're subscribed, you start to receive the messages other people post, and you can reply to them or send your own to `sgml-l@uicvm.uiuc.edu`.

A useful feature of *LISTSERV* is that it keeps copies of all posts to most lists, so you can retrieve the log files if you missed some discussion. Most log files are monthly except on very high-volume lists: the filename is the list name and the filetype is the letters `LOG` followed by the numeric month and year (for example the December 1994 Typography Discussion List log file is `TYPO-L.LOG9412`) You can get an index of the logs for a specific list by sending the command `index` followed by the name of the list to the relevant *LISTSERV* address, for example to see what logs are available for `TYPO-L` you would send

```
index typo-l
```

to the address `listserv@irlearn.ucd.ie`.

You can also search the logs for keywords by using the `LISTDB` program. This is available interactively only for users directly logged on to BITNET computers, but Internet users can send queries by email to the relevant *LISTSERV* address in the form:

```
//    Job Echo=No
Database Search DD=Rules
//Rules DD  *
search riada in irtrad-l since 1 may 1994
index
/*
```

where you follow the command **search** with the keywords of your choice, then **in** and the name of the list (here **irtrad-l** and optionally the restriction **since** followed by a date. Further details and other commands can be got from any *LISTSERV* machine (e.g. **listserv@bitnic.educom.edu**) by sending the request

```
GET LISTDB.MEMO
```

Other list managers

There are many other list-servers which operate in a similar way on Internet machines, notably **majordomo**, **ListProcessor** (at many sites) and **mailbase@ mailbase.ac.uk**, but they are not peered, so you have to make sure your requests go to the right address. The **subscribe** command applies to most of these programs as it does to the original *LISTSERV*.

An overall *List of Lists* was started many years ago by Rich Zellich but is now maintained by Vivian Neou at SRI International and is available by anonymous FTP to **sri.com** in **netinfo/interest-groups.txt** or by sending a 1-line mail to **mail-server@sri.com** saying **send interest-groups**

The list covers both *LISTSERV* and non-*LISTSERV* lists: the subscription method for non-*LISTSERV* lists is in most cases similar to the *LISTSERV* ones with the exception of those which are maintained by hand. In these cases, you send a mail message to an address formed by taking the address of the list itself and adding **-request** to the username part. For example, to subscribe to the list on commercialization and privatization of the Internet, **com-priv@psi.com**, you would send mail to **com-priv-request@psi.com** asking politely to be added to the list (don't forget these subscriptions are handled by humans, not programs). One other common exception is lists maintained by the *Mailbase* service, which uses the command **join** instead of **subscribe**.

Usenet news

Usenet News is an information service which runs over almost all the big networks, including the Internet. It is composed of messages (called 'articles'), which are circulated or distributed automatically to all sites who choose (or pay) to receive them.

The articles are grouped into 'newsgroups' according to topic. There are many thousands of these, some worldwide, some restricted to countries or specific sites. The newsgroups are named hierarchically, as described on p. 17.

To read news, you need a 'newsreader', a program which connects to your nearest news server computer and displays the newsgroups and articles. The traditional Unix-based newsreaders such as *nn*, *rn*, *trn*, or *tin*, are all character-mode programs used on plain terminals. For graphical systems there are *xvnews* for X Windows, *WinQVT/Net* News, *Free Agent* and the *Trumpet Newsreader* for PCs, *InterNews* or *TheNews* for Macs and many others.

Web browsers can also read news using the **news:** URL, and some (*Netscape* and *InternetWorks*, for example) can also let you post articles of your own. Following a hypertext reference in a HTML file (Chapter 9) to a newsgroup or using the ***Open URL*** function (p. 99) to type in one of your own, will display a list of articles in the newsgroup specified.

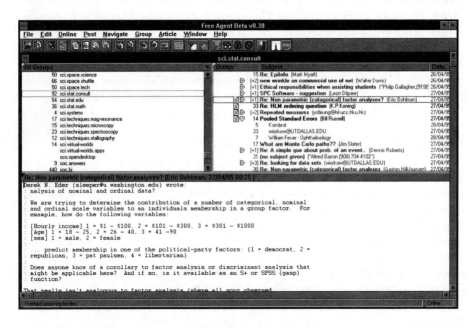

Figure 4.1   Reading Usenet news in *MS-Windows* with *Free Agent*

Unlike email, where messages are directed at you personally (or through a mailing list), news articles are like a bulletin board, pinned up publicly for anyone to see. You can read them, reply to the sender, post a follow-up article (or a new one) of your own, or forward a copy to someone via email: the only thing you can't do is delete them. News articles have a limited life: most news host operators expire articles after a fixed time (a few days, a week, a month, depending on how much disk space they have). If you want to keep a copy of an article for reference, you can save a copy to a file on your own disk.

Telnet: logging in elsewhere on the network

To log into another machine on the Internet, you have to have an account on that machine. This is fairly common in the research field, where scholars often share access to several machines around the world. For most users, however, the biggest use of Telnet is to log into remote databases like library catalogs, or into their own machine while they are traveling elsewhere. Subject to organizational restrictions, most people on the network are happy to let visitors to their office use a terminal for a short while to connect to their home machine to read mail or do other work. Some organizations, particularly in the educational field, make a point of extending this courtesy to visitors to meetings or conferences with Internet access specifically for this kind of activity (some, alas, do not). There are also public-access Internet providers who will let visitors use short-term accounts for a small sum (or even free), and there are even some cafés in places where Internet-minded people congregate, who have terminals on the premises, for example the CyberCafé in London's Monmouth Street (WC2), who have their Web page at `http://www.cybercafe.org/cybercafe/gallery/gallery.html`.

Apart from the username and password, all you need is the name of the machine you want to connect to (or its IP address). You then click the Telnet program and give the computer's name or IP address, or type the command

```
telnet address
```

(replacing the *address* with the name or IP address). Telnet will connect to that machine, and respond with the regular `login:` prompt. From there, you login and work just as if you were in your own home or office, except that you are subject to whatever equipment you are using locally to connect through. When you are finished, you log off in the normal way, and type `quit` to return control to the local machine. If a Telnet session gets stuck, perhaps because of network congestion, and you want to abort it, the normal escape is to press Ctrl] and then type `quit`.

Many university libraries provide open-access Telnet services to let people elsewhere browse through their library catalog, and use Telnet in the same way themselves to access other catalogs. A list of these is maintained by Peter Scott in the FTP archives of the University of Saskatchewan, `ftp.usask.ca`, in directory `pub/hytelnet` along with the *HyTelnet* program, which provides a convenient front-end for people using Telnet access to many Internet sites, especially libraries. For a demonstration, Telnet to `access.usask.ca` and login as `hytelnet` (no password): there's also a Web version at `http://www.usask.ca/cgi-bin/hytelnet`.

Other services accessible using Telnet include databases of weather and other dynamically-measurable phenomena, and a variety of rôle-playing simulations (sometimes dismissed as games by those who have not experimented with them).

FTP: downloading files from the Internet

A vast quantity of software and other information of all descriptions can be obtained from public repositories on the Internet and other networks. Most of the original and subsequent development of the Web system was carried out using software developed by individuals and teams who have made their programs freely available in this way for others to use.

The File Transfer Protocol (FTP) is the normal method of retrieving software from archives and repositories on the Internet. If you have a Web browser running already, you can use it to retrieve files by FTP (p. 100), but in order to get a Web browser in the first place, you will need to get it by FTP manually, unless you buy a commercial version or are supplied with the software by your ISP separately on disk, CD-ROM or tape. This section explains how to retrieve files manually.

The FTP program allows you to connect your computer to another computer elsewhere on the Internet, and send or receive files to and from the disks attached to that machine. Normally, as with Telnet, you need an account with a username and password to use other people's computers, but there is a special case called **anonymous FTP**, which allows anyone anywhere on the Internet to have access to file storage areas where publicly-available software and other information has been placed so that you can download it.

To retrieve files using anonymous FTP, you need to know something about what you want to download:

1   the name of the machine where the files you want are held;
2   the name of the directory or folder in which the files are stored;
3   the names of the files themselves.

In most cases this information is something which you are told by other people in electronic mail messages, or which you read in newspapers, magazines, or Usenet newsgroup articles, or in information pages accessible through Web, or in this book! It is common for users to exchange details between themselves such as 'you can get file **xyz** by anonymous FTP from **abc.def.edu** in directory **pub/net/fred**'.

If you have only the machine name or IP address, you can still use FTP, because it lets you change directory and list the files and subdirectories, so you can follow any obvious-looking paths to find what you are looking for.

Failing this, you can search the world's FTP archives using a service called *Archie*, which will help you find where things are stored (pp. 58–60).

Equipped with this information, you can then run the FTP program by clicking your FTP icon and entering the name of the computer you want to connect to, or typing the command `ftp` followed by the name or IP address of the computer.

In either case you will need to enter the special username **anonymous** whenasked for the username (on VAX/VMS systems running Multinet you have to type **login anonymous** instead). When you are asked for a password, you enter your email address (this does not display on the screen as you type it, in accordance with the normal practice for security of passwords).

Here's an example of a user called **jane** logged on to a workstation called **fish. ocean.edu** who wanted to retrieve some files from an anonymous FTP server called **foo.bar.org**. The session would start with the following dialog: the user's input is in bold and I've shown the password grayed out, so you can see where it is (normally it would be invisible):

```
fish% ftp foo.bar.org
Connected to foo.bar.org.
220 foo.bar.org FTP server (SunOS 4.1) ready.
Name (fish.ocean.edu:jane): anonymous
331 Guest login ok, send ident as password.
Password: jane@fish.ocean.edu
230 Guest login ok, access restrictions apply.
Welcome to the anonymous ftp server at foo.
Please read the notices in README
ftp>
```

Once logged in, FTP displays

```
ftp>
```

to prompt you to type one of the commands shown below. To finish, type the command `quit`. If you have problems connecting, such as the error message

```
fop.bar.org: unknown host
```

then it means you have either typed the name wrongly, or you have been given the wrong name, or that machine does not exist (or it may exist but it's not on public access). If you get the message

```
ftp: connect: Connection timed out
```

it means that the name is valid but the connection has failed, possibly due to some part of the network being temporarily congested or offline. In this case all you can do is try again later.

FTP commands to retrieve files

Once you are connected, you can use the following commands to navigate the directory structure and retrieve files.

cd (Change Directory)

Opens the specified subdirectory for access, for example:

```
ftp> cd pub/net/fred/wedit
250 CWD command successful
ftp>
```

The user changed directory to pub/net/fred/wedit (she knew the name already, probably as a result of being told, or of having used the dir command). The code 250 indicates a successful action for the Change Working Directory (CWD) instruction.

dir (Directory)

Lists the names of files and subdirectories in the current directory, for example:

```
ftp> dir
200 PORT command successful.
150 ASCII data connection for /bin/ls
(143.239.996.43,2726)
(0 bytes).
total 1649
-r--r--r-- 1 fred staff     4563 Oct 19 17:45 README
dr--r--r-- 1 fred staff       15 Oct 18 11:07 source
-r--r--r-- 1 fred staff   176352 Oct 19 17:39 wedit.doc.ps
-r--r--r-- 1 fred staff    87263 Oct 19 17:14 wedit.sit.hqx
-r--r--r-- 1 fred staff    38275 Oct 19 17:44 wedit.tar.Z
-r--r--r-- 1 fred staff    10946 Oct 19 17:22 wedit.doc.txt
-r--r--r-- 1 fred staff    49872 Oct 19 17:37 wedit.zip
226 ASCII Transfer complete.
1032 bytes received in 2.9 seconds (0.35 Kbytes/s)
ftp>
```

In this case, the user typed dir and got a directory listing of six files and a subdirectory belonging to Fred (Unix shows directories by prefixing their read/write permissions with a d). Filename conventions and encodings can be deduced from the filetype and are explained in more detail on pp. 61–68 but it's not hard to see that one file is clearly important, as it's called README. There is also what looks like documentation in plain text form (**wedit.doc.txt**) and a *PostScript* file (**wedit.doc.ps**) which probably contains the same documentation in typographic form. The other three files are (respectively) a Macintosh, Unix, and PC version of some software. There is also the subdirectory **source** which probably contains programming source files for this program.

binary (specify Binary files)

Tells the remote computer that the files you are going to download are binary (non-text) files, such as programs or compressed archive files. This is essential in order to download such files correctly, for example:

```
ftp> binary
200 Type set to I.
ftp>
```

The user intends to download a binary file. The code 200 signifies that the type of file has been set to Image (I), which is correct for binary files. If after downloading the binary files you want to download some text files, use the command **ascii** (see below) to reset the type of file to ASCII.

ascii (specify ASCII files)

This is the corresponding command to **binary**. It sets the type of file to **A** for downloading plain text files, and is used after you have been downloading binary files (see above) when you want to download some text files. ASCII is the default, so if all you want is text files, there is no need to type this command.

lcd (Local Change Directory)

Changes the working directory on your own machine to the directory name you type. This is usually used just before you download a file you want placed in that directory, for example:

```
ftp> lcd /users/jane/web
Local directory now /users/jane/web
ftp>
```

The user changed the local directory to /users/jane/web.

get (Get files)

Retrieves the file whose name you type and stores it on your local disk, for example:

```
ftp> get README
200 PORT command successful.
150 Binary data connection for README
(143.239.996.43,2530) (4563 bytes).
226 Binary Transfer complete
local: wedit.zip remote: wedit.zip
4563 bytes received in 0.01 seconds (2.2e+03 Kbytes/s)
ftp>
```

The user retrieved the documentation file **README**. You have to wait while the file downloads: on slow lines or with large files this can take several minutes.

prompt (turn prompting on or off)

Turns prompting on if it was off, or off if it was on: prompting is used automatically when you download multiple files (see below) to ask you in turn if you really want each file. To turn it off, type

```
ftp> prompt
Interactive mode off
ftp>
```

if you are certain that you want all of the files, and don't want to have to say 'yes' to each in turn. To turn prompting back on, type the **prompt** command again.

mget (Multiple Get)

Downloads all files matching the wildcard specification you type. Wildcarding is the use of special characters such as the asterisk (*) to represent a portion of the filename which can match any sequence of characters, for example:

```
ftp> mget wedit.*
200 PORT command successful.
150 Binary data connection for wedit.doc.ps
(143.239.996.43,2530) (176352 bytes).
226 Binary Transfer complete
local: wedit.doc.ps remote: wedit.doc.ps
176352 bytes received in 0.023 seconds (2.1e+03 Kbytes/s)
150 Binary data connection for wedit.doc.txt
(143.239.996.43,2530) (10946 bytes).
226 Binary Transfer complete
local: wedit.doc.txt remote: wedit.doc.txt
10946 bytes received in 0.016 seconds (1.9e+03 Kbytes/s)
150 Binary data connection for wedit.sit.hqx
(143.239.996.43,2530) (87263 bytes).
226 Binary Transfer complete
local: wedit.sit.hqx remote: wedit.sit.hqx
```

```
87263 bytes received in 0.019 seconds (2.3e+03 Kbytes/s)
150 Binary data connection for wedit.tar.Z
(143.239.996.43,2530) (38275 bytes).
226 Binary Transfer complete
local: wedit.tar.Z remote: wedit.tar.Z
38275 bytes received in 0.012 seconds (2.5e+03 Kbytes/s)
150 Binary data connection for wedit.zip
(143.239.996.43,2530) (49872 bytes).
226 Binary Transfer complete
local: wedit.zip remote: wedit.zip
49872 bytes received in 0.015 seconds (2.4e+03 Kbytes/s)
ftp>
```

The user downloaded all files beginning with `wedit.` (regardless of how the filename ended).

quit

Terminates an FTP session and returns to your local prompt, for example:

```
ftp> quit
221 Goodbye.
fish%
```

The user finished the FTP session. Her computer responds with the local system prompt.

Note that the exact wording of the responses may vary slightly from machine to machine, depending on the version of the FTP program being used.

Downloading files from LISTSERV and NETSERV archives

LISTSERV and *NETSERV* are separate non-Internet services: they run on mainframes connected to another large network called BITNET and its partner networks outside the USA such as TERENA (Europe, formerly EARN), NET-NORTH (Canada) and GULFNET (Arabian Gulf). Users on these networks can access files interactively, but Internet users can also retrieve files from *LISTSERV* and *NETSERV* by sending requests in email messages.

You need to know in advance the name of the BITNET computer which holds the files you want: there is no global index of these files which you can search, as there is on the Internet with the `archie` command (see next section). Nevertheless, if you know (perhaps from information in email discussions or Usenet newsgroups) that you need to get a specific file, the mechanism is very simple: send an email message to *LISTSERV* or *NETSERV* at the relevant machine saying

```
get filename filetype
```

(there can be more than one command in each message). Some files 'belong' to specific mailing lists, and in these cases you need to add the name of the list to the GET command: `get filename filetype listname`. Sending the single-word command `index` will return you an index of all files held on the *LISTSERV* or *NETSERV* machine you send it to. Native BITNET addresses only have a username and nodename, like `MARY@LAMB` (sometimes quoted in IBM mainframe format as `MARY at LAMB`). To send email to such an address, follow the instructions in Panel 4.1 on p. 43.

Archie: finding where to retrieve files from

If you do not know the location of the files you are looking for, there is a database of frequently-used FTP archives which can be searched with a service called *Archie*. This can be used as a simple command, or you can log into an *Archie* host to conduct more complex searches. The command can also be set up for use from within a Web browser if you also have access to a server, by using a script (pp. 250–257).

To use the *Archie* service with the `archie` command, the *Archie* front-end (client program) has to be installed on the computer you are using. If the computer you use for access to the Internet is not your own, and typing `archie` does not work, you should ask the systems manager to install it for you. If it's your own computer, you can get an *Archie* client from many FTP servers (for PCs, for example, there is David Woakes' *WSArchie*).

To find the storage location of a program whose name you already know, you type `archie filename` so if you were looking for a chess program, for example, you could type `archie chess` and the *Archie* system will search its indexes and display all the entries it has for that name (which in this case is several dozen, so I've just kept a few for illustration):

```
Host rena.dit.co.jp

  Location: /pub/GNU/games
    DIRECTORY drwxr-xr-x    1024 May 31 07:54 chess
```

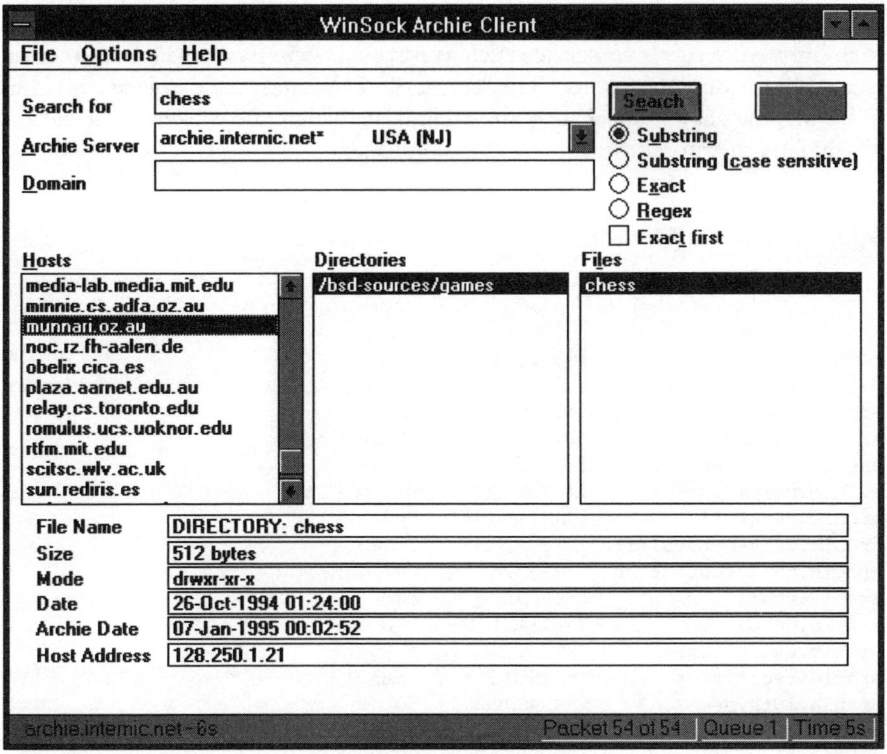

Figure 4.2 An Archie Windows client being used to find a file

```
Host scitsc.wlv.ac.uk

  Location: /pub/infomagic/source.code.cdrom/bsd_srcs/games
    DIRECTORY drwxr-xr-x    512 Feb 8 1994 chess
                                                    Location:
/pub/infomagic/usenet.cdrom/sources/games/volume1
      FILE -r--r--r--   66557 May 20 1987 chess

Host svin02.info.win.tue.nl

  Location: /pub/bsd-sources/games
    DIRECTORY drwxr-xr-x    512 Jul 4 1993 chess
```

For each 'hit', the computer name (the host) comes first, followed by the directory location that you would use cd to get into. Each entry is introduced with its type, DIRECTORY or FILE, followed by the protection, size, date, time, and name, in standard Unix format. *Archie* searches only Unix file repositories, but these are not restricted to Unix software: on the contrary, all kinds of software is stored there.

If your computer does not have the **archie** command, you can use Telnet to connect to your nearest *Archie* site and run the search from there, or point your Web browser at an *Archie* service such as **http://www.pvv.unit.no/archie** (see p. 99 for how to do this). The names of *Archie* sites worldwide are listed in Table 4.1: the geographical areas shown indicate which one is likely to be closest to you (and therefore fastest for you to connect to).

Table 4.1   *Archie* sites

> Source: **archie.doc.ic.ac.uk** *(systems marked with an asterisk are those mentioned in Brendan Kehoe's Archie client software as suitable servers)*

Archie system	IP address	Area
archie.doc.ic.ac.uk	146.169.2.10	UK *
archie.hensa.ac.uk	129.12.21.25	United Kingdom
archie.uni-linz.ac.at	140.78.3.8	Austria
archie.univie.ac.at	131.130.1.23	Austria
archie.funet.fi	128.214.6.102	Finland *
archie.univ-rennes1.fr	129.20.128.38	France
archie.th-darmstadt.de	130.83.128.118	Germany
archie.ac.il	132.65.16.18	Israel
archie.unipi.it	131.114.21.10	Italy
archie.uninett.no	128.39.2.20	Norway
archie.rediris.es	130.206.1.2	Spain
archie.luth.se	130.240.12.30	Sweden
archie.switch.ch	130.59.1.40	Switzerland
archie.cs.mcgill.ca	132.206.51.250	Canada *
archie.uqam.ca	132.208.250.10	Canada
archie.unl.edu	129.93.1.14	USA (NE)
archie.internic.net	198.49.45.10	USA (NJ)
archie.rutgers.edu	128.6.18.15	USA (NJ)
archie.ans.net	147.225.1.10	USA (NY)
archie.sura.net	128.167.254.179	USA (MD) *
archie.twnic.net	192.83.166.10	Taiwan
archie.ncu.edu.tw	192.83.166.12	Taiwan
archie.wide.ad.jp	133.4.3.6	Japan
archie.hana.nm.kr	128.134.1.1	Korea
archie.sogang.ac.kr	163.239.1.11	Korea
archie.au	139.130.4.6	Australia *

To login to an *Archie* site, type **telnet** followed by the name of the computer as given in Table 4.1. When it connects, login as **archie** (there is no password). To search for a program, use the command **prog** *filename* where *filename* is the name or part of the name of the file that you are looking for. *Archie* will search its database for any entry containing the word you typed, and display a listing in the same format as shown earlier. To disconnect when you have finished searching, type **quit** to disconnect.

Filenames and filetypes and what to do with them

The huge variety of files, filenames, and filetypes that you encounter on the network can be a bit confusing to start with. Fortunately there are some simple guidelines which make it much easier.

Most computer filing systems allow you to divide a filename into one or more parts, usually separated by a dot (period or full stop). The first part is the name of the contents (a program, data, text, whatever) or an abbreviation to make it quicker to type. The remaining part(s) describe information about the file, such as what type of file it is, which version it is, or how it is stored. Some systems like MS-DOS and VMS classify files by their filetype (the bit after the dot), others like Unix and Macintosh let you divide up filenames like this but don't assign any particular meaning to the filetype: it's there for your convenience. For this reason, if you use a graphical windowing system, you may only see a descriptive name displayed (the one you click on to run the program) rather than the real filename. However, if you have to download files coming from other systems, it is important to understand how these names are constructed and what they mean: some common examples are shown in Table 4.2. Most information and software providers try to make the meaning and usage of a file as obvious as possible from its name, without going to excessive lengths, but to understand all the abbreviations, you need to know what they mean.

Table 4.2   Examples of filenames and filetypes

Filename example	Type of information
readme.txt	Something important in a plain text file
INSTALLATION	Installation instructions in a plain text file
*.ps	Formatted documentation for a PostScript printer
*.exe	DOS or VMS executable program
*.zip	PC compressed file archive stored using PKzip
*.tar.gz	Unix Tape Archive stored using GNU Zip
*.sit.hqx	Mac StuffIt archive encoded with BinHex
*.shar.Z	Unix Shell Archive, compressed (multi-file)
*.gif	Graphics Interchange Format file
*.html	WWW file using HyperText Markup Language

There are a few restrictions related to the operating systems. On IBM-style PCs running MS-DOS or *MS-Windows*, the filename is limited to eight characters and the filetype is limited to three characters. IBM mainframes running VM or MVS have a limit of eight characters for each of the filename and filetype (and they use a space to separate them instead of a dot). Most other modern filing systems have a limit which is so big you are unlikely to run up against it (256 characters overall is a common limit). Systems like Apple Macs which allow spaces in filenames cause a problem for systems which do not, so it is common to find spaces replaced by an underscore or dollar character, which is acceptable in most systems. This means that a file on a Mac called 'Sales Report 1995' would have to be named something like `Sales_Report_1995` if it is to be usable on non-Mac computers. Although many computers do not distinguish between upper- and lowercase letters in file naming, Unix and Mac systems both do, so you need to take care when typing filenames for these systems.

Handling different filetypes

Why all these different types of files? The Internet is made up of millions of different computers, all interconnected. Unfortunately, there's no way that inventors, manufacturers, researchers, programmers, and users are all going to agree on one single master plan which solves all computing filename problems. Fortunately, the Internet, and WorldWideWeb in particular, offer a lot of ways of hiding the discrepancies between systems from the people who use them. The people who set them up, though (and that includes you, if you become an information provider), need to know something about what goes on behind the scenes.

There are three problems in sending files over the network:

1   many software systems are not just single programs but large collections of all sorts of files;
2   some kinds of file in their raw form can take up a lot of space and therefore take a long time to transmit or receive;
3   some parts of the network may inadvertently or carelessly corrupt files which contain certain codes.

The first problem is eased by packaging many files together into a single file called an archive, which can be dearchived by the receiver, extracting the files back to their original form. To improve the second situation, compression routines have been developed to encode files using mathematical techniques which pack the information as densely as possible. In their compressed state, files take much less time to send over a network, but are not directly usable: they have to be decompressed first. The third solution involves an additional re-coding of a file which uses only a set of characters which are known to be immune to corruption.

There are therefore three types of operation which may have been performed on a file that you retrieve, rather like three layers of wrapping paper:

1   lots of files may have been packaged together into a single archive file;
2   as an archive file can be quite large, it may have been compressed in some way;
3   finally, it may then have been encoded to make it less prone to being garbled.

The filetype (the part of a filename after the first or second dot) usually means something important about the way in which the file has been stored. The following is a list of the filetypes frequently encountered in the Web, and what you should do if they imply some form of action like dearchiving, uncompressing, or decoding. The command examples given are for Unix or DOS where relevant: equivalents on other systems are usually very similar. Because archiving followed by compression is so common, there are several popular programs which do both at the same time: these are identified as a separate category.

Archive formats

The term 'archive' here has nothing to do with the other meaning of the word, referring to the long-term storage of material in a repository, but simply means a way of storing many files together as one.

.tar

Tape Archive is a Unix method of archiving files, but there are **tar** programs for PCs, Macs, VAX/VMS and other systems as well. To dearchive ('detar') these files, first see if the files in the .tar file have directory names included with them: do this by listing the contents with

```
tar tvf filename.tar | more
```

(t for 'typeout', v for 'verbose', f for 'use this file, not the tape drive'). Use Ctrl-C to stop the listing when the word --More--(n%) appears at the bottom of the screen (this avoids having to wait while long listings scroll past). If directory names are shown in the listing (i.e. if there are slashes in the filenames), move the file to your home or root directory and make that your current directory:

```
mv   filename.tar   /
cd   /
```

If there were no directory names, create a suitably-named directory, move the file into it and make that your current directory:

```
mkdir   dirname
mv   filename.tar   dirname
cd   dirname
```

Then extract the files with the command

```
tar xvf filename.tar
```

See p. 64 for details of how to uncompress files which end with .tar.Z .

.sh, .shar or .csh shell scripts

These are files of Unix commands (a bit like `.bat` files in MS-DOS or `.com` files in VMS) which can be executed like a program. Because they can contain data and programs as well as the commands to unwrap them, they are sometimes used as a means of archiving. To dearchive them, use the shell command

```
[c]sh filename
```

There is also a VMS SHAR for use on DEC VAX/VMS systems.

Compressed files

.gz

GNU *Zip* is a file compression routine available for Unix and PCs. For straightforward decompression, type

```
gunzip filename.gz
```

The `.gz` file will be deleted and replaced with the decompressed file which was inside it. As with `.z` files below, this will often be a `.tar` file requiring subsequent dearchiving.

.Z

This is the standard Unix compression method, but `.gz` (see above) is becoming more common. To decompress a file ending in `.z`, type

```
uncompress filename.Z
```

The `.z` file will be deleted and replaced with the decompressed file which was inside it. In many cases, files distributed on the network end with `.tar.z`, so do this decompression first, then do the dearchiving of the resultant `.tar` file afterwards. There are uncompressing programs also available on most other systems.

zcat

The `zcat` command works just like `uncompress`, except that it leaves the original `.z` file on disk afterwards, instead of deleting it.

Archive-compressed files

.exe

This could be either a DOS or VMS program, or a PC self-extracting compressed archives done using a Zip form of archive compression. It's impossible to tell which just from the filename: the only way to find out is to run it and see. Self-extracting means you don't need to have a copy of **pkunzip.exe** or **uzip.exe** to do the job. Instead you just type the filename followed by a space and **-d** (to ensure that the files unwrap into their right directories).

.boo

This method is used mainly for PC and some Amiga software. To unwrap a BOO archive, you need a copy of the **deboo.exe** program. Type

```
deboo filename.boo
```

BOO archives may be UUencoded as well (p. 67), so the file may end with **.boo.uue** or **.uueboo** (with or without the dots): in this case use **uudecode** first.

.zoo

ZOO is also used mainly for PC software. To unwrap a ZOO archive, you need a copy of the **zoo.exe** program. Type

```
zoo extract filename.zoo
```

.sit

StuffIt is a commercial file compression and archiving program for the Apple Macintosh, but *UnStuffIt* is publicly available free of charge. To unwrap a **.sit** file, double-click the *StuffIt* icon and then open the **.sit** file with the file dialog box. *StuffIt* compressed archives are often *BinHex*ed (p. 67) for network (particularly email) transmission: such files end with **.sit.hqx**. Most versions of unstuffing programs include a menu option to handle the *BinHex*ed file first and then unstuff the archive automatically.

.sea

Self-Extracting Archive for Apple Macs. This works like the **.exe** files for DOS and VMS in that you just double-click the file to run it, and it unpacks itself. As with **.sit** files, these are often found with the filetype **.sea.hqx** which means they must be handled with *BinHex* first (automated in modern versions of *UnStuffIt*).

.cpt

Files compressed with *Compact Pro* for the Apple Mac. The sequence to unpack is the same as for *UnStuffIt* (`.sit` files, see above).

.zip

A combined archive-compressed file used mainly in MS-DOS and *MS-Windows*. There are several zipping and unzipping programs, both commercial and public-domain, but the most popular are Phil Katz's *PKzip* and *PKunzip* (shareware if used privately) and the public-domain `zip` and `unzip` (or `uzip`). Before you unzip a file, check first to see if subdirectory names have been stored in the file along with the compressed files themselves: type

```
pkzip -v filename
```

This will display a list of files. If they have directory names with them (i.e. if there are slashes in the filenames), make sure you are in the root directory of your hard disk (by typing the **cd** \) and then type

```
pkunzip -d filename
```

(making sure you type the full directory and filename if the `.zip` file itself is not in the root directory). This will unzip the file and place all the uncompressed files in the right directories. If there were no directory names in the file listing, create a suitably-named directory, make it your current directory and then unzip the file:

```
md   dirname
cd   dirname
pkunzip   filename
```

(making sure you type the full directory and filename if the `.zip` file itself is not in the root directory). This will unzip the file into that directory. The public-domain `unzip` program does not need the `-d` option as it honors directories by default. If some of the files already exist (for example if you have done this before with an earlier version of the same file), you will be asked if you want to overwrite them: answer Y or N to each as appropriate. It's also possible to force all the files to be overwritten without asking, by using the command: `pkunzip -d -o filename` (o for 'overwrite'), but you should only use this if you know what you are doing.

Encoded files

.hqx

This is a coding method called *BinHex*, and the file needs to be decoded with the `hexbin` routine. This method is most common on Apple Macintoshes, where the decoding is usually handled by the file uncompression and dearchiving programs such as *StuffIt* (p. 65).

.uue

UUencoding is very common for archive or other binary files such as is sent by electronic mail or posted on Usenet newsgroups. Files ending in `.uue` can be decoded with the `uudecode` or `uud` programs: just type

uud[ecode] *filename*

You can identify UUencoded mail messages and newsgroup posts by the presence of a line at the top saying something like

```
begin 666 mythesis.zip
```

followed by many lines of apparently random characters. There are also variants of UUencoding known as *VVencode*, *XXencode*, *YYencode*, and *ZZencode* which encode files ever more robustly, so that they can survive transit through some of the more idiosyncratic email gateways. These programs follow the same pattern of usage as *UUencode*.

MIME email messages

MIME stands for Multipurpose Internet Mail Extensions, and is a method of letting email programs encode files which are *not* in plain text format (e.g. wordprocessor files, images etc.) so that they transport correctly across email networks. You have to have a MIME-compliant email program to decode these messages, so you shouldn't send them to people unless you know they have such software.

There is however a very useful pair of programs called *mpack* and *munpack* which are utilities for encoding and decoding (respectively) binary files in MIME format. The canonical FTP site for this software is `ftp://ftp.andrew.cmu.edu:pub/mpack/`. To decode a message sent to you in MIME format, even if your mailer is not MIME-compliant, save the message as a separate file, quit your mailer, then type `munpack` *filename*.

Multimedia formats

There are seven common formats used in the Web for still images, movie clips and sound files:

- **.gif** (Graphics Interchange Format) for inlined imaged, especially line art and icons;
- **.jpg** (Joint Photographic Experts Group) for external images, especially photographs;
- **.xbm** (X Windows BitMap) for icons;
- **.mpg** (Motion Picture Experts Group) for video;
- **.mov** (Movie) for video in QuickTime format;
- **.au** (AUdio) sound files;
- **.wav** (Wave) sound files.

Most of the utility programs mentioned in this list are freely available for personal use as public-domain, shareware, freeware, or other freely-distributable software, and can be downloaded from many FTP archives (use *Archie* to find them). If you want to continue using shareware, or want it for corporate use, you will need to contact the authors to discuss licensing. The programs are usually available in uncompressed, unarchived, uncoded form, so that you don't need to have a copy already to unwrap them with.

If instead you get copies from your supplier or from friends or colleagues on disk, be sure to check them for viruses first, before you use them. Software that you download from regular, trusted, public FTP archives on the Internet is almost always virus-free because archive maintainers are very careful about what they make available, and there are so many people downloading it that any problems get spotted and corrected very fast: the same cannot necessarily be said of software coming from individuals' private disks or from private (non-Internet) bulletin boards.

There are many other forms of archiving, compression, and encoding: these are just the most commonly-used for Web software. If you encounter others which you don't know how to handle, your service provider or computer services center should be able to help you. *The Web directory of acronyms and abbreviations* [Flynn 1994] contains a long list of filetypes and their uses: if you come across one you don't recognize, try looking it up by pointing your browser at http://www.ucc.ie/cgi-bin/acronym.html?xyz replacing *xyz* with the filetype you are inquiring about. See p. 99 for details of how to point your browser at a specific service like this.

Finding your way around the network

The sheer size of the Internet can make the task of finding your way round a little daunting for new users. Like a foreign country, it is in fact reasonably well signposted, but the signs themselves are in a language which needs learning before you can use it. If you get lost, asking directions is always a good idea, and on the Internet you have a choice between asking people or asking machines.

● Asking machines means using some software to send a request to a computer which has been set up to answer specific requests for information.

● Asking people means finding those who are know something about the field that you are enquiring about. The two biggest group communications applications on the network, mailing lists and Usenet newsgroups, are good meeting-places for people with common interests.

Finding someone's email address

Because of the way in which the Internet is constructed, there is no single authoritative directory service which can be guaranteed to locate a user and give you the right email address. There are however several online services and directories you can query, and an international pilot project (X.500) to establish a real distributed directory.

NetFind

Netfind combines a variety of accesses to information services to try and locate a user's address. The easiest way to access it is via a gateway from the Gopher service, so you can point your browser at (for example) `gopher://ds.internic.net: 70/11/.ds/.whitepages` and pick the Netfind service. When asked for the search terms enter the surname first, then one or more keys like the name of the city or organization and the country, for example

`Enter your search terms: `**`flynn cork ireland`**

Netfind will do its searching and return (with any luck) several possible entries for people who match the keywords you typed. You can also obtain client and server software independently to run on your own machine (mail `netfind@xcaret.com` for more details).

The Usenet white pages

This list, maintained at MIT, holds the names and email addresses of users who have posted articles to any of the Usenet newsgroups. If it is likely that the person you're looking for reads and posts news, or mails to a mailing list which is echoed in the news system, then their name and address will probably be here. Send a 1-line email message to `mail-server@rtfm.mit.edu` saying

```
send usenet-addresses/name
```

where *name* is the surname of the person you are looking for. This will return a list to you by email of all matches for *name*, from which you can try to identify the address.

Four11

Four11 is a commercial user directory service at `http://www.four11.com`. You can try it out for free: membership brings additional benefits such as expanded listings, in-depth searches using a search agent, *PGP* key services, and your entry linked to your own home page.

The whois command

The information in WHOIS databases tends to be organizational, rather than personal, so it's at its most useful for finding the street addresses or phone numbers of organizations on the Internet, and the names of the network managers or support staff at each site. You just type

```
whois name
```

where *name* is the surname, site name, or company name you are looking for:

```
whois caltech.edu
whois gadgets
whois clinton
```

NETSERV UDS (User Directory Service)

This is a directory of users on BITNET (including TERENA [formerly EARN], NETNORTH, GULFNET, and others). Although it registers only users on BITNET machines, many of these are also on the Internet, and anyone on any network can query the directory by email. You need to know what site the person works at: to get this, send a 1-line email message to `netserv@bitnic.educom.edu` saying `get bitearn nodes`. This will return you a list of all sites: these are short (maximum eight characters) abbreviations for each of the machines connected to BITNET. When you have identified the right one, send another message to the same address, saying `query service sitename` where *sitename* is the abbreviated name of the site. You will get back the address of the computer which handles directory registrations for that site. The final stage is to query that machine by sending a third message to `netserv@site` saying `uds get .name:string` where *string* is the surname or a string of characters from the surname of the person you are looking for.

X.500

This is the emerging international standard for networked directories. Projects in many countries are cooperating to establish the service. Not everyone is participating, so coverage is patchy, although some entire countries have put details of thousands of users into their directories.

There are two ways to look up a user: you can use Telnet to connect to one of the sites running the public directory enquiry software such as `nameflow.dante.net` and login as `de` (no password): you are then prompted for name, department, institution, and country; or you can point your Web browser at one of the Web-to-X.500 gateways such as `http://x500.tu-chemnitz.de:8888/M` and use the on-screen form-fill application (your browser must be capable of handling HTML Level 3 forms to do this).

One way of finding email addresses which is becoming very common is to check if there is a Web or Gopher server at the person's organization, if you know the name of it. A good guess is to use `whois` to find the organization's domain name, and then prefix it with `http://www.` and see if it provides a Web server with a name directory.

Other services

There are two other services which are useful once you have located a user's email address: `finger` and `ping`. The `finger` program retrieves information about individuals or their computers. The `ping` program tests to see if a specific machine is up and running on the network.

To finger an individual, you type `finger` followed by their email address. This will tell you the last time they logged in (or if they're actually logged in at the time, how long they've been connected), whether they have new mail waiting, and the contents of their `.plan` and `.project` files (if they have them). However, many sites consider this a security hole, and have disabled the `finger` server on their machines, so you get no response. If you type only the @-sign and the computer name, without any username, you may get a complete list of everyone logged in at that site at the time.

To ping a site, you type `ping` followed by the name of the computer you are enquiring about, for example `ping rtfm.mit.edu`. This program simply contacts the computer to check that it is alive. On DEC VAX/VMS computers running Multinet, you have to type `multinet ping` instead (and get ready to halt it with with `Ctrl` `c` because this version of `ping` carries on testing repeatedly).

Finding a Web service

As with directories, there is no formal authoritative source for a registry for Web servers. However, OpenMarket, Inc., and First Virtual, Inc. operate a 'New on the Net' registry (`http://directory.net` and `http://www.fv.com/access/`), and the Yahoo server carries a list of places people register and announce their servers (`http://www.yahoo.com/Computer/World_Wide_Web/Announcement_Services/`). there is also the list of known Web servers from (`http://www.w3.org/hypertext/DataSources/WWW/Servers.html`).

One way of finding out if a site you are interested in runs a Web server is (as described above) to prefix their expected domain name with `http://www.` and see if you get a response by pointing your browser at this address. For example, if you suspect that Widgets, Inc. in the USA runs a Web server, check with the `whois` to see if `widgets.com` exists: if so, then `http://www.widgets.com` is probably a good starting-point.

Mailing lists and Usenet newsgroups

If you're looking for some specific information which you can't find by going to a Web server, FTP archive, or name directory, you can ask people involved in the field via the hundreds of mailing lists and thousands of Usenet newsgroups. You can subscribe to these and read what people have to say, then phrase your request accordingly. If you're not planning on remaining subscribed, you should observe the conventional courtesies described in pp. 268–272: while most users are happy to help those who are lost, you need to be aware that they are answering your questions voluntarily, not because it's their job.

Most mailing lists and newsgroups have a **FAQ**, a list of Frequently-Asked Questions, which is designed to help the newcomer by answering the most common queries without them having to post an individual message. Those FAQs relating directly to newsgroups are posted regularly in their respective group and to the group `news.answers`, and can also be downloaded by FTP from `rtfm.mit.edu` in the `pub/usenet-by-hierarchy` directories. For mailing lists, send a request to the list address asking if there is a FAQ and if so, where it may be obtained from. If the mailing list does not accept posts from unsubscribed users, you will have to subscribe first (see details in pp. 47–49).

Chapter 5

Using a WorldWideWeb browser

○ Graphical and character browsers

○ Installing a browser

○ Facilities and navigation

This chapter assumes you have a computer (or access to one) with a full connection to the Internet so that you are ready to start working with the Web. The only program you need to get started is a browser (client), although there are a few other utility programs which you might want to handle external graphics and sound or movies.

What browser you use may be determined for you, if you are using an account on someone else's machine (via a dial-up account, for example). If you are installing one for yourself, you may want to try out several before you settle on one you will use regularly. There is a list of all of them and where to get them below.

If you've already got a browser installed and working, you can jump to p. 95 for a tour of the facilities available, but you need to be aware that other browsers may present the information you see differently (see Table 5.1 and the subsequent details).

Different kinds of browser

Web browsers fall into two categories: 'graphical' and 'character'. The graphical ones can use a range of typefaces in their display, and can handle pictures and sound as well, but are restricted to use in graphical user interfaces (e.g. *MS-Windows*, Apple Macintosh, or Unix/X). A character browser displays typewriter-style text only (although they can download graphics and sound for later use elsewhere), but they can be used from a wider variety of terminals, including terminal windows in graphical user interfaces. This chapter shows most of the popular graphical and character browsers.

With a graphical browser, you use a mouse to point and click at things you want to see, like hypertext references or images. A character browser uses the arrow keys or a reference number and the [Enter] key to select them instead. Graphical browsers run directly from your desktop computer, so they require a direct connection to the Internet, whereas character browsers usually run on your service provider's computer, and you can use them from any indirect connection (although you can get character browsers for your own computer to run using a direct connection as well, if you don't use a graphical interface).

You can use FTP to get a browser from many FTP servers worldwide, and some of them are now available on CD-ROM, or can be licensed in commercial versions. If you want to download one of the publicly-available ones, you should use *Archie* to find the site closest to you (pp. 58–60), but in case you can't find a closer site, the canonical 'home' site is given in each case.

In the descriptions which follow, each browser is illustrated displaying its authors' home page. Most browsers for Unix and VMS are available in both **source code** and **binary** form for many models of computer. Source code is raw programming: you need to have access to a compiler, usually for the 'C' language, in order to build the program; binary means precompiled, ready-to-run. Versions for MS-DOS, *MS-Windows* and Apple Macintosh are almost always supplied in binary form.

Table 5.1   Summary of WorldWideWeb browsers

Name	Source	Platforms
Air Mosaic Express	ftp.spry.com	MS-Win, Mac, Unix/X
Albert	gopher.ufl.edu	VM/CMS
Arena	www0.cern.ch	Unix/X
Cello	fatty.law.cornell.edu	MS-Win
Chimera	ftp.cs.unlv.edu	Unix/X
Emacs w3-mode	ftp.cs.indiana.edu	anywhere Emacs runs
GWHIS Mosaic	Quadralay	Unix/X
InternetWorks	ftp.booklink.com	MS-Win
Lynx	ftp2.cc.ukans.edu	DOS, VMS, Unix
MacWeb	ftp.einet.net	Mac
MidasWWW	freehep.scri.fsu.edu	Unix/X
NCSA Mosaic	ftp.ncsa.uiuc.edu	MS-Win, Mac, X
NetScape Navigator	ftp.netscape.com	MS-Win, Mac, Unix/X
OmniWeb	ftp.omnigroup.com	NeXT
perlWWW	archive.cis.ohio-state.edu	Unix
Samba	www0.cern.ch	Mac
SlipKnot	ftp.netcom.com	MS-Win
tkWWW	ftp.aud.alcatel.com	Unix/X
url_get	ftp.cc.utexas.edu	Unix
Viola	ora.com	Unix/X
VMS	vms.huji.ac.il	VMS
WinWeb	ftp.einet.net	MS-Win
WorldWideWeb	www0.cern.ch	NeXT
WWW	www0.cern.ch	Any linemode

Character-mode (non-graphical) browsers

The original WWW program

This was written by Tim Berners-Lee and the original Web project team at CERN. It can be compiled for almost any system with a C compiler and a full Internet connection, and works with any kind of terminal, even those without a character-addressable screen. Because of this, it does not use arrow-key or mouse controls: instead, hypertext links appear instead as numbers in square brackets after the phrase to which they refer, and you type the number and press the [Enter] key to follow the link.

The source code can be downloaded from www0.cern.ch in pub/www/src (you'll need WWWLibrary.tar.Z and WWWLineMode.tar.Z) and there are binaries for DEC (Alpha, OSF–1, DECstation, and VMS), HP, Mac, MS-DOS, Linux, MS-Windows, IBM (RS6000 and VM/CMS), SGI, and Sun (SunOS and Solaris) on the same machine in pub/www/bin.

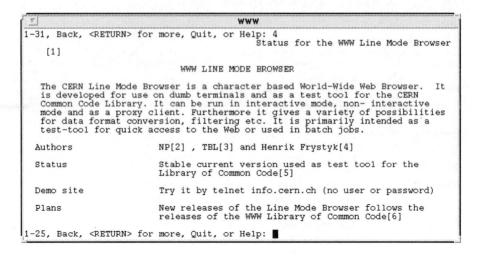

Figure 5.1 The CERN WWW line-mode browser

Lynx

Lynx is the most popular of the character-mode browsers, and it can be used on most systems accessed via character-based terminals or terminal emulators, (VT100 series, *Xterm*, *ProComm* or *Windows Terminal* on PCs, or *Zterm* or *VersaTerm* on Macs, for example). It was written by Lou Montulli at the University of Kansas (now with Netscape Communications Corporation). There is also a native version for MS-DOS called *DosLynx*.

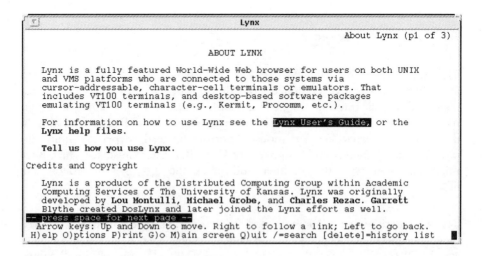

Figure 5.2 Lynx

Lynx uses the arrow keys for navigation, and provides highlighting of the hypertext links, with bold, reverse video, or underline for other forms of character emphasis. The *DosLynx* version can display external PC graphics. Download it from `ftp2.cc.ukans.edu` in and below `pub/WWW/lynx:` binaries for AIX, OSF, Sun4, Ultrix, and VMS are in the same directory. Binaries and source for *DosLynx* are in `pub/WWW/DosLynx`.

Emacs `w3-mode`

This is a major mode for the *Emacs* editing system which lets you use the Web without leaving the editor. This way you can retrieve and download information for reference or inclusion in other files using simple cut and paste even without a graphical operating system. The *Lucid Emacs* version under *X Windows* also enables the display of graphics. *Emacs* also has several HTML editing modes, so it can be used by information providers as an editing and file creation tool as well as a browser (p. 120).

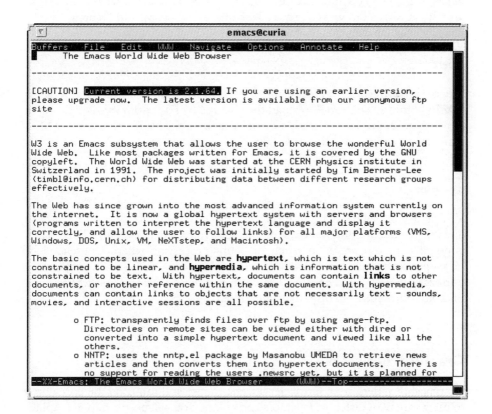

Figure 5.3   Emacs `w3-mode`

W3-mode was written by Bill Perry at the University of Indiana (now with Spry, Inc.) and is available from ftp.cs.indiana.edu in pub/elisp/w3 or from many other public archives for almost any machine that full *Emacs* will run on: Unix, MS-DOS, MS-Windows, DesqView/X, NeXT, OS/2, Windows NT, AmigaDOS.

perlWWW

This is a terminal browser for Unix written in *Perl* (so you need a copy of *Perl* to run it). The author says it is out of date but remains available if anyone wants to do further work on it. Available from archive.cis.ohio-state.edu in pub/w3browser.

SMG

A browser for VAX/VMS systems running the Multinet implementation of TCP/IP. You need the UVMTH runtime library as well if you want to use the binary, otherwise you'll have to recompile it yourself. You can download it from vms.huji.ac.il in vms_client. This browser also works in Hebrew.

Albert

The only fullscreen browser available for IBM VM/CMS mainframes: it requires a 3270 terminal. You can download the package by FTP from www.ufl.edu in directory pub/vm/www. There's a demonstration available if you use tn3270 to connect to nermvs.nerdc.ufl.edu.

url_get

This is a commandline program written in *Perl* for Unix to retrieve a Web document directly into standard output, or redirected into a file. This makes it possible to use *url_get* in batch or script processing where unattended or bulk operation is needed. Download it from ftp.cc.utexas.edu in directory pub/zippy/url_get.tar.Z. Details can be viewed at http://wwwhost.cc.utexas.edu/test/zippy/url_get.html .

Graphical browsers

Graphical browsers are controlled with the mouse and can often be configured to use a variety of different typefaces and colors. You will need external graphics programs for still pictures and movies, and a sound program for audio files to take full advantage of the multimedia capabilities of the Web, but these are usually either supplied with the program or are available from the same sources as the programs themselves.

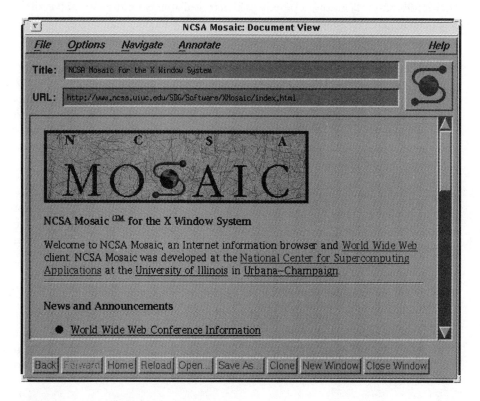

Figure 5.4   Mosaic (X Windows version)

NCSA Mosaic

Mosaic became the best-known of the graphical browsers because of its advanced facilities which have become the standard by which other browsers are judged. The NCSA's is the original free *Mosaic* which runs on Apple Macintosh, PC/MS-Windows and Unix/X Windows computers, but there are now commercial versions under development or being marketed under license via Spyglass Inc. from IBM (for OS/2 Warp), FTP Software, Inc., Microsoft (for Windows95), O'Reilly and Spry, as well as separate developments by some of the original authors, such as *Netscape*.

Originally written by Marc Andreessen, Rob McCool (now both with Netscape Communications Corporation) and Chris Wilson (now with Spry, Inc.) plus others in the development team at the National Centre for Supercomputing Applicationsat the University of Illinois at Urbana-Champaign, USA. Download the program from `ftp.ncsa.uiuc.edu` under the `Web/Mosaic` directory, or from many other sites (ask *Archie*). For the *MS-Windows* version, you also need Microsoft's 32-bit Windows upgrade, which is available from the same FTP sites that keep *Mosaic*. There is a mailing list for users (Appendix C).

PMosaic

PMosaic is a specially-tailored version of Mosaic for Persian and Arabic display. The software (binaries only) is available from `ftp://gpg.com/pub/PMosaic/`.

MacWeb

MacWeb from MCT Corp is available from `ftp.einet.net` in directory `einet/mac/macweb`. MacWeb requires that your Macintosh be configured with System 7 and *MacTCP* 2.0.2 (2.0.4 recommended). Like its companion, *WinWeb*, it is very light on system resources.

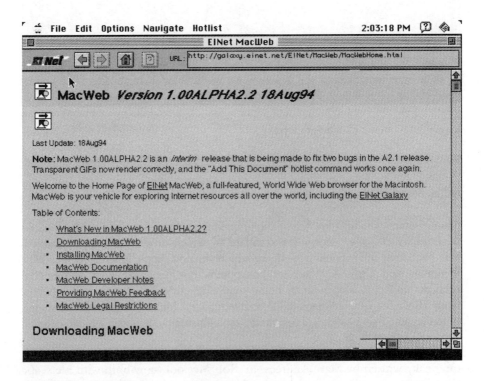

Figure 5.5   MacWeb

There are some nice features like blank line suppression (some early HTML files try to use multiple <p> tags for visual control of whitespace: MacWeb users can specify whether multiple blank lines should be suppressed or allowed); an auto-popup hotlist; user-definable colors and element styles; and the ability to import *Mosaic* hotlists.

Panorama

Panorama is an SGML browser made by SoftQuad with powerful style sheet abilities which communicates with *Mosaic* (for example) in order to retrieve the relevant DTD, style sheet(s) and navigator (table of contents) definitions. In addition, it can follow links to other documents using *HyTime* (a hypertext and time-based application of SGML), and to specific locations within other documents, by asking Mosaic to fetch the corresponding document using its URL. You can find a copy of Panorama at `http://www.oclc.org:5046/oclc/research/panorama/panorama.html`, and details of *HyTime* at `http://www.sil.org/sgml/gen-apps.html#hytime`.

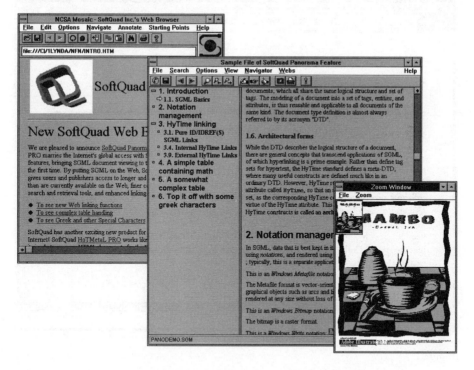

Figure 5.6 SoftQuad's *Panorama* SGML Web viewer working with NCSA *Mosaic*

Panorama Pro is a full-blown SGML browser; it can be used to open local files which are the tip of a web (known in *HyTime* as a Hub document) as well as other SGML files, DTDs, style sheets, and navigators across the Web, using your own Web browser to resolve the URLs. The display is far richer than other Web browsers, supporting arbitrary formatting and display for any element (any element can be a URL, for example, or a table); formatting based on context-sensitivity; color; prefixed and suffixed text; formatting based on attribute value; and on whether something is the first, last, non-first, etc. occurrence of an element in its structure. This is the first time that a fully SGML-sensitive browser has been made available for use on the Web, and it illustrates the enormous potential of this direction in development.

Cello

A browser for *MS-Windows* from Cornell University Legal Information Institute (LII). Features include boxed highlights and configurable colors. Download from `fatty.law.cornell.edu` in `pub/LII/cello`.

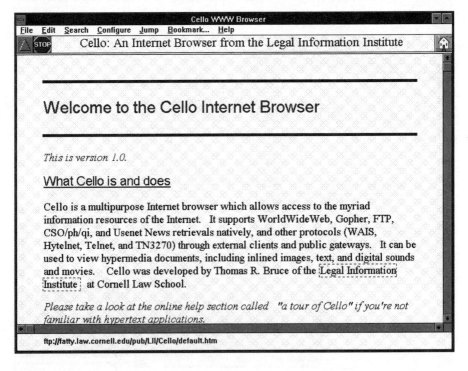

Figure 5.7 *Cello*

Cello has a home page at `ftp://fatty.law.cornell.edu/pub/LII/Cello/default.html` and a mailing list `CELLO-L` (run by ListProcessor: subscription requests to `listserv@law.cornell.edu`—see p. 49 for how to subscribe).

NeXT

The original development work for Web at CERN was done on a *NeXT*, but this browser (which was also intended as an editor) is not currently being supported, although you can still download it from **www0.cern.ch** in directory **pub/www/src**. The current CERN graphical product is the HTML3 browser *Arena*.

WinWeb

Browser for *MS-Windows* from the same stable as *MacWeb* (MCT Corp) and is available from **ftp.einet.net** in directory **einet/pc/winweb**. *WinWeb* has extensive color and font configuration and built-in buttons for searching the *Einet Galaxy* information database.

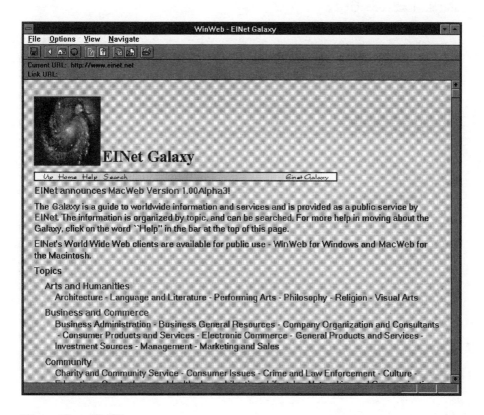

Figure 5.8   *WinWeb*

Both *WinWeb* and *MacWeb* run lighter than most browsers, and provide a very configurable interface to the Web.

OmniWeb

Omni Development Inc's *NeXT* browser can be downloaded using an existing browser from `http://www.omnigroup.com/Software/OmniWeb/OmniWeb.app.tar.gz`. It requires an image filter for graphics: Omni supplies *OmniImageFilter* but *ImageViewer* or *ImageAgent* will also work. Their home page is at `http://www.omnigroup.com/Software/OmniWeb/`.

InternetWorks

InternetWorks from Booklink Technologies is the easiest to install of all *MS-Windows* browsers, as it asks the configuration questions up front, instead of requiring the configuration file to be edited. Complete color and font management, asynchronous image loading and display (p. 193) and support for Usenet News and the `mailto:` **URL**.

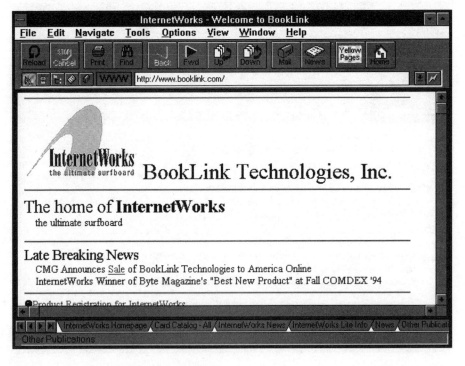

Figure 5.9 *InternetWorks for MS-Windows*

The *Lite* version is available free from `ftp.booklink.com` in `lite` but this version does not support news and email.

Netscape Navigator

This is a commercial browser written by some of the original authors of *Mosaic*, now in business as Netscape Communications Corporation. It has many sophisticated features, including asynchronous image loading (p. 193), support for the `mailto:` URL, access to Usenet News with the ability to post articles, the saving of hotlists as HTML files and a button bar providing direct links to some of the major information systems.

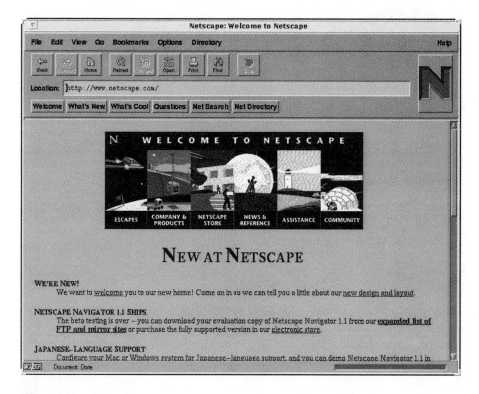

Figure 5.10   *Netscape*

The software can be downloaded for private individual use without charge from `ftp.netscape.com` in the `netscape` directory (it runs on *MS-Windows*, Mac, and Unix/X so there are subdirectories for `windows`, `mac` and `unix`). *Netscape* supports some proposed new formatting extensions to HTML but these currently only work for other *Netscape* users. There is a mailing list for users (Appendix C).

Arena

This graphical browser is being developed (currently) at CERN by Håkon Lie and others, in cooperation with Dave Raggett, the author of HTML3. It supports many of the proposed features of HTML3, including mathematics, tables, and the dynamic flowing of text around images.

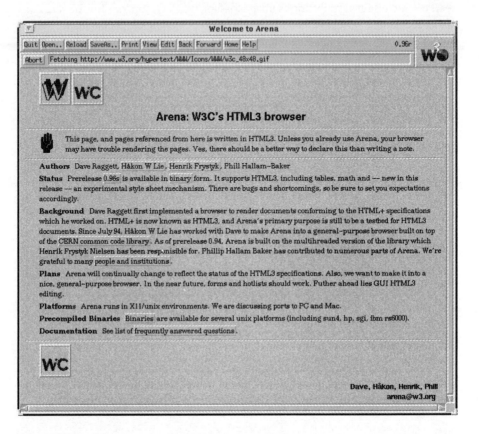

Figure 5.11 *Arena*

Arena is for Unix/X only and can be downloaded from **www0.cern.ch** in **pub/ www/arena**. The software is still under development, so not all the buttons are active.

Emacs w3-mode

Lucid Emacs and *XEmacs* enable the display of graphics (Figure 5.12) and *Emacs* also has several HTML editing modes, so it can be used by information providers as an editing and file creation tool as well as a browser. *Emacs'* editing abilities (mentioned earlier) make it a useful tool when combined with the browser and its existing facilities such as RMAIL and GNUS.

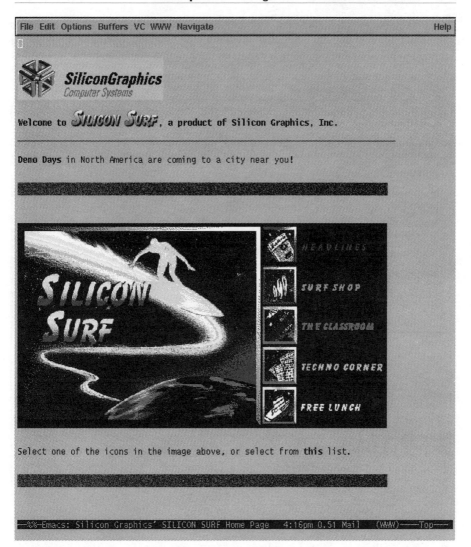

Figure 5.12 *Emacs* as a graphical browser in X Windows

Chimera

A modular browser by John Kilburg at the University of Nevada, Las Vegas, for UNIX/X machines. *Chimera* uses the Athena widget set, so *Motif* is not needed, and it supports forms, inline images, TERM, SOCKS, proxy servers, Gopher, FTP, HTTP, and local file accesses. *Chimera* can be extended using external programs: new protocols can easily be added and alternate image formats can be used for inline images (e.g. *PostScript*, JPEG etc.).

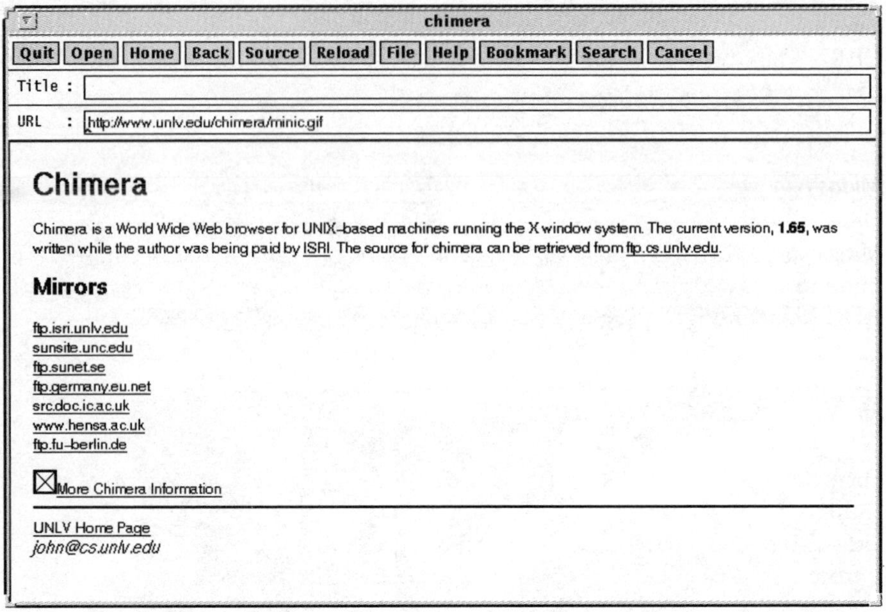

Figure 5.13   *Chimera*

It is available at `ftp.cs.unlv.edu` in the directory `pub/chimera`. There is a site for a partial list of mirrors and other information at `http://www.unlv.edu/chimera/`. The author has compiled and run *Chimera* on Sun Sparc (SunOS 4.1.x) and IBM RS/6000 (AIX 3.2.5) but it should run on anything with X11R[3–6], *imake*, and a C compiler. *Pbmplus* or *netpbm* is required.

WebWorks

A commercial family of Web applications from Quadralay Inc., including *Mosaic*, an HTTP server, search system, and document translator. Details of the products are on `http://www.quadralay.com/products/products.html`.

tkWWW

Currently the only browser for Unix/X apart from *Emacs* `w3-mode` which also does editing. Requires the use of the `tk/tcl` toolkits, which have to be compiled separately.

Download *tkWWW* from `ftp.aud.alcatel.com` in `tcl/extensions`. To add graphics support you also need the `xli` package.

Samba

CERN's Mac browser, available for download from www0.cern.ch in pub/www/bin.

MidasWWW

Midas is a Unix/X browser available from freehep.scri.fsu.edu in freehep/networking_email_news/midaswww. Binaries are available for AIX, Alpha, HPUX, SGI, and Sun4.

Air Mosaic Express

Spry, Inc.'s commercial version of *Mosaic* for *MS-Windows* is claimed to be faster and more robust than the NCSA's, with a demonstration version available which lets you retrieve up to five pages from sites other than Spry's own server. Download it from ftp.spry.com in the demo/AirMosaicDemo directory.

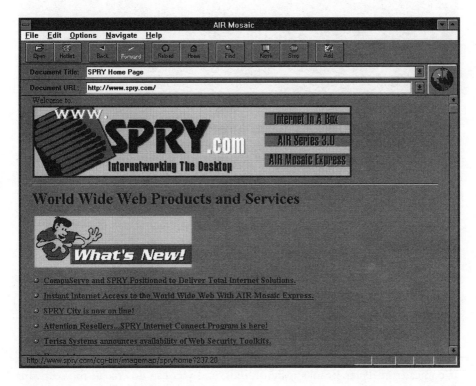

Figure 5.14   *Air Mosaic Express*

SlipKnot

A package for *MS-Windows* providing a graphical browser which runs over an indirect dial-up connection to a Unix shell account. It explicitly does not use SLIP, but instead passes messages to a copy of *WWW* or *Lynx* running on the Unix machine, and uses **xmodem** to transfer the files received back to the PC.

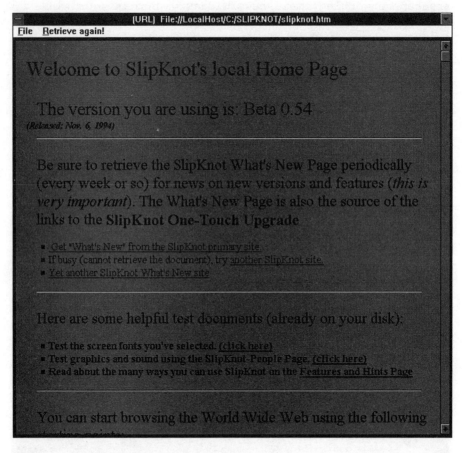

Figure 5.15 *SlipKnot*

This is a convenient way of getting a graphical browser when you don't have access to a full SLIP account. The login and startup can be completely automated. It comes from Peter Brooks (MicroMind), and you can download the software from **ftp.netcom.com** in **/pub/pbrooks/slipknot**.

AMosaic

For the Commodore Amiga, based on the NCSA's *Mosaic*, but developed and maintained independently by a team from the Institute for Theoretical Physics of the State University of New York at Stony Brook. Download from `max.physics.sunysb.edu` in `pub/amosaic`. *AMosaic* requires Amiga OS 2.0 (preferably 3.0), plus AmiTCP, MUI 2.0 and ZGIF (which you can get from `max.physica.sunysb.edu/pub/amosaic/support`).

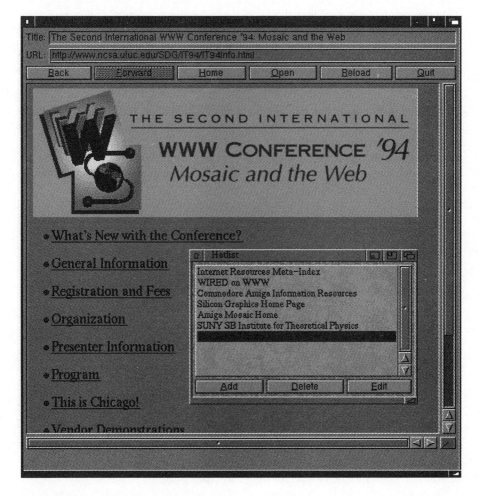

Figure 5.16 *AMosaic* for the Amiga

ViolaWWW

A Unix/X browser from Pei Y. Wei at O'Reilly & Associates, based on the *Viola* scripting language, providing an extensible toolkit for developing hypermedia applications with extra features such as multiple columns and collapsible lists. It is in source form, and needs `imake` to manage compilation. Download Viola from `ftp.ora.com` in `pub/www/viola`.

Using a remote browser by Telnet

If you cannot retrieve or install a browser for some reason, or if you just want to try out the Web without getting your own browser first, you can use Telnet to connect to some public demonstration copies of *Lynx* and *WWW*.

The canonical one is CERN's own *WWW*, `telnet.w3.org` (128.141.201.214, no username or password needed). For users outside Europe, there is *Lynx* running at `ukanaix.cc.ukans.edu` (login as `kufacts`) or at `www.njit.edu` (login as www). Elsewhere in Europe, there are browsers at `info.funet.fi` (Finland), `sun.uakom.cs` (former Czechoslovakia), `vms.huji.ac.il` (Israel) and `fserv.kfki.hu` (Hungary). Login for all systems (where needed) is www, no password. Most of these services are run as a public gesture by the sites concerned, but may not be available at all times.

Installation and configuration

If you have downloaded browser software from the network, or been supplied it on disk or tape, it may be in a compressed, coded, or archived form to save space. Software supplied on disk or tape usually comes with an automated installation routine (usually called `install` or `setup`) which does the necessary unpacking and moving of files for you. This process will be familiar to anyone who has installed PC or Mac software from floppy disk or CD-ROM before.

Software obtained from the network you usually have to uncompress, decode, or dearchive by yourself before you can install the programs: details of how to handle the most common methods of compression, coding, and archiving are in pp. 61–68. When this has been done, there will be one or more files of documentation with names like `README`, `readme.1st` or `INSTALL` which describe any further action you need to take before running the setup program.

The information that you need to provide during installation varies depending on the operating environment you are working in. The basic networking information that you set up in installing your IP software (your IP address and that of your Domain Name Server and IP gateway) will be recognized by the browser automatically, but you may have to edit a configuration file to enter your email address and the names or IP addresses of your email server, Usenet news server, and other network service addresses. Figure 5.17 shows a part of the *MS-Windows Mosaic* configuration file (`mosaic.ini`) containing this kind of information. If you are installing a browser for *MS-Windows* which comes with a `.ini` file, that file should be copied into the `\windows` directory after editing, before you can run the browser. *Netscape*, *InternetWorks*, and some other browsers let you configure operation from the browser display so that you don't have to edit a file to do it.

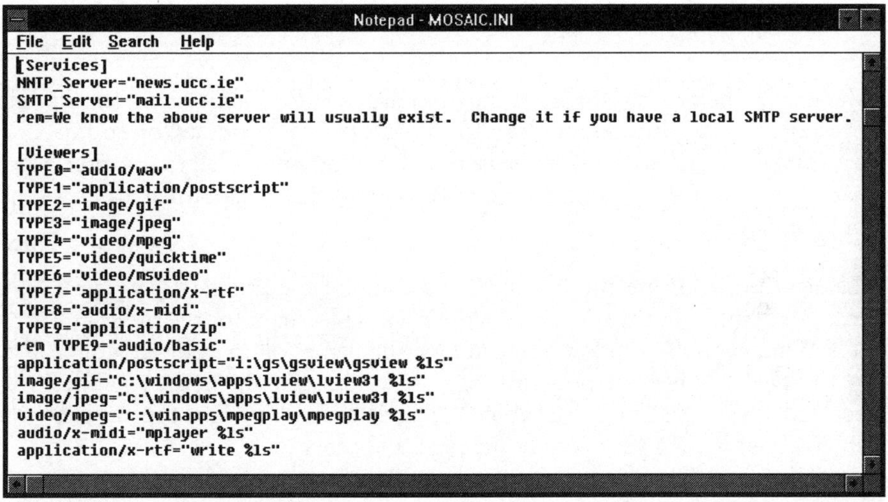

```
Notepad - MOSAIC.INI
File   Edit   Search   Help
[Services]
NNTP_Server="news.ucc.ie"
SMTP_Server="mail.ucc.ie"
rem=We know the above server will usually exist.   Change it if you have a local SMTP server.

[Viewers]
TYPE0="audio/wav"
TYPE1="application/postscript"
TYPE2="image/gif"
TYPE3="image/jpeg"
TYPE4="video/mpeg"
TYPE5="video/quicktime"
TYPE6="video/msvideo"
TYPE7="application/x-rtf"
TYPE8="audio/x-midi"
TYPE9="application/zip"
rem TYPE9="audio/basic"
application/postscript="i:\gs\gsview\gsview %ls"
image/gif="c:\windows\apps\lview\lview31 %ls"
image/jpeg="c:\windows\apps\lview\lview31 %ls"
video/mpeg="c:\winapps\mpegplay\mpegplay %ls"
audio/x-midi="mplayer %ls"
application/x-rtf="write %ls"
```

Figure 5.17   NCSA *Mosaic* for *MS-Windows* configuration

One thing that you should set up yourself is the Uniform Resource Locator (**URL**) of the home page you want the browser to display each time it starts up (URLs are described on pp. 95–103). The convention is to have an environment variable called WWW_HOME containing this, although some browsers also allow you to specify it in the configuration file. Most browsers also come with a default value, set to point to their authors' or suppliers' own welcome page. The documentation should explain which value takes priority when the browser starts. You will probably want to change the default after having seen it a few times. To set this variable to your own value, type a command like:

Unix (Bourne shell)

```
set WWW_HOME=http://www.acme.org/welcome.html
export WWW_HOME
```

Unix (C shell)

```
setenv WWW_HOME http://www.acme.org/welcome.html
```

MSDOS and MS-Windows

```
set WWW_HOME=http://www.acme.org/welcome.html
```

VMS

```
define WWW_HOME "http://www.acme.org/welcome.html"
```

You may want to edit the relevant commands into your system startup file (`.login` for Unix, `autoexec.bat` for MS-DOS/MS-Windows, or `login.com` for VMS) so that it takes effect every time your computer is started. Apple Macs have no facility for environment variables, so this information has to go in the configuration file.

Character browsers are run by typing the name of the program (e.g. `lynx`, `www` etc.). For graphical browsers you double-click on the icon for the program (or in an X Windows shell window you can type the name followed by an ampersand, e.g. `arena &`). When the program starts, it will retrieve the home page that you specified when installing it (see above). The details in Part Two explain how you can go about writing your own home page and other files.

If the browser does not run when you do this, or runs but immediately halts, perhaps with an error message, then you need to re-examine how it has been installed, and whether all the files and services it expects to find are in the places where it expects to find them. Look carefully at the error message, if one is displayed, as it will usually give a clue as to what is amiss. Some of the most common problems are:

- The program itself may be corrupted, or may be the wrong version for your operating system, or there may be a major conflict between it and some other program you are running at the same time.
- If you downloaded the program from the network using FTP, did you remember to set the type of file to Binary beforehand? If not, you'll have to download it again.
- If you get non-response on a PC or Mac, disable any memory-resident auto-start programs like TSRs or INITs and reboot the computer before you try again: it may be that some internal setting of one of them is interfering with the network or memory setup. When you have the browser running, re-load the TSRs or INITs one by one until you find the fault.
- Check that your network connection is stable and active: you should be able to check with the `ping` or `ftp` programs that you are connected to the outside world correctly.

If you still get no response, then you'll have to call in some outside help. Try to have full details ready of the make and model of your computer and operating system, the type of network connection and network software, and the name and version of the browser you are trying to run. The authors and supporters of free browser programs are usually happy to field questions about installation and configuration of their own programs, but they get a lot of email and calls, so it's only fair to examine the problem thoroughly before contacting them direct. You can also post a query to one of the newsgroups or mailing lists for Web discussions (Appendix C), but be sure to give all the relevant information about your setup, to make it easier for people to help you: don't just say your browser won't run.

How to use a Web browser

Once your browser is running, you can start navigating through the WorldWideWeb. The explanations in this section refer to all browsers, although there are fractional differences between the exact names used by each browser to describe the various functions they have available. Where a specific browser does not offer a particular function, it is indicated. There is a list at the end of this chapter of the keystrokes use by character browsers for the functions mentioned.

The first two things you should find out (and this holds true for any program) are 1) how to get help and 2) how to get out of the program. In a graphical browser, there is the [Help] button (by tradition the righthandmost item in the menu bar at the top of the screen) and the [Quit] or [File/Exit] buttons. In a character browser it varies: for *Lynx* and *Emacs* w3-mode, help is the question-mark ([?]) and in *WWW* it's the command help or the letter [h]; but in all three you type [Q] to leave the program.

In the rest of this section, we're going to look at the three major function groups: navigation (finding your way around the Web), file-handling (doing things with the document which is on display) and referencing (keeping track of where you are and where you've been). We'll also see what options there are to let you tailor the appearance and behavior of your browser to make it fit your own way of working.

Navigation: the Uniform Resource Locator

When your browser starts up, it will retrieve and display the 'home page' specified in its configuration file (or as given by the value of the WWW_HOME environment variable: see p. 93). If you haven't given a value of your own for either of these, the browser will retrieve and display its developers' welcome page. The way that browsers know what document to fetch is by using a URL or Uniform Resource

Locator. This is the network 'address' of a document (or graphic, or sound, or video clip). As we're going to need to refer to them quite a lot from now on, we'll start with a summary of what they look like.

The URL

The URL is a way of telling a browser 1) how to retrieve a document, 2) what computer to retrieve it from, 3) whereabouts on that computer it can be found, and 4) anything that needs doing to or with it before or after it is retrieved. This means there are several parts to a URL: the method of retrieval, called the protocol or 'scheme'; the server name of the computer; the directory and filename of the document; and any optional search terms or labels. Here's an example, the project description of the WorldWideWeb itself:

```
http://www.w3.org/hypertext/WWW/TheProject.html
```

In this example, the protocol is the bit ending with the colon; the server name is the bit between the double slash and the first single slash; and the directory and filename are everything after the first single slash (there are no spaces in a URL). There are a couple of exceptions to this pattern which are mentioned below, but directories, filenames, and hostnames of computers should be familiar to you from applications like email, Telnet, and FTP (pp. 17–18).

The protocol refers to the method by which an information provider has made information available. FTP is one method, Telnet is another, so are WAIS and Gopher. HTTP is HyperText Transfer Protocol, the Web's 'own' way of serving up information, but Web browsers will work with many different protocols.

The protocol is important because it tells your browser how to initiate contact with the machine where the information lives: there's no point in trying to retrieve by Telnet a file which someone has made available by FTP. The common protocols are:

http:

The Web's 'own' protocol, the one used for retrieving information from a HTTP server. This could be text written in HTML, still pictures, sound files, motion video, or just plain text: a HTTP server knows how to recognize filetypes and precedes the transmission with a line telling your browser what kind of file is coming, so that it will know what to do with it. Examples:

```
http://kufacts.cc.ukans.edu/
http://gatekeeper.dec.com/archive/pub/DEC/DECinfo
http://www.hcc.hawaii.edu/dinos/deinonychus.gif
```

`ftp:`

Any file on an anonymous FTP server can be retrieved. If you are retrieving software packages in files with compressed, archived, or encoded filetypes like those described on pp. 61–68, you need to use your browser's *Load to disk* function to tell the browser to store the file on disk, rather than trying to display it on the screen. Example: `ftp://src.doc.ic.ac.uk/computing/gnu/emacs-19.29.tar.Z`.

`gopher:`

The Web supports retrieval from the Internet Gopher system, so anything which is available through Gopher can be got through your browser. Example: `gopher://sunet.se/`

`mailto:`

This is not a retrieval method, but a way of sending email to a specific address (perhaps to send your comments on something, or the contents of a form you have filled in online). Sending mail this way is not supported in all browsers. Example: `mailto:listserv@irlearn.ucd.ie` (an exception: `mailto:` has no slashes after the colon).

`news:`

News articles and newsgroup listings can be retrieved, and some browsers allow posting of articles as well (notably *Netscape*). However, as individual articles eventually expire from most news servers, it is only meaningful to refer to a newsgroup, not a specific article. Example: `news:comp.infosystems.www.announce` (an exception: no slashes after the colon).

`telnet:, rlogin:` and `tn3270:`

A hypertext link can point to interactive services like library catalog systems, remote databases and even multi-user simulation systems. A Web browser will start the Telnet program (in another window if a windowing system is being used), and you can then log on with the relevant username (and password, if any).

Example: `telnet://opac:public@library.unseenu.a-m.dw`, where the username and password come between the double slash and the server name, separated by a colon, and with an 'at' sign between the password and the server name.

file:

This lets you specify a local file on your own disk, not available by using a server. Example: `file:///work/jobs/resume.html` (exception: no network name, just directory and filename). Some browsers use `localhost` to refer to your own machine, even if they are not running under Unix.

Some services which run on a different 'port' than normal need the port number after the server name, separated by a colon, for example `http://www.acme.org:4030/private/web.html`. A **port** is a TCP/IP concept which allows individual services (like Telnet, FTP, HTTP, etc.) to be separately addressed. The allocated port for HTTP is 80, so you only need to specify otherwise if a server is running on some other port.

Many of the machines used to serve information use Unix, so upper- and lower-case letters are significant. Forward slashes are used for all directory and filenames, even if the file is coming from a VAX/VMS or PC system. There is a more detailed discussion of URLs and some additional features in pp. 178–182. Now let's see how to use them.

Following the links

As we saw in Figure 2.1 on p. 8, each highlighted word or phrase on the screen is a hypertext link, either to another place in the same document, to some other document in the Web, or to another object such as a graphical image, sound, or video clip. To activate any of these links, use the ***Follow Link*** function:

In a graphical browser

Use the mouse to move the on-screen pointer onto a highlighted link and press the mouse button once (the left button if there's more than one).

In a character browser (*Lynx*)

Select a link with the arrow keys and press the Enter or Return key.

In an editor browser (*Emacs*)

Press f (forward) or b (backward) to select the link, then press the Enter or Return key.

In a line-mode browser (*WWW*)

Type the number which shows in [square brackets] after a link, and press the Enter or Return key.

This retrieves the object which the link points to, and displays it or plays it. *Mosaic* and some other graphical browsers allow you to create an additional window to display another document in, so you can have several documents displayed simultaneously. As we will see in Chapter 9, it is the URL coded into the markup of the document which causes the word or phrase to be highlighted and which provides the address of the object to be fetched, but this is entirely transparent to the user.

If the document is longer than one screenful, you can use the mouse and the scrollbars at the side to move up and down through the text. In *Lynx*, the plus and minus keys display the next and previous screenfuls: in *Emacs* **w3-mode** it's [Del] and the spacebar; in *WWW* you press [Enter] for the next screen and [U] (up) for the previous one.

Some documents contain images which are links. They are highlighted with a border to show they are links, so clicking on one of these has the same effect as if it had been a piece of text. Character browsers can do this as well, even though they can't display the image, because the substitute text which shows where the image occurs will become a link. A more advanced case of this is the image map, where different parts of an image have been set up as links to different documents. In this case, point and click at the part of the image which interests you, and it should retrieve a document relevant to that bit of the picture.

Pointing at a specific document

You can retrieve any other document in the Web (specifically, one which is not mentioned or highlighted in your current document) at any time by using the ***Open URL*** function, and typing the URL in the space provided (at the top or bottom of the screen, or in a dialog box which pops up). If you are using a system which allows 'cut-and-paste' between different applications, it is possible to mark and copy a URL from some other place (an edit file, mail message, Usenet newsgroup article, or terminal window) and paste it into the dialog box instead of having to type it by hand. Most graphical systems allow this, as does *Emacs*, which also allows completion of the URL from your global history list (p. 105) to minimize typing.

If you give a URL without a filename at the end of it (so that it ends with the server name or a directory name and a trailing slash), most servers will return a list of files to choose from, or an index or other default file specified by the owner or operator. There are details of how to make this work for your own files on p. 244.

Although the URL specification allows the use of `file://` as a retrieval method, some browsers have a separate ***Open Local*** function, which pops up a file dialog where you can select the name of a local file on your disk instead of one accessed through a server on the network.

FTP in a Web browser

If you are retrieving a non-HTML file, such as a program or data from an FTP server, you obviously don't want it displayed, but stored on disk instead. To do this, use the **Load to disk** function *before* you activate the link or use the **Open URL** function. When the file is retrieved, instead of displaying it, you will be asked to give the name you want it stored on disk as.

When you connect to an FTP server from your browser, each file and each subdirectory becomes a hypertext link, so clicking a file will start retrieving it, and clicking on a subdirectory name will display a list of files in that subdirectory. The difference between files and subdirectories is marked on the screen with different icons, or (in a character browser) with the words FILE or DIR.

Monitoring progress and halting retrieval

While your browser is fetching a file, it may display a counter of the number of bytes (characters) received so far, and the total number of bytes in the file, so you can monitor progress. In the case of *Mosaic*, *Netscape*, and some others, a symbol or corporate logo animates in the corner of the window while file retrieval is in progress.

If retrieval is slow, perhaps because of network congestion or an unexpectedly large file, you can stop it, leaving the display unaltered. To do this, use the **Abort transfer** function (*Netscape* has a red dot button for this; in *Mosaic* you click on the 'Wired World'; in *Lynx* you press Z).

Backwards and forwards

All browsers remember the sequence of documents you visit, so they have a **Back** function to return you to the previous link. If you repeat this, you will progressively go back until you get to the page you started with. If you use this to go back, you can use the **Forward** function to return down the path you just went back up, but if you diverge from it, then the remaining documents of the previous path are no longer memorized. There is also a **Home** function which jumps back to your home page immediately.

Loading and reloading

Graphical system retrieve inlined graphics along with (or immediately after) the document they appear in. As graphics can sometimes be very large, you can turn them off with the **Delay images** function, so only the text will appear on the screen, with the places for the graphics represented by a symbol.

Panel 5.1   What to do when a URL doesn't work

When a URL (say, `http://foo.bar.com/pub/users/joe/docs/info.html`) doesn't work you can try the following, listed below roughly in the order of difficulty, easiest first:

1   Reload, in case there was a very brief temporary problem with making the connection;

2   Examine the URL for components with time significance, and if found, change them. For example, change `http://www.ux.edu/catalog/classes/fall94/list.html` to `http://www.ux.edu/catalog/classes/spring95/list.html` (of course we usually aren't lucky enough to have it this easy);

3   Take off the filename and directory name, to see if Joe has some kind of index: `http://foo.bar.com/pub/users/joe/`. This will load `index.html` [or some such file] in the `joe/` directory, if it exists. Otherwise it will show a listing of the files available for public access, or if the directory is not public, will give a message to that effect;

4   Take off everything but the root server name to see whether the site has a welcome page: `http://foo.bar.com/pub/` or `http://foo.bar.com/`;

5   Try the same thing without the trailing slashes: `http://foo.bar.com/pub` or `http://foo.bar.com`;

6   Many hosts are creating new `www.` machines and moving all Web documents there. So try changing `foo` to `www`: `http://www.bar.com/pub/users/joe/docs/info.html` and `http://www.bar.com/`;

7   Use a search engine to find the parent organization of whoever created the resource, and try to find the resource through the links from the main page of that organization;

8   Find a person who might know the current status, and ask them.

Steps 1–6 take a little more time than doing a library catalog search. Step seven takes a bit longer, and step eight generally takes a day or two if the person responds to email. Still faster than [postal mail], but the main problem is that success is by no means assured. After 1–6 are exhausted, seven might yield no results and eight might be impossible. So the problem still exists.

[I am grateful to Carlos McEvilly (`cim@lanl.gov`) for permission to reproduce these helpful hints. Carlos is author of the *How to make great WWW Pages* [McEvilly n.d.] document.]

If you turn graphics on again, you have to request the document to be reloaded (fetched again) with the **Reload** function. This is also useful if you are developing your own files, and editing one in another window: each time you save the file, you can use your browser's **Reload** function to get the new version redisplayed. On an indirect connection, you can also use it to have the document redisplayed if there has been communications interference which has messed up your screen, although most terminal systems also have a **Refresh** function, usually Ctrl L or Ctrl W.

URLs which do things

Not all documents are static. Some are generated on the fly from programs which will accept further input from you via a dialog box. These are often called 'searchable' documents, although the document itself is not usually the thing you want to search, it's more likely to be a database of some kind, and the document is just the front-end which lets you type in a value or word to use. When you retrieve a document like this, it will explain what you can do, and a dialog box will become active on the screen where you type the relevant word or phrase and click OK or press Enter. In the case of *Lynx*, you have to press [s] before you type the search term; in *Emacs* you have to press Enter and in *WWW* you must type find or [f].

If a document contains a form for you to fill in, position the cursor in each field as you work through it by using the mouse or the Tab key. In some *X Windows* implementations, the BackSpace key does not work in form-fill documents: use the Delete key instead. In character browsers, you have to activate each field by pressing the Enter key on it before typing the text you want to enter. At the bottom of the form there will be a Submit button or link which sends the form away to be processed.

What to do if it goes wrong

If you make a mistake in typing a URL, you will get an error message when the browser tries to retrieve it. If the mistyping was in the name of the server machine, and the name you typed does not exist, the network name lookup mechanism will fail to find it, and the browser will display something like

```
Failed DNS lookup on wwq.acme.org
```

You need to check the correct server name, and then repeat the *Open URL* operation as above, giving the right name.

If you got the server name correct, but made a mistake in the directory or filename, the browser will display an error message from the server saying it couldn't find the file you asked for:

```
404 Not Found
```

(there is a list of HTTP status codes in Appendix D). Again, you need to repeat the process with the correct name. It is of course possible that the owner of the file (or the owner of the server) has removed the file or renamed it. If it is supposed to be available for public retrieval and you cannot find it, the best thing is to mail the owner or server operator and ask where the file has gone or what its new name is. If this fails to provide the solution, you can post a query on the relevant mailing list or Usenet newsgroup asking what has happened to it.

Lynx offers a useful service for this kind of error when you are following a link from within a file: if a `<link>` element giving the email address of the person responsible for the file existed in the document header, mail is sent to that address warning that a user attempted to follow a link which failed.

If the URL is correct but there is a network fault between you and the server, the browser will try for a specified period of time or number of attempts, and then if it still can't get through, will give up and say so. The period of time is usually something that can be set in the configuration file when you install the browser.

It is also possible that the owners of certain files have arranged for security checks, so that they can only be retrieved by people from particular network addresses, either because the files contain private information, or because they are not intended for public use for some other reason (there may be a charge for accessing the information). In this case, your browser will display a message from the server saying that you are not authorized to retrieve this file.

File handling

Once you've got a document on-screen, there are several things you may want to do with it apart from read it and follow the links:

Saving a document

The **Save As**... allows you a choice of several formats to save the document in: usually the original HTML file, complete with markup, ready for re-use; or plain text, with all the markup removed, either formatted or unformatted; or as a *PostScript* file for typographic printing (*Emacs* and *Lynx* offer the alternative of *LATEX*: *WWW* just does plain text). A file dialog lets you give the directory and filename you want the text stored in.

Printing a document

Similar options to saving a document are also available to let you print it with the **Print**. Graphical browsers may also allow you to preview the page image before confirming the print operation, and let you specify page size, margins, and other print-configuration options.

There are other options for printing, external to the browser, such as the several conversion routines mentioned in pp. 294–295. The question has been raised as to how you can print a document and all its links, but there is the problem of where to stop: many documents are heavily linked to others elsewhere which in turn are heavily linked. . . you would eventually end up printing the entire planet's collection of Web files!

Don't forget that if you are using a character-mode browser running on another computer over an indirect connection, 'printing' means using the printer attached to *that* machine, not yours. If you want local printing in this case, you need to download or otherwise capture the file or image and then print it on your own printer.

The quality of printed Web files, even from graphical browsers is not good. It is certainly sufficient as a draft or as a working copy, but to get professional-level typesetting you should use a conversion routine to turn the HTML source code into a form suitable for a high-end DTP system such as *TEX* or *FrameMaker*. Some experimental services are planned to allow you to send a document or its URL to an email server, which will return you a *PostScript* file ready to print, but details are not yet available.

Mailing a document

You can also send the current document to someone else by email with the ***Mail to.*** . . . The choice of formats is again similar to those for saving and printing. A dialog box will let you give the email address and the subject line. On direct-connection PC, Mac, and Amiga systems you need to ensure that you have a mail user agent or `sendmail` program installed and that your configuration file contains a valid IP address for a mail gateway which will accept the message for transmission.

Viewing the source file

The ***Source view*** function lets you see the HTML source of the document. This is very useful if you want to find out why something displays as it does, or read the source code to identify and retrieve an inline graphic URL as an external file so it can be saved for re-use. However, if you want to re-use a file in this way, you should check that you are not breaching any copyright restrictions.

Finding a word or phrase

In a long document you might want to locate a particular word which could be a long way down the file. The ***Find*** function lets you type in a word to search for in the current document. There may also be a ***Find next*** function to allow repeated searches for the same word. This is not the same function as what is called a 'searchable document': see p. 102.

Editing the document

Some browsers have an **Edit** function to let you edit the file locally, perhaps before printing or mailing it. If the document has come from somewhere other than your own machine, though, you cannot the save it back where it came from: only the file owner or server operator can do that.

References

Because people often want to store a URL reference so they can refer to it again, several functions exist for recording and retrieving lists of documents visited, or the URLs referenced within a document.

History files

As explained on p. 100, browsers maintain an internal list of documents visited in the current session. The **History** functions let you save this list or append it to an existing list, so that you have a record of your travels. *Mosaic* programs keep a permanent global history file automatically, storing a record of every document you ever visited.

Hotlists

The **Hotlist** functions let you maintain a separate list of documents you know you will want to revisit frequently, and pick from them whenever you need to. You can use these functions to add, delete, or modify the details displayed. As hotlists can grow quite large over time, there are conversion routines to turn them into HTML files in their own right, so they can be opened either using the **Open Local** function, or installed in a server for others to access as well. A nice feature of *Netscape* is that it saves hotlist URLs as a HTML file, so they can be re-edited later into other files more easily.

Annotations

Mosaic programs let you create a local file of comments, called annotations, which you can make with the **Annotate** function. This lets you add comments of your own which will be displayed whenever you open that document again.

The FAQ

As with most widespread Internet topics, the Web has its own list of

Frequently-Asked Questions (FAQ) for new users, maintained by Thomas Boutell. You can access the most recent version in hypertext form at `http://sunsite.unc.edu/boutell/faq/www_faq.html` or you can retrieve a copy by anonymous FTP to `rtfm.mit.edu` in `pub/usenet/news.answers/www/faq` or by sending email to `mail-server@rtfm.mit.edu` saying `send usenet/news.answers/www/faq/*`. The FAQ can be accessed directly from the *FAQ* function of *Netscape* without you having to type the URL.

Mailing developers and authors

As mentioned on p. 103, Lynx will automatically use the `<link>` element if it holds a `mailto:` URL whenever it encounters a link which cannot be activated: the address is presumed to be that of the author of the file. In addition to this, *Mosaic, Lynx, Netscape*, and *Emacs* `w3-mode` have a *Mail developers* function to let you report bugs or other problems with the program.

Listing URLs

WWW has a *List references* function (the `list` command) which displays a list of all the URLs referenced in the current document, and allows you to choose one to follow.

File information

Lynx and *Emacs* `w3-mode` have a *File info* function (an ⌑ in `w3-mode`; the ⌑ key in *Lynx*) which displays all the information available about the current file: size, URL, owner, etc.

Reading and posting Usenet News

Although all browsers can use the `news:` URL method to display articles from a Usenet newsgroup, and some (e.g. *Netscape*) can post articles as well, they don't handle things in the same way as dedicated newsreader programs which offer many more facilities for controlling how you read and respond to articles.

Options

We saw (pp. 92–95) that there are often settings you can make to determine how your browser looks and performs. Most configuration files use self-explanatory names for the settings, so changing them is not a problem. For these changes to take effect, you usually have to exit and restart the browser.

Graphical browsers also let you change some of the settings from menu items on the screen while the browser is running. The selection of fonts and colors, toolbar options, and hotlist pages is entirely a matter of personal need and taste, but if you want to customize your browser, the following functions exist in many of the menus, although not all browsers offer all of them.

● Fonts: selection of the fonts usually affects the structural elements of a document: plain text, the six levels of headings, emphasis, strong emphasis, block quotations, different kinds of list, and the fixed-width display of preformatted text.

● Color: background and foreground color are the most common choices, but *WinWeb* for example lets you select color for each font as well.

● Toolbar and status line: the row of icons below the menu headings and a status line at the bottom of the screen may be independently enabled or disabled.

● Home page: the default page displayed at startup may be set and reset.

● The display of the current URL and/or title may be turned off or on.

● The way in which hypertext links (anchors) are displayed according to whether you have ever visited that document or not may be influenced (color or underlining changes, for example).

Chapter 6

How it works

- ○ The client–server mechanism
- ○ Text and markup
- ○ SGML and HTML
- ○ Editing for Web files

This chapter is for those readers who need to understand the details of what is going on behind the scenes. It also lays the ground for the next part of the book, where we look at how you go about writing and providing your own files for other people to use.

The first section covers the concept of client–server information retrieval and how browsers interact with servers. We then look at the idea of markup and how to specify the construction of a file. Finally, a section on editors that can be used in the creation of files for the Web.

Clients and servers

When we looked earlier at the uses of the Internet, we saw that they involve an exchange of information between a provider and a consumer. In the case of humans, either party can provide or consume information: users of mailing lists and Usenet newsgroups are constantly asking and answering questions. In the case of the exchange of information between computer programs in an information system like Web, however, only one is normally the provider and one the consumer. The consumers are the users, whose programs act as interpreters between them and the computer, translating requests into a formalized language: the job of the provider's program is to serve up information on demand from its repository. This relationship has been formalized into the 'client–server' methodology, and it is widely used in networked information retrieval.

In the case of Web, the browser programs are the clients. The servers are hidden from view, but are programs running on thousands of machines across the network, each serving the clients with files from their own repositories or filestores. To make it work, there has to be an agreed language or protocol for use between client and server which operates behind the scenes every time you click on a hypertext link on your screen.

We have already seen on pp. 95–103 that a URL describes the method of access for files in the Web: this method is the protocol, and the client uses it to send a formatted request to the relevant machine address requesting transmission of the file specification which forms the rest of the URL, with any optional details. The server receives this, identifies the client's address (which got sent automatically along with the request), finds the file and transmits it back to the client.

Each protocol is a formal definition of how to negotiate the exchange of information between client and server. In the case of the Web, many protocols can be used, but one in particular, called **HTTP** (*HyperText Transfer Protocol* [Berners-Lee, Fielding and Frystyk 1994]) specifies how a client may request a file from a Web server and how the server is to transmit it.

Two features of HTTP are worth noting at this stage: the way in which an HTTP server identifies what kind of file is being transmitted, and the kind of connection between client and server that is used to handle the request and the transmission.

HTTP servers have in their configuration a list of types of file which are defined in *MIME* [Borenstein and Freed 1993], the Multipurpose Internet Mail Extensions specification. This lets the server notify the client with a header (modeled on those used in email standards) that the file which follows has a specific type of content, so that the client can take the appropriate action. A MIME content-type header looks like this:

```
Content-type: text/html
```

The filetype is described with a major and a minor content-type, separated by a slash. In the case of the Web's 'native' format of information, HTML (HyperText Markup Language), the content-type is text/html or text/html, version=2. 0. In most cases this typing is done automatically, because the server checks the filetype of each file requested against its configuration list of MIME types, and transmits the appropriate header. If you are writing a script, however, you need to include this manually (see pp. 250–257 for details of how to do it). There is a reference list of the standard MIME types in Appendix D.

Browsers use the same table to identify which external applications are to be used for files retrieved which are not text/html. The configuration file might, for example, specify a program to be run when a *PostScript* file is encountered by giving the name of the *GhostScript/GhostView* viewer:

```
application/postscript          c:\gs\gs261\gsview
```

The other point is that the connection between HTTP client and server is only maintained for the duration of the request (in one direction) and the transmission of the file (in the other direction). Unlike Telnet or FTP, where the line is held open all the time until the session ends, and can change in state depending on whether the user is transmitting or receiving, a HTTP connection is known as 'stateless': a client sends a request and then shuts up. When the server receives the request, it finds the file and sends it back, and that's it. Once a request has been sent, a client itself does indeed change state internally, in that it sits and waits for a response from the server, but the connection between them is not held open during this period. In networking terms this means that a HTTP connection is lighter on network resources than an equivalent (say) FTP connection, although it remains to be seen whether or not the phenomenal growth in HTTP traffic overall becomes a cause for concern in the provision of capacity.

Universal text

If you have worked on more than one type of computer or used more than one type of program, you will probably have noticed that not all information is stored in the same way. Most programs store information in a manner specially designed for them, because of varying needs for speed, compactness, or some other criterion. Frequently this is a form of storage which uses special codes developed solely for that specific program. Coding the information has also been a convenient way for manufacturers to prevent users from moving their information to or from a competitor's product, an understandable but somewhat short-sighted method of market protection which has now largely backfired as users demand more flexibility.

Using this kind of storage works fine if you can guarantee you will never have any need to transfer the information to another make of program or computer, but it is clearly not a good way to keep information which is going to be used on all kinds of makes and models of computer all over the world, where you have no idea what hardware or software the user has. In this case, using one specific set of private codes would be the surest way to cripple a networked information project at birth. Although Web software can handle a wide variety of file formats, the format most commonly used between HTTP server and client is the most widespread public format of computer information there is: plain text.

For largely irrelevant historical reasons, there is currently (1995) only one univer-sally accepted way of representing plain text in a form which can be used on *any* computer. This is a specification established over the years by various standards authorities and now known (with minute variations) as ISO 646 (International Reference Version) or ASCII (American Standard Code for Information Inter-change). It defines 128 characters: codes 0 to 31 and 127 are for the computer's own internal control purposes and codes 32 to 126 are the 94 printable characters (Table 6.1).

Despite its other drawbacks, which we will see below, the overriding advantage of plain text is that it can be transferred onto almost any kind of computer with no need for conversion. The only major exception is IBM mainframes, which use a set of characters called EBCDIC, but translation to and from ASCII is provided for automatically in most cases.

Identifying text with markup

While plain text of the ASCII or ISO 646 variety is adequate for continuous prose written in English, it contains no symbols for many of the letters essential in other languages, especially accents. Equally importantly, there are no visible symbols for marking the structure of a document: nothing to show headings, paragraphs, lists, graphics, or any of the common attributes of a piece of text apart from linebreaks, tabs, and spaces.

For many decades, computer users and programmers had to devise their own methods of making these things evident: hence the private coding systems mentioned earlier. Wordprocessors and other text-handling systems use a wide variety of printing and non-printing symbols to mark the text to indicate changes

Table 6.1 The ISO 646 IRV or ASCII character set

Num	Character	Num	Character	Num	Character	Num	Character
000	null	032	space	064	@	096	'
001	start of heading	033	!	065	A	097	a
002	start of text	034	"	066	B	098	b
003	end of text	035	#	067	C	099	c
004	end of transmission	036	$	068	D	100	d
005	enquire	037	%	069	E	101	e
006	acknowledge	038	&	070	F	102	f
007	bell	039	'	071	G	103	g
008	backspace	040	(	072	H	104	h
009	horizontal tab	041	)	073	I	105	i
010	linefeed	042	*	074	J	106	j
011	vertical tab	043	+	075	K	107	k
012	formfeed	044	,	076	L	108	l
013	carriage return	045	-	077	M	109	m
014	shift out	046	.	078	N	110	n
015	shift in	047	/	079	O	111	o
016	data link escape	048	0	080	P	112	p
017	device control 1	049	1	081	Q	113	q
018	device control 2	050	2	082	R	114	r
019	device control 3	051	3	083	S	115	s
020	device control 4	052	4	084	T	116	t
021	negative acknowledge	053	5	085	U	117	u
022	synchronize	054	6	086	V	118	v
023	end transmission block	055	7	087	W	119	w
024	cancel	056	8	088	X	120	x
025	end of medium	057	9	089	Y	121	y
026	substitute	058	:	090	Z	122	z
027	escape	059	;	091	[	123	{
028	file separator	060	<	092	\	124	|
029	group separator	061	=	093	]	125	}
030	record separator	062	>	094	^	126	~
031	unit separator	063	?	095	_	127	delete

in appearance: these symbols are known as 'markup', using the term borrowed from the activities of printers' proofreaders. They range from the dot-lines used by early programs like *RUNOFF* and *Wordstar* through the hidden control codes of most modern wordprocessors or DTP systems to the sophisticated programming commands of systems like $T_{E}X$ and *PostScript*.

While these work fine on the screen and on paper, almost none of them describe *what* you are doing, only how it looks. In a heterogenous network environment like the Internet, there is no way to know what display facilities your readers have, so using a system which only describes appearance is pointless: you need to be able to describe the *function* of elements of your document, like 'this is a heading' and 'this is an item in a list', and leave the rendering largely up to the abilities of the user's client (browser).

Structural and visual markup

Almost all wordprocessor and DTP systems use what has been termed visual markup: the control codes are instructions about how the text should appear, with no indication of what part it plays in the document. Section headings, for example, are given a certain positioning, font, and size, but with no indication that they were actually headings: as far as the program is concerned, they are just a bunch of dots on the screen or the paper. Almost the sole exceptions for many years were *RUNOFF* and *LATEX*, where the emphasis was on logical markup [Lamport 1988] or structural markup. As an example, section headings in *LATEX* are typed in such a way as to identify what their rôle is:

```
\subsection{Identifying text with markup}
```

and only given an instantiation (positioning, font, and size) when processed for display or printing on a particular occasion. This way, the structural information (the fact that some text is a subsection heading) is inviolably preserved in the file, and the visual information (the appearance on a particular occasion) can be stored separately, in a style file.

Purely visual markup is enormously useful in short or transient documents, non-repetitive formats like display advertisements, and in matter requiring a high degree of visual intervention to create, but logical markup offers other facilities particularly suited to portability and multi-platform use, to long or complex documents, and to text which may need to be re-used in other ways than the original requirement. It is far more effective to say 'typeset subsection headings in Pandora 14/16pt bold flush left' in a style file once only (because your subsections are already identified in the text) than to have to manually edit the appearance for several dozen subsection entries, even with repeat-replace in a good editor. Although the concept of programmable logical markup in plain text files has been around for over 15 years, many DTP systems and wordprocessors have been slow to adopt it in their style files, preferring to dispense with the facilities it makes available for long-term usage in favour of concentrating on the facilities for modifying the appearance (what one writer has called 'instant textual gratification').

To allow better control over the identification of content and structure as well as appearance, a generalised language was developed in 1985 to allow a document to be marked up in a way that could be formally specified and tested, and which would allow files to be moved between different computers without the need for format conversion and the consequent loss of information. This was the Standard Generalized Markup Language (**SGML**: ISO 8879), which is a language for defining how a document is constructed. In SGML, each element of the text (headings, paragraphs, lists, etc.) in a particular type of document is defined as 'belonging' somewhere: for example, list items belong in a list, not in a section header. A description of a document type can be used both to enforce compliance with a specific structure (like making sure the management summary is not left out of a report), or to describe an existing structure (like which speakers say which lines in a play). After a slow start SGML is rapidly becoming accepted as the most adaptable way devised so far to improve the reliability and usability of text documents.

Markup for the Web

After all this, it will come as no surprise to find that the 'native' structure of documents for Web was defined using SGML. A Document Type Description (**DTD**) called HyperText Markup Language (**HTML**) is used, which defines what textual elements are available and how they fit together to make a document. HTML was developed by the inventor of the Web, Tim Berners-Lee, and others, and is now in its second version, HTML 2.0, revised by a Working Group of the Internet Engineering Task Force (IETF). The specification of the HTML 2.0 DTD can be found at `ftp://ds.internic.net/internet-drafts/draft-ietf-html-spec-02.txt` (plain text: there's a `.ps` version in *PostScript* as well). The work of the Working Group is documented at `http://www.ics.uci.edu:80/pub/ietf/html/`.

A more advanced version called HTML3 is under development, which will include many features like mathematics and tables, which were not part of the original HTML.

The second part of this book describes the elements and features of HTML files and how to write them and use them. There are advance details of the HTML3 proposals in Appendix B. If you want to know more about SGML itself, an interim report of the Text Encoding Initiative (**TEI**), which has developed a DTD for encoding texts for the Humanities, contains a chapter called *A Gentle Introduction to SGML* [Burnard and Sperberg-McQueen 1994], and this is a good starting-point: it is available at `http://etext.virginia.edu/bin/tei-tocs?div=DIV1&id=SG`. You can read more about the TEI project itself at `http://www.ucc.ie/info/net/tei.html`. The NCSA maintain a resource on SGML for the Web at `http://www.ncsa.uiuc.edu/SDG/Software/Mosaic/WebSGML.sgml`.

When you write using use structural markup, you are freed to a large extent from having to concern yourself with the minutiae of final appearance while you are actually doing the writing: unless you are William Morris you are more likely to be concerned with *what* you are saying rather than how your publisher will have it finally typeset, and in any case those decisions may not have been made yet, or may be unmade later. You do of course need to set things up to be easily readable the first time you create a new type of document, but thereafter you should be able to re-use the same format for other documents of the same type, and concentrate on the more serious business of writing. For Web files, the fonts and formatting are in any event usually handled by the browser program at the reader's end, not by the author, making the need to format and reformat the text on your own screen largely irrelevant. However, to handle this efficiently, you need the services of an editor program which understands HTML.

HTML 2.0 has been developed with two ends in mind: to allow people to create valid files for the Web, and also to let them model or cope with the 'legacy' documents containing older forms of HTML from an earlier period. In the section which follows, it is worth bearing in mind that an SGML editor can be used either way, the approach being controlled by the setting of the parameter entities `HTML.Recommended` or `HTML.Deprecated` in the DTD file.

Editing software

Before we look at Web files in detail, what can we use to edit them? They are all plain text, so there are no funny characters, and you can if you wish use almost any editor or wordprocessor you care for, provided it can load and save plain ASCII text files. This can on occasions be a very real benefit, if you are away from base, stuck with local software you are not familiar with, but with access to a plain text editor: it is tedious to edit HTML files 'in the raw', but it is perfectly possible, and some people actually prefer it.

Choosing an editor

Your choice of editor often comes down to what you are comfortable with. My own work usually means I need an editor which makes it fast to write and edit very large amounts of text, with lots of facilities for finding, moving, changing, and interpolating text in different windows, cutting, and pasting between files on a variety of systems and from many sources, using keystrokes for speed, rather than having to lift my hands off the keyboard to use a mouse. However, many people in the text-processing field regularly use five or six different editing systems for other purposes.

The other factor influencing choice is the kind of text you deal with. Some authors may deal with small amounts of continuous text in single files on one computer; yet others work with lots of fonts and typographic display options; others again need detailed scientific or mathematical facilities or the complex requirements of a multilingual *apparatus criticus* for scholarly editions.

No one editor or wordprocessor is therefore inherently 'better' or 'worse' than another, although devotees of particular programs will often defend their favorite against criticism with religious fervour.

The editors listed here fall into two main groups: those which understand HTML fully and those with only a partial understanding. Most of them are for graphical systems, but there are several text-only ones: however, only those programs which understand HTML fully can actually use a graphical system to affect things like font choice and size for your local display while editing.

Having said that, I do strongly recommend you use an editor that is compliant with SGML (and therefore with HTML), because it will mean far less trouble in the future maintaining and re-using the files you create. It's also easier and faster if you use an editor which understands what you are trying to do, even if it does mean spending a little time learning how it works. There is a list of SGML editors and other software in Steve Pepper's *Whirlwind Guide to SGML Tools* [Pepper n.d.] at `ftp://sgml1.ex.ac.uk/pub/SGML/sgml-tools.info/`.

If you do use a non-compliant editor, you can send your document for checking by using the form at `http://www.hal.com/~connolly/html-test/service/` `validation-form.html`. Mark Gaither has assembled a *HTML Check* toolkit at `http://www.hal.com/~markg/HaLSoft/html-check/index.html` which contains a copy of the public domain *sgmls* parser and all the files needed to run validation checks on your HTML files.

There is also the *WebLint* system at `http://www.unipress.com/web-lint/` which checks your HTML file for errors when you supply the URL, and the *htmlchek* program, which checks both HTML 2.0 and HTML3 files as well as those with the Netscape proposed extensions (`http://uts.cc.utexas.edu/` `~churchh/htmlchek.html`).

HTML-compliant editors

These editors understand HTML: that is, they can read the DTD and work out what elements belong where and how they can fit together.

Author/Editor

SoftQuad's SGML editor works well with HTML and is available for MS-Windows, Apple Mac, and Sun Sparc. Version 3.0 has extensive font-handling and formatting capabilities, including graphics on systems with OLE capability.

The parser (the tool which turns the HTML DTD into a set of rules for the editor) is available separately, so that if you use Author/Editor on a corporate-wide basis, you can provide managed version control, rather than letting every user roll their own. An add-on system called *Sculptor* lets you customize *Author/Editor* to fit it to your organization's standards (it also provides a very good scripting language).

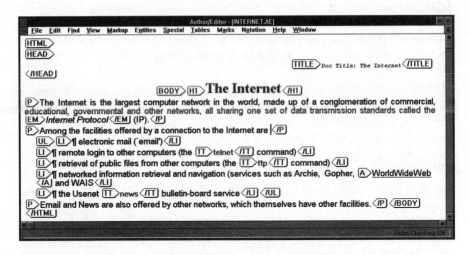

Figure 6.1   SoftQuad's Author/Editor used for HTML
This shows the markup revealed

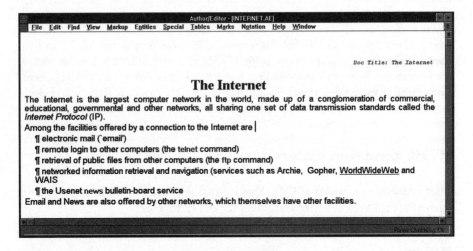

Figure 6.2   SoftQuad's Author/Editor used for HTML
This shows the markup hidden

HoTMetaL

SoftQuad as well: a cut-down version of Author/Editor distributed free on the network for use with HTML files only. This does not have all the facilities of *Author/Editor*, but provides a good way of getting into structured editing. Available for MS-Windows and SunOS 4.1.3 (a Mac version is due as well) from `ftp:/ /ftp.ncsa.uiuc.edu/Web/hotmetal/`. A commercial version with facilities more like *Author/Editor* is available as *HoTMetaL PRO*.

SGML Author for Word

This is an add-on tool for Microsoft *Word for Windows* for creating SGML files, including HTML. It includes an autotagger in the form of a filter, which converts Word files to SGML by mapping Word document templates to the elements. This does mean that you have to know something of SGML and HTML to set it up, in order to associate the styles with elements, but this can be done using a visual interface which comes as part of the package.

WordPerfect SGML Edition

WordPerfect SGML Edition (available August 1995) is SGML embedded in WordPerfect 6.1 for Windows. It gives all the functionality of WordPerfect but operating in an SGML-aware fashion. It will ship with several DTDs already compiled, and you can also import your own. The SGML options are activated by an extra function in the **Tools** menu which then makes a whole host of SGML facilities available to you. You can use the **Save As...** to save an SGML file and can also import SGML files. Humanities at Princeton and Rutgers Universities for these impressions in a report from a recent demonstration presentation.

Web Wizard

Add-on macros for Microsoft *Word* by Eric van Herwijnen from NICE Technologies of Capitola, California. This preserves the Word visual environment as much as possible and produces fully-conformant HTML files. An evaluation copy is available: download it from `ftp.webcom.com` in `nicetech/Downloads`.

WebAuthor

This is another editor with a browser-like view using Microsoft's *Word for Windows*. *WebAuthor* is a product of Quarterdeck Corporation and allows you to import existing HTML files into Word for revision, and also lets you create new documents from scratch. Once imported, files can be saved in Word format (as a master copy) and can be exported into HTML files. *WebAuthor* includes a parsing routine which validates HTML files, and also has limited support for some non-HTML 'extensions' (at the expense of compliance).

GriF Symposia

GRIF have recently (April 1995) introduced an extension of their SGML editing capability to allow documents to be edited over the Web. *Symposia* is a structured editor combining their existing WYSIWYG tools with support for TCP/IP, so that collaborative work from people in different locations can be carried out using the Internet. It will be available for Unix, Mac and MS-Windows, and a free version without support for Sun and HP workstations can be downloaded from `http://symposia.inria.fr`.

Phoenix

The University of Chicago Biological Science Division's Office of Academic Computing is producing an experimental editor called *Phoenix* (for *X Windows* under SunOS and Solaris), which can be downloaded from `http://www.bsd. uchicago.edu/ftp/pub/phoenix`.

HTMLtext

WYSIWYG editor for Unix/X with inline image support and the ability to fix up non-conformant files. By Nick Williams, available from `ftp.cs.city.ac. uk` in `pub/htmltext`. It requires the Andrew Toolkit to compile. Details in `http://web.cs.city.ac.uk/homes/njw/htmltext/htmltext.html`.

Emacs `psgml`

GNU software (freely distributable) by Lennart Staflin. Works with *Emacs* for Unix, X Windows, MS-DOS, MS-Windows, VMS, and Apple Mac (the Mac version is not from the GNU stable and is maintained separately), available from many FTP servers worldwide.

Partially compliant editors

These systems offer keystroke access or menu access to HTML tags, but don't actually check the validity of what you do when you use them. If you're already familiar with HTML, or sure of what you're doing, they are very useful for a quick edit of a file you only want to make small changes to without seriously disrupting the structure.

HTML HyperEdit

This comes from Asymetrix Corp for *MS-Windows*: it has a beginner/advanced mode switch, good customization and a reasonably complete set of tags (Figure 6.3).

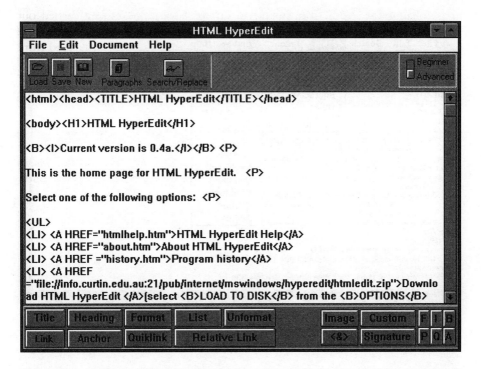

Figure 6.3 *HTML HyperEdit* for *MS-Windows*

HTML Writer

This *MS-Windows* program is the easiest to use and has the least cluttered screen (Figure 6.4), with the elements selectable from menus, but the unfortunate habit of leaving the cursor outside the element, rather than between the start-tag and end-tag.

HTML Assistant

Another *MS-Windows* program, with most of the HTML elements controlled by their own button at the top of the screen (Figure 6.5).

Word for Windows template

Georgia Tech has produced a set of template macros for Microsoft *Word for Windows* to help with the production an maintenance of HTML files. Details and links to the software are at `http://www.gatech.edu/word_html/release.html`

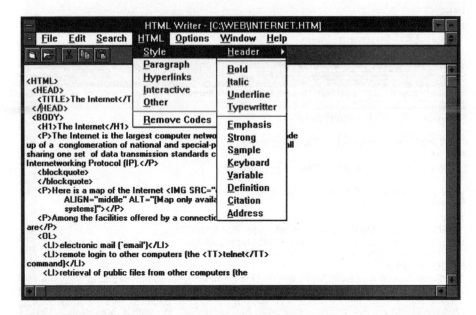

Figure 6.4   *HTML Writer*

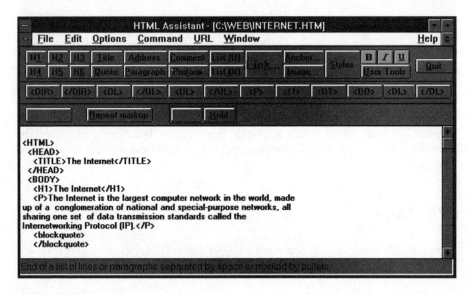

Figure 6.5   *HTML Assistant* for *MS-Windows*

Webmagic

SGI produce this graphical editor to partner their *WebFORCE* server. Although it concentrates mainly on embedding large colour graphics into HTML files, it also handles text editing in a structured manner well, and comes very close to being a fully conformant editor.

SHE

Simple HTML Editor for the Mac, requires *HyperCard* or *HyperCard Player*. Supports the non-HTML tags of *Netscape*, spawns browser for preview, many editing extras. `ftp.lib.ncsu.edu` in `pub/software/mac/simple-html-editor.hqx`

BBEdit HTML extensions

Two sets of extensions for the Mac editor *BBEdit*: one is from the University of York, England, at `ftp.york.ac.uk` in `pub/users/ld11/BBEdit_HTML_Tools.sea.hqx`. Details at `http://www.york.ac.uk/~ld11/BBEditTools.html`.

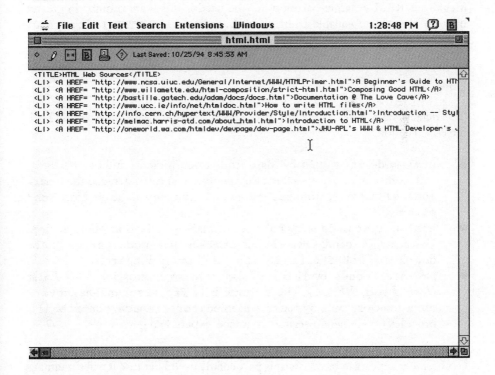

Figure 6.6 *BBEdit* extensions for HTML (Mac)

The other one is by Carles Bellver of the Universitat Jaume I, Spain. You can find more information at the *BBEdit* HTML extensions' page `http://www.uji.es/bbedit-html-extensions.html`. The extensions package itself can be downloaded from `ftp.uji.es` in `pub/mac/util/bbedit-html-ext.sea.hqx`.

PC-Write HTML macros

PC-Write (formerly from QuickSoft, Seattle, now distributed by Starlight Software) is one of the best-known and most robust small shareware DOS file-editor/wordprocessors. I wrote the macros which you can find (with a copy of the software) in `http://www.ucc.ie/pub/sgml/pcw4.zip`. It also runs in *MS-Windows* as a text window.

HTML Editor for the Mac

This is a semi-WYSIWYG editor for a Macintosh SE/30, Mac II, or other Macintosh with a 68020-compatible CPU, System 7 or higher and at least 2 Megabytes RAM. A larger partition may be needed if you are running in greater than 16 bit color. Available from `cs.dal.ca` in `giles/HTML_Editor_1.0.sit.hqx`.

Emacs

(For details see p. 120.) There are three sets of macros for helping with HTML file construction:

- `html-mode` was written by Marc Andreessen (original author of *Mosaic*), with contributions from many other people. You can download the `html-mode.el` macro file from `zaphod.ncsa.uiuc.edu` in the directory `Web/elisp`.
- `html-helper` mode is a similar set of macros by Nelson Minar at Reed University (Portland, OR). The file `html-helper-mode.tar.gz` can be downloaded from `ftp.reed.edu` in the directory `pub/src`.
- `hm--html-menus` by Heiko Münkel, contains macros for *Lucid Emacs* (*Lucid Emacs*, *XEmacs*). The software is at `ftp.rrzn.uni-hannover.de` in directory `pub/systems/unix/editors/lemacs/contrib`. This provides for element insertion at novice, expert, and guru levels.

GNU *Emacs* appears in both lists: it is particularly useful because it will simultaneously act as an HTML editor and Web browser, as well as let you read your email, Usenet newsgroups and IRC chatlines, compile and test software, including CGI scripts, and let you edit files from other machines directly via FTP, and it works both in windowing systems and in plain terminal mode. If you are in the network information-provider business, this can be a significant productivity tool: the only drawback is the large amounts of memory and disk space it needs to do all this.

Now that both *WordPerfect* and Microsoft *Word* have nailed their banner to the SGML flagstaff, it is reasonable to expect that many other wordprocessors for desktop systems would be expected to follow with similar products.

Part Two

How to make WorldWideWeb files

- O   HTML: the rules of the game
- O   Simple HTML markup
- O   Hypertext links, URLs, and graphics
- O   Tables, forms, and math
- O   Controlling appearance

Chapter 7

Introduction to HTML

O   HTML: the specification

O   The mechanics of markup

O   Basic file structure

This part of the book describes in detail what HyperText Markup Language (HTML) is and how it works. It forms a tutorial on creating and maintaining these files for the WorldWideWeb, with exercises at the end of each chapter. By this stage you should be familiar with the concepts of the Web and hypertext, and you will already have encountered some of the aspects of HTML, so I suggest you read these chapters at your computer, where you can practice and experiment as you read.

You don't have to have a server of your own running to do this: most browsers have an *Open Local* function which lets you display a file from your local hard disk exactly as it would if you had retrieved it from a server on the 'net.

Why a formal specification?

HTML was conceived by the inventor of the WorldWideWeb, Tim Berners-Lee, and was further developed by Dan Connolly, Dave Raggett and a team of volunteers. Early on it was recognised that users, developers, and authors needed to have a reference point for HTML so that there was agreement about the meaning and usage of the language. This team now forms the **Internet Engineering Task Force** (**IETF**) Working Group on HTML who have finalized the revised standard, called HTML 2.0.

Like any new application, HTML is still evolving. You may come across references to several versions:

● The original HTML (1.0), which is obsolete.
● This book refers to HTML 2.0, the official specification.
● HTML+ was the proposed successor to HTML 1.0 and is now obsolete, but many of its proposals have been used as the basis for HTML3.
● Work on HTML3 is under way. I have included details in Appendix B but not all of it is yet implemented. The *Arena* browser (p. 85) from CERN is acting as a testbed for some of these facilities. The reference manual is also under development [Raggett 1995].

You can read the Web version of the specification at (`http://www.w3.org/hypertext/WWW/MarkUp/MarkUp.html`): this reference includes links to the HTML Document Type Description.

Because different browsers are written for systems with differing facilities, the definitions in HTML 2.0 are classified into three levels. These are intended as a guide to authors as to how well their intentions will be reflected in the rendering of their files, because not all browsers support all features of HTML, and the way in which they display a file can vary considerably.

In the earlier stages of browser development, it was taken as a principle that if a browser did not support a particular feature, it would not cause an error, but simply pass on as if the feature was not there. The obvious example is graphics: character browsers don't do graphics, but if they encounter a file with an illustration, they should simply ignore it gracefully, rather than fail.

● Level 0 includes all the basic structural elements. A document which uses only these elements should display in its entirety in all browsers.
● Level 1 adds highlighting and graphics. These elements will only display in

browsers which support them, but all the rest of the file will display correctly in all browsers.

● Level 2 adds fill-in forms. A form in a document will only display in browsers which have this capability: the remainder of the file will display according to the principles of Levels 1 and 0.

The HTML DTD also includes some hidden facilities to make HTML texts usable with software for the print-impaired. These are in the form of SGML Document Access (SDA) fixed attributes in support of easy transformation to the International Committee for Accessible Document Design (**ICADD**) DTD. ICADD applications are designed to support usable access to structured information by print-impaired individuals through Braille, large print and voice synthesis.

The ICADD community has a mailing list `icadd@asuvm.inre.asu.edu` (run by *LISTSERV*: p. 47), and there is an experimental transformation service at `http://www.ucla.edu/ICADD/html2icadd-form.html` with a Braille output option.

How HTML markup works

We have seen (pp. 115–116) that HTML uses textual markup to identify the structure of your document. It does this by using keywords called **tags** to surround portions of your text, so that the computer can recognize the **elements** which make up your document. If this is the title of your document:

```
My first attempt at an HTML file
```

just putting it on a line by itself doesn't actually mean 'hello, I'm the title', because there's nothing there which can tell the computer that it *is* a title. HTML lets us identify the title of a document as an element called 'Title' by enclosing it in tags:

```
<title>My first attempt at an HTML file</title>
```

Notice a few things about the way these element tags are used:

● Tag names always go inside **angle brackets** (< and > , like mathematical less-than and greater-than signs) so that the computer can recognize them as different from the flow of your text.
● An element is marked with a **start-tag** and an **end-tag**. The text surrounded by them is called the **content** of the element.
● The tag name is the same in both start-tag and end-tag, but the end-tag has a slash (/) after the opening angle bracket.

The names of the elements are predefined in HTML: you can't make up your own. They are 'case insensitive', so typing TITLE or TiTlE means just the same thing. There's a diagram of the overall structure in Figure 7.1 and a list of all the elements with a summary of their meaning and use on the reference card at the back of the book. The diagrams appear in the sections where each element is introduced, showing where the element fits into the DTD as a whole, and what other elements it can contain.

Elements fall into one of three classes:

1   'structural', like paragraphs, lists, section headings, figures, and tables: these are also called 'block-oriented' elements because they contain blocks of text.
2   'descriptive' or 'content-oriented', because they describe the reason *why* certain words are significant, such as emphasis, an index entry, a citation, or a hypertext link
3   'visual', because they are a part of the external appearance, such as centering, or a new typeface, rather than having some intrinsic meaning.

In HTML, most elements are structural: there are also many descriptive elements, but very few visual ones, because the objective is to concentrate on content and meaning, rather than how it happens to look on any one user's machine.

The word 'tag' is used to describe the individual start- and end-tags; the word 'element' refers to the whole element, including both start- and end-tags and the text content between them.

Empty elements

A few elements are defined as **empty**: they only have a start-tag and they don't have any content. For example, <br> is used to mark special line-breaks (browsers do their own formatting of normal text, so this is only needed when you want to force a line-break to occur). There isn't any text to surround, so there's no end-tag:

```
Mary had a little lamb:<br>
The doctors were surprised.
```

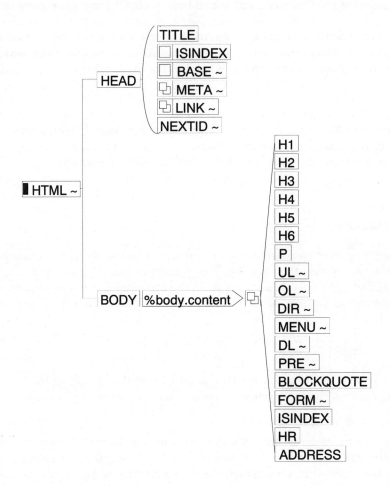

Figure 7.1   Overall structure of a HTML 2.0 file
For details of these diagrams and the symbols, see Panel 7.1 on p. 135

Omitting tags

It is possible to omit the end-tag for some elements in restricted circumstances (a trick called **minimization**). For example, when one paragraph is followed directly by another, like this:

```
<p>...information about travel habits was gathered from a
sample of shoppers using a questionnaire.</p><p>The
responses were analysed using the P-Stat package...</p>
```

it could equally well be typed with the end-tag omitted from the first paragraph:

```
<p>...information about travel habits was gathered from a
sample of shoppers using a questionnaire.<p>The responses
were analysed using the P-Stat package...</p>
```

because the start of the second paragraph is completely unambiguous (if a new paragraph is starting, the previous one *has* to end). However, it is good practice to insert the end-tag unless you know from experience when HTML allows you to omit it. If you are using an editor which understands HTML, then this is handled automatically (see pp. 116–125 for details about editing software).

Attributes

Some start-tags can hold additional information. These items are called **attributes**, and they occur *inside* the angle brackets of the start-tag, after the tag name. They are used to make finer distinctions about the meaning or use of an element, or to hold important information which is not to be displayed as part of the text. For example:

```
<pre width="72">
```

The `width` attribute specifies that the preformatted text defined by the `<pre>` element should be displayed with a maximum line length of 72 characters per line.

Attributes are separated from the element name and from each other by a space. They usually take the form of *keyword="value"* pairs, as in the above example, although in some cases you can use the keyword on its own (this is explained later where it occurs).

Character entities

Because files have to be portable between systems, HTML uses only plain text: the characters A–Z, a–z, 0–9 and punctuation, which can be used on all computer systems. Accents, symbols and other glyphs which are not in this set of characters are represented using ISO 8859–1 mnemonics (see below). These cover the symbols used in the more common European languages that use the Latin alphabet, and avoid the confusion caused by different manufacturers of hardware and software using their own private sets of character codes.

The mnemonics are called **character entities** and are abbreviations preceded by an ampersand and followed by a semicolon. For example, you can get an e-acute (é) in a HTML file by using `&eacute;`. Table 8.1, on p. 169, lists the ones valid for HTML 2.0.

Panel 7.1   CADE structure diagrams

I'm going to be using these diagrams quite a bit to illustrate how the elements of an HTML file fit together. They come from a system called CADE (Computer-Aided Document Engineering) made by Microstar, implemented in their *Near&Far* program. The 'family-tree' structure is used to indicate which elements belong inside which other elements, and thus show where they can be used.

The 'root' element in our case is always `<html>`, signified by the black rectangle to its left. The connector bracketing shows what each element can be made up of: square bracketing means that the order of the elements is significant; curved bracketing means it is not; angled straight-line bracketing simply means you can choose arbitrarily from among the allowed elements, as your needs determine.

Elements are preceded by a symbol which indicates how many times an element can be used (occurrence indicators):

Compulsory: ☐ —An open square means the element is compulsory, but may occur only once;

Optional: ■ —A filled square means the element is optional, but if present, it may only occur once;

Compulsory but repeatable: ▣ —An overlapped filled square means the element is compulsory but may occur more than once;

Optional and repeatable: ▣ —An overlapped open square means the element is optional, but may occur any number of times.

Elements with no symbol are compulsory (first group above). Ultimately, most elements end up containing text. CADE diagrams use five symbols to show what content an element can have:

PCDATA: ▤ —Processable character data: text which may include further element markup and character entities;

RCDATA: ▨ —Replaceable character data: text which may contain character entities but not element markup;

CDATA: ▨ —Character data: plain text which may not contain any markup or character entities;

ANY: ▧ —Any text: PCDATA or further occurrences of elements;

EMPTY: ☐ —Empty: the element may not have any content.

An element name followed by a tilde (∼) means that the element can have 'attributes' (p. 134) which modify its meaning. Some more complex constructions, such as the definitions in HTML3, use Inclusions (the ◯ symbol) and Exclusions (the ⊘ symbol) to prevent some elements containing unwanted material, such as paragraph matter within mathematics. SGML also has a shorthand way of referring to a group of elements, called a 'parameter entity': these are shown in the CADE diagrams preceded by a percent sign. This avoids having to display the full content definition of a frequently-used element (like a paragraph) every time it gets referred to.

Basic file structure

A lot of files in the Web today were created without the help of tools like HTML editors, before it became clear that there's a bit more to making Web files work effectively than just sticking in an arbitrary bunch of tags wherever they seemed to do the most good. At one stage, some developers (for otherwise sound commercial reasons) started inventing their own element tags, and the legacy of these is still with us. Most browsers are very tolerant of malformed files, which means that it is possible to use (some people would say misuse) HTML as if it were some kind of wordprocessing system, where any old thing goes so long as it looks vaguely right. In fact, the best results come from precise and careful use of the right tags in the right places, so we're going to concentrate here on getting your documents to work as efficiently for you as possible.

Chapter 8

Simple document markup

○ Paragraphs and section headings

○ All kinds of lists

○ Fonts, accents, and symbols

○ Block quotation

Before you can start typing a document, you have to give it a kind of skeleton or template into which you can put the text. There are two main parts to an HTML file which give it this basic structure, preceded by a single line declaring the document type as HTML.

1   an HTML **header**, containing information *about* the file;
2   the **body**, which contains the text itself.

This structure is shown in the diagram in Figure 7.1 on p. 133.

The skeleton looks like this when viewed in a plain text editor:

```
<!doctype html public "-//IETF//DTD HTML//EN//">
<html>
<head>     </head>
<body>  </body>
</html>
```

You can see the document type declaration at the top. All the rest of the file is enclosed in the `<html>...</html>` tags. Within this, the document is divided into the head and body. The `<head>...</head>` tags enclose the header, which identifies the file title and any relationships the document has with the world outside. The `<body>...</body>` tags surround all the rest of your text. Notice that the head and body are separate, non-overlapping sections, entirely contained within the `<html>` element.

The document type declaration

This identifies the type of file with a special kind of tag called a **markup declaration**, which has an exclamation mark after the opening angle bracket:

```
<!doctype html public "-//IETF//DTD HTML//EN">
```

You should always use this line as the first line of every HTML file, exactly as given here (until the version changes and you add extra markup). If you're editing files with a plain text editor or wordprocessor, you may want to keep this line in a separate template file which you can copy in each time you create a new file.

This line is used by HTML editors and other software to locate a copy of the correct DTD so that they can understand what elements are usable in your file. Fully-compliant editors handle this automatically, and may not even display the declaration, although they will insert it when the file is saved to disk.

If you're using a copy of the HTML DTD in the same directory as the files you are editing, you can use the form

```
<!doctype html system "html.dtd">
```

■

Exercise 8.1   Creating a new file

For these exercises, you need to have some information you want to put into the Web. One good starting point would be to create your own personal page, with information about yourself—a kind of extended business card. You might even want to make it into a Web version of your résumé or *curriculum vitae*. How you phrase it and what information you put in it is entirely up to you: the objective is to become familiar with using HTML.

Use your editor to open a new file. Insert the document type declaration as the first line (unless you're using something like *HoTMetaL* or *Author/Editor*, which use a built-in or precompiled version automatically, and don't display it). Then add the <html> and </html> tags. Save the file with a name of your choosing, but ending with .html (or .htm if you're on a PC).

■

The HTML header

An HTML file should be self-documenting: that is, it should contain some information about itself, so that you can identify the file without having to read through it all. You do this with the header, in which you can specify the title of the file and a variety of other information about it.

A header with a title must occur in every file. It's equivalent to a running head in a printed document. Here's an example of a header with a title:

```
<head>
<title>How to make $1,000,000</title>
</head>
```

There are other optional elements which can be included for additional information which we'll come to on pp. 202–205. The structure of a header is shown at the top of Figure 7.1 on p. 133.

■

Exercise 8.2   Adding a file title

Insert a <head> element between the <html> and </html> tags, and put a <title> element inside it containing a description of what this file will be. Keep the title under a line long so that it won't overflow the display box used by some browsers to show it.

■

The <title> element is a kind of label for recording the function of the file: it is not a part of the document text. Most browsers show the file title at the top of the screen, separate from the text, either off to the right-hand side or in a separate panel labeled 'Title' or something similar (p. 143), so it should be short enough not to overflow the display: a few words is usually enough. To display a heading at the start of your text you use a different element which we'll see in the next chapter.

The text body: paragraphs and headings

All of the file after the header is enclosed in the `<body>`...`</body>` tags. This is where all your text, illustrations, forms, tables, and hypertext references go. The body of most documents consists of a mixture of elements: some are simple one-line items like section headings, subheadings, and illustrations; others are blocks of text like paragraphs and lists, but a lot depends on the nature of the material and how you want to present it. The structure of the text body and the elements you can use in it is shown in Figure 7.1 on p. 133.

■

Exercise 8.3   The text body

Insert the `<body>` element between the `</head>` and `</html>` tags. As the overall structure up to now is common to all files, you might want to create a macro to insert this kind of skeleton for you (if your editor handles macros: they're a kind of miniature program of prerecorded keystrokes which you can get the editor to play back with a single key).

■

Paragraphs

Inside the body of a document, the most common element is the paragraph. HTML defines a paragraph with the `<p>` element, for example:

```
<p>If you are ordering for shipment abroad,
please add $30 to cover air freight and insurance
charges.</p>
```

HTML does not recognise blank lines or indentation as the sign of a new paragraph in the way that wordprocessors or DTP systems do, but uses the `<p>` element to enclose each paragraph. Browsers pay no attention to multiple spaces, tabs, or linebreaks, but treat them all as a single space (except in one special circumstance which we'll come on to later) because it is the markup which defines where elements like paragraphs begin and end. The paragraph above could equally well have been written as

```
<p>
If you are ordering for shipment abroad,      please
add
$30  to  cover
air freight and           insurance charges.         </p>
```

The effect in a browser display would have been just the same in both cases:

> If you are ordering for shipment abroad, please add $30 to cover air freight and insurance charges.

You can take advantage of this relaxed attitude to spacing if you are using a plain text editor rather than an HTML-sensitive one, because it allows you to include as much extra spacing as you want to make things easier to edit on the screen, without having to worry about whether it will format properly in the user's display. Paragraphs can contain plain text with the markup elements shown in the diagram in Figure 8.1.

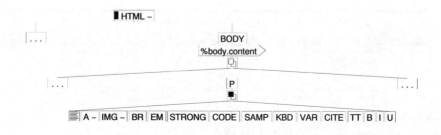

Figure 8.1   Element contents of a paragraph

Exercise 8.4   Adding text in paragraphs

Use the `<p>...</p>` tags to insert a few paragraphs of text in the body of your document. Don't worry about their order or placement at the moment: you can always move them around later.

Panel 8.1   Displaying a local file

If you've created a file while reading this, you probably want to see what it looks like when displayed. Graphical editors let you specify fonts and layout while you are editing, but these may not match the various ways in which browsers interpret the markup.

Run your browser and use the **Open Local** function to display your file. If you're using a windowing system, you can have the browser display in one window and your editor in another, and use the browser's **Reload** function to redisplay the file each time you make changes (don't forget you'll have to save the file in your editor before trying to load it in the browser).

Using a character system, you'll have to save the file and exit from your editor, then run a browser as a separate command and open the file for display. If you're using Emacs in character mode, however, you can split the screen into two text windows and run the `w3-mode` browser in one half and the `psgml-mode` editor in the other half.

Section headings

Sectioning is used to divide a document into some form of logical groups, and each section or subsection usually has its own heading. HTML allows you up to six levels of section heading, using the `<h1>` to `<h6>` elements.

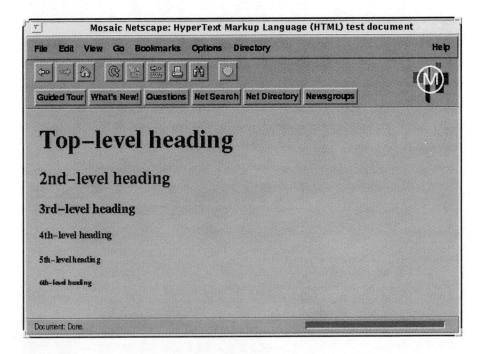

Figure 8.2   Levels of section heading in *Netscape*

The top-level heading is used to represent the major divisions of your text, and the first one in the file normally contains some kind of title which applies to the whole document. The text is enclosed in `<h1>...</h1>` tags, and this conventionally makes it display in large bold type in a graphical browser, although some allow the user to select the exact font, size, and style to suit their own taste. In a character browser it is positioned, outlined, or highlighted in some other way.

Further levels of section headings are done with `<h2>`, subsections with `<h3>`, subsubsections with `<h4>` and so on with `<h5>` and `<h6>`.

Graphical browsers display different highlights, sizes, colors, or positions of type for the different levels of headings, conventionally getting smaller or less bold as the depth of sectioning gets greater (Figure 8.2). In some browsers the user can change how the headings display. *Mosaic*'s section headings for `<h4>` to `<h6>` actually use smaller type than that used for the normal text of paragraphs. Here's an example of a top-level heading:

```
<h1>Jill Doe's own page</h1>
```

If the file title said 'Autobiography', this would display in a graphical browser something like:

Autobiography

Jill Doe's own page

and in a text browser like *Lynx* (which shows `<h1>` elements in capitals, centered, and puts the title at the top on the right) as:

Autobiography

JILL DOE'S OWN PAGE

In character browsers, with a smaller range of typographic variation available, other visual techniques are used for headings, such as centering or capitalising (*Lynx*), or surrounding or underlining with asterisks, dashes, or dots (*Emacs* `w3-mode`).

The top-level heading `<h1>` is usually the first element after the `<body>` start-tag, so that it displays at the top of the screen when the document is retrieved. Headings always come between paragraphs, not within them: putting a heading element inside a paragraph is not meaningful for the reader (an HTML-compliant editor won't let you do this anyway). All that a browser will do is split the paragraph in two and display the heading between the two halves.

Exercise 8.5   Inserting headings

Insert a `<h1>` element immediately after the start-tag for the body, before your first paragraph, and type in it the text that you want displayed as the top heading.

Insert a `<h2>` element between your first and second paragraphs and type a second-level heading in there.

What happens if you omit the first-level heading entirely?

Second-level headings (and all the rest) are done in the same way, for example:

```
<h2>Chapter 1 - Born to rule</h2>
```

This produces this kind of output when displayed in graphical form:

Autobiography

Jill Doe - My Life

Chapter 1 - Born to rule

and in a text browser as:

Autobiography

JILL DOE - MY LIFE

Chapter 1 - Born to rule

The elements you can use inside a heading are exactly the same as those you can use inside a paragraph: these are shown in Figure 8.1.

Section headings in HTML represent section levels, not section numbers, so <h3> means 'heading level 3', not 'section number 3'. Although there are six levels of heading provided for, each level can occur as many times as necessary. There is no automated section-numbering in HTML 2.0, but if you need section headers numbered, you can insert the numbers along with the text of the heading.

Panel 8.2   Style guide

Although it is easy to put tags around your headings and paragraphs, and to write a simple document with a header and a body, there are some basic practices which experience has shown to make good sense. This is not to say that you *have* to do things this way—there are always plenty of reasons why not—but the following guidelines appear to meet the approval of readers of all kinds of material, not just Web hypertext.

- Keep files to a reasonable size. Users on slow connections do not appreciate having to wait many minutes to receive a file when they may only want to refer to a few sentences. Unfortunately, it's impossible to give an optimum length for a file, because even long files can load fast when you're in the same building as the server, and even short files can be slow if you're the other side of the world. As a rule of thumb, when working with corporate or campus information systems, I try not to create files over 10 screens long (based on the default 22 lines of 80 characters, used in a standard terminal window), simply to avoid the reader getting lost in the verbal jungle. Most are much shorter, a very few are a little longer (whole articles, for example). I have also seen recommendations that no HTML file should be longer than one screenful, but this is perhaps unduly restrictive.
- If you are creating a long document, split it into separate files on section boundaries and make the first page a table of contents. We'll see in Chapter 9 how to reference one file from another.
- Make the file title meaningful and try to keep it under a line long so that it doesn't overrun the window in which it gets displayed, or get in the way in browsers which use the top line of a 25-line screen for it.
- Try to keep headings less than one line long as well: top-level (<h1>) headings in a graphical browser can take up a lot of space when a large bold font is used.
- Keep paragraphs reasonably short, preferably less than a screenful each. Although what constitutes a 'screenful' varies enormously (especially as many users read Web documents in a resizable window), try the following guide: a standard 25-line, 80-character screen means 2,000 characters when full, or about 250 words (at an average of 6 characters per word plus spacing and margins), but such solid slabs of text tire the eyes: to keep the reader's interest, try about 16 lines as a maximum, roughly 160 words.
- Write clearly, without overlong sentences or complex grammatical constructions, unless you are writing for a specialist audience who are accustomed to a particular style or content.

Making lists

Everyone makes lists: they're a handy way of marshalling your thoughts and a common way of providing instructions or a record of events. Lists tend to be used in several ways: there are three main groups:

● **ordered lists**, where the items are numbered in sequence because the order is important;
● **unordered lists**, where the items don't have a particular sequence: these are sometimes marked with a symbol called a 'bullet', and are sometimes referred to as 'bulleted lists' (like this one);
● **definition lists**, where each item is made up of a term followed by one or more subparagraphs of definition.

There are elements to define all of these in HTML, and they can be nested within each other. Lists are block-oriented elements, so they occur between paragraphs, not within them.

There is in fact a fourth type, labeled lists, where the items are numbered or lettered for reference purposes, but where the order is not important. HTML 2.0 does not provide for this explicitly, as the subparagraphs of a definition list can be used, with the labeling provided by hypertext.

Ordered lists

This is an example of an ordered list:

> 1 Undo the two screws holding the coverplate.
> 2 Gently lift the coverplate from the back.
> 3 Latch the coverplate open using the hook inside on the left.
> 4 Remove the soundproof wadding from over the blower motor housing.

The numbering is automatic in HTML, so if you delete or insert items, they get renumbered automatically by the browser when the file is next displayed. An ordered list is a sequence of <li> (list item) elements completely enclosed in the <ol> (ordered list) element. An ordered list is written like this:

```
<ol>
<li>Undo the two screws holding the coverplate.</li>
<li>Gently lift the coverplate from the back.</li>
<li>Latch the coverplate open using the hook inside on the
left.</li>
<li>Remove the soundproof wadding from over the blower motor
housing.</li>
</ol>
```

There's a diagram of what elements can go inside a list item in Figure 8.3.

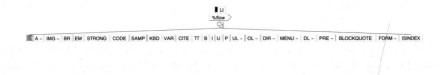

Figure 8.3   Element contents of a list item
            This applies to all lists which use <li> *(ordered, unordered, menu, and directory lists)*

Exercise 8.6   Ordered lists

Add an ordered list between two of your paragraphs, or between a paragraph and a section heading. Insert a few items in the list, then save the file and display it using your browser.

Edit the file to change the position of some of the list items, then save the file and reload it in the browser: check that the items get renumbered automatically.

Unordered lists

An unordered list has bullets or asterisks instead of numbers, for example:

- 2lb (4 cups) sugar
- 8oz (8 squares) dark chocolate
- 1/2pt (8 fl.oz) evaporated milk
- 2oz (1 stick) butter

The same `<li>` tags are used for the list items, but in this case, the tag used to surround the whole list is `<ul>` (unordered list):

```
<ul><li>2lb (4 cups) sugar</li>
<li>8oz (8 squares) dark chocolate</li>
<li>1/2pt (8 fl.oz) evaporated milk</li>
<li>2oz (1 stick) butter</li></ul>
```

This makes it easy to change the kind of list later: just change the `<ul>` tags for `<ol>` ones (the fudge tastes pretty good, too...).

Both ordered and unordered lists can have an attribute of **compact** which browsers can interpret as meaning the list items will be short, so the space between items can be reduced. Like other attributes, the word **compact** goes inside the angle brackets after the tag name, separated by a space:

```
<ul compact><li>sugar</li>
<li>chocolate</li>
<li>milk</li>
<li>butter</li></ul>
```

In a character browser, because of the fixed line-height, there is less scope for such compression, although *Emacs* **w3-mode** does show the difference by using a different bullet and spacing. The elements which can make up the content of a list item in an unordered list are the same as for a list item in ordered, menu, or directory lists (Figure 8.3).

■

Exercise 8.7   Unordered lists

Add an unordered list in a similar way to how you did the ordered one in the last exercise (or just change the `<ol>` tagging of that list to `<ul>`). Save the file and reload it in the browser and see the difference in the way the two kinds of list are displayed.

■

Definition lists

Definition lists are designed to handle cases where each list item is made up of the term being defined or explained as well as one or more paragraphs of definition. This is common where the items are categories rather than just simple entries.

In this case, the whole list is a <dl> (definition list) element. Typically, each term is given as a <dt> element (definition term), followed by one or more <dd> (definition discussion) elements, but they can be used on their own or in other combinations.

The idea is that within the <dl> element, <dt> and <dd> elements normally occur in pairs. In fact you can have several <dt> elements together (where multiple terms are being defined as synonyms, perhaps) as well as several <dd> elements defining them. You can see from the diagram in Figure 8.4 that the most significant structural difference is that the <dt> element cannot contain another structure like a list or form, because it functions only as a title, while the <dd> element can contain any element in the normal flow of text: the content is the same as that for the list item (Figure 8.3). Here's an example of such a list:

```
<dl>
<dt>Managerial grades</dt>
<dd>Senior and junior managers are expected
to dress in conventional blue business suits with white
shirts and suitable ties during office hours,
particularly while meeting clients.</dd>
<dd>Any departure from this norm will be
taken very seriously as it reflects on the standing of
Widget Computers Inc.</dd>
<dt>Salaried staff below managerial
level</dt>
<dd>Employees must dress neatly but need not
wear suits. Unusual or extravagant clothing is
inappropriate to the position of these employees within
the company.</dd>
<dd>When meeting clients, conventional blue
business suits with white shirts and suitable ties
<em>must</em> be worn.</dd>
<dt>Programmers and HTML hacks</dt>
<dd>Back-office staff can wear anything they
want, provided it falls within the bounds of
decency.</dd>
<dd>In any case, we depend on these people so
much to keep our systems running that we'll make almost
any exception they insist on.</dd>
</dl>
```

which results in the following display:

> ### Managerial grades
>
> > Senior and junior managers must wear conventional blue business suits with white shirts and suitable ties during office hours, particularly while meeting clients.
> >
> > Any departure from this norm will be taken very seriously as it reflects on the standing of Widget Computers Inc.
>
> ### Salaried staff below managerial level
>
> > Employees must dress neatly but need not wear suits. Unusual or extravagant clothing is inappropriate to the position of these employees within the company.
> >
> > When meeting clients, conventional blue business suits with white shirts and suitable ties **must** be worn.
>
> ### Programmers and HTML hacks
>
> > Back-office staff can wear anything they want, provided it falls within the bounds of decency.
> >
> > In any case, we depend on these people so much to keep our systems running that we'll make almost any exception they insist on.

The `<dd>` element can contain any text, as well as other elements including separate paragraphs and lists (but not headings); the `<dt>` element can contain only text and inline markup. The `<dl>` element can have a **compact** attribute like other lists, to imply that it should be formatted more tightly.

Exercise 8.8   Definition lists

Add a definition list to your file. If it's your résumé that you're typing, this might be a good way to list your employment history, with the name of the company or the job title as the `<dt>` element and the `<dd>` element for describing the job. Check the display in your browser.

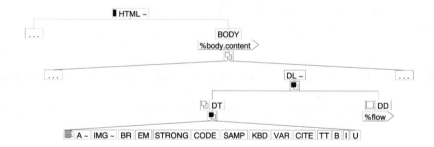

Figure 8.4   Contents of the definition list element

Other list elements

HTML also defines two other list elements, `<menu>` and `<dir>`, for handling menus and directory listings. In both cases the individual items in their content are enclosed in `<li>` tags, as for ordered and unordered lists, and both can take the `compact` attribute implying closer formatting.

Menu lists

A menu list is intended for items which each fit on one line, so browser authors can implement alternative formatting. Because a menu implies choices which the user can select, it is suited to lists of short selections for hypertext links (Chapter 9 for how to do these):

Search menu

Pick one of the following:

- Try the last search again with a new keyword
- Change the database you want to search
- Return to the main menu

which is produced by the following code:

```
<p>Pick one of the following:</p>
<menu>
<li>Try the last search again with a new keyword</li>
```

```
<li>Change the database you want to search</li>
<li>Return to the main menu</li>
</menu>
```

When we come to look at making fill-in forms, this can be used as a convenient way to represent selections from a list of options. The elements which can make up the content of a list item in a menu list are the same as for a list item in ordered, unordered, or directory lists (Figure 8.3).

Directory lists

The `<dir>` element is intended for items containing fewer than 20 characters each. The HTML specification suggests that the items in a directory list may be arranged in columns, although this does not seem to have been implemented in any known browser. This means that a much more horizontally-compressed display should be possible, so that

```
<dir>
<li>Paris <li>London <li>Berlin
<li>Madrid <li>Dublin <li>Moscow
<li>New York <li>Tokyo
</dir>
```

could result in a display such as:

```
Destinations


    Paris       Madrid      New York
    London      Dublin      Tokyo
    Berlin      Moscow
```

The elements which can make up the content of a list item in a directory list are the same as for a list item in ordered, unordered, or menu lists (Figure 8.3). Notice that in this example, I've omitted the end-tags from the list items, as lists are among those cases where the only element permitted inside them is the list item, so there is no ambiguity. The same would apply to ordered and unordered lists and to menu lists. In definition lists the end-tags `</dt>` and `</dd>` can be omitted in the same way.

Exercise 8.9   Menus and directories

Experiment with menu and directory lists and see how they display in your browser. A résumé is probably not a likely place to find them, but if you're creating files as part of a larger system which gathers input from the user or provides choices of what document to visit next, they may make a more logical choice than ordered or unordered lists.

Lists: some overall comments

You can have any type of list within any other type, but if it involves nested ordered lists, the subsidiary numbering or lettering scheme is a function of the browser: under HTML 2.0 you do not have any means of specifying how a browser numbers or letters the items. Some browser authors have indicated that they may include configuration options to handle how you prefer to see such nested lists displayed. Here's a part of a nested list, showing a definition list containing an ordered list containing a menu list:

Changing the settings

Configuration

Swarf Brothers' numerically-controlled lathes are shipped with factory settings (see the manual for details). To change these settings, follow this sequence:

1   Open the front panel by turning the knurled knobs on the sides toward you.
2   Move the blue control switch to **Standby**.
3   Adjust the settings as shown in the manual. The settings which you can change from this position are:

   ●   Maximum speed;
   ●   Maximum distance of bit travel;
   ●   Shear level for the automatic cut-off;
   ●   Default communications parameters for the serial interface.

4   Move the blue control switch to **Run** and close the front panel.

The code to produce such a nest looks like this:

```
<dl>
<dt>Configuration</dt>
<dd>Swarf Brothers' numerically-controlled
lathes are shipped with factory settings (see the
manual for details). To change these settings, follow
this sequence:
<ol>
<li>Open the front panel by turning the
knurled knobs on the sides toward you.</li>
<li>Move the blue control switch to
<b>Standby</b>.</li>
<li>Adjust the settings as shown in the
manual. The settings which you can change from this
position are:
<menu>
<li>Maximum speed;</li>
<li>Maximum distance of bit
travel;</li>
<li>Shear level for the automatic
cut-off;</li>
<li>Default communications parameters
for the serial interface.</li>
</menu></li>
<li>Move the blue control switch to
<b>Run</b> and close the front
panel.</li>
</ol>
</dd>
</dl>
```

■

Exercise 8.10   Nested lists

Try your hand at a nested list. If you used a definition list for your employment history, and you had several positions with one employer, you could use an ordered list in the <dd> element to show the jobs in order.

■

Emphasis, fonts, and formatting

So far we have looked at tags which describe structure or content. Browsers use this information to decide how to lay out and display a file, so you (as author) do not need to specify how this is done, because you cannot know or tell what hardware and software the user has got. There are many occasions, though, when you need to be able to influence some part of the user's display in order to emphasize or distinguish words or phrases.

There are also occasions when you need to mark certain words or phrases as having some special quality, for example citations, fragments of computer or other code, or sample input or output. These may not necessarily need or receive special typographic treatment, but once marked correctly, they are useful for retrieval by indexing routines, textbase programs, or formatting systems.

The whole business of exerting further control over the user's display is one which is receiving close attention, and is discussed in more detail in Chapter 11.

Some of these elements may only be obvious to the user if they have a graphical browser which can use different typestyles. Plain-text terminals cannot do this, so character browsers may simulate the changes by using highlighting, underscores or asterisks to make the text stand out.

Emphasis and font changes

If you need to make some words more obvious in the text, it might be because you want to emphasize them, or because they have some other special meaning. Either way it normally means changing the kind of type used to display them, bold and italics being the two most common variations. HTML provides several methods for doing this: *emphasis or italics*, **strong emphasis or bold type** and underlining. There are also several other ways to define special meanings for words and phrases which are explained in pp. 163–164.

Emphasis and italics

Regular emphasis of a word or phrase is done with the <em> element:

```
Remember, <em>send no money now!</em>
```

which usually produces italics in a graphical browser:

Remember, *send no money now!*

although some browsers let you change the exact font used. In character browsers, italic or slanted type is not normally available, so some other form of highlighting may be used, such as reverse video or high-intensity letters, or the conventions established by email, where the words are surrounded by underscores:

> Remember, send no money now!

When you want something italicized for reasons other than emphasis, there is an `<i>` element. The choice between them allows you to distinguish between real emphasis and simple font change:

```
Italic type is slanted <i>like this</i>.
```

The difference between `<em>` and `<i>` may or may not be apparent on a graphical browser screen, depending on what fonts they have installed, but if you are using your text for other purposes (perhaps for a database, or paper publishing), it is a useful way of differentiating usage:

> Italic type is slanted *like this*.

Strong emphasis and bold type

Strong emphasis is done with the `<strong>` element:

```
Unsuccessful candidates are <strong>not</strong> eligible
for a refund of expenses.
```

which typically displays in bold type in a graphical browser:

> Unsuccessful candidates are **not** eligible for a refund of expenses.

(although as with `<em>`, users may be able to change the font they see). In character browsers, following email convention, the words may appear highlighted in some way or surrounded by asterisks if the characteristics of the terminal being used do not allow for highlighting:

Unsuccessful candidates are **not** eligible for a
refund of expenses.

Along similar lines to the distinction between <em> and <i>, there is a <b> tag for occasions when you want bold type for purposes other than strong emphasis:

In bibliographies, the volume number of a serial
publication must be given in <b>bold type</b>.

so that you can keep the usage clear:

In bibliographies, the volume number of a serial publication
must be given in **bold type**.

Underlining

Underlining became common in the days of the typewriter, when there was no other way to do emphasis. It is extremely rare in printing, where italics are available. Many wordprocessors and DTP systems users still have it available, although its use in anything other than typewriter type usually looks ugly and is best avoided. There are occasions, though, when it makes a useful alternative if you are already using italics for other reasons. The <u> element was proposed in an earlier version of HTML 2.0, and as a result is still implemented by many browsers. If you want to use underlining, therefore, you should be aware that it may not always work, and that it is not valid in the HTML 2.0 DTD.

In these examples, terminal input by the user is shown
<u>underlined</u>.

If you are using a validating (SGML-compliant) editor, it may not let you insert the <u> element if it is not in the version of the DTD which is in use.

Where you have one element which affects font control embedded inside another, it is normal in wordprocessors and DTP systems for the type changes to be 'commutative', that is, they inherit their style from the next outer element, so

This is <b>bold type <i>with italic and
<u>underlining</u></i></b>.

would be expected to produce:

This is **bold type** *with italic and <u>underlining</u>*

Not all browsers support this. If you embed elements in this way, take great care to insert the end-tags in the right (reverse) order if you are typing them manually in your editor, as element start- and end-tags are not supposed to overlap. The following would be an invalid use:

```
This is <b>bold type <i>with italic
<u>and underlining</b></i></u>.
```

Exercise 8.11   Emphasis

Use the emphasis and strong emphasis elements (or bold and italics) and underlining to make any changes to your file where the reader's attention needs to be brought to particular words or phrases. Try nesting the elements to see what your browser supports.

Fixed-width type

Because of the extensive use of Web for computer-based documentation, there are several ways of showing fixed-width (typewriter) type. However, as with the tags for emphasis (italics) and strong emphasis (bold), users on plain-text terminals only get typewriter-style letters anyway, so they won't be able to see any difference.

There are two main elements for explicit typewriter type, one for inline usage (words in the middle of a paragraph) and one for display usage (blocks of text).

Inline typewriter type

Email addresses and file or machine names in the text of a paragraph are typically displayed in fixed-width type using the `<tt>` element:

```
To find all files ending with <tt>.html</tt> in your
disk area
```

which would display as:

> To find all files ending with `.html` in your disk area

Preformatted blocks of typewriter type

Examples of preformatted fixed-width text (like a computer program, for example) can go in a `<pre>` element. The content of this element can have many lines, and this is the one case I mentioned earlier where the linebreaks, multiple spaces and blank lines *will* be honored exactly as you type them:

```
<pre>
\parindent=<i>1em</i>
\parskip=<i>\baselineskip</i>
\parfillskip=<i>\parindent plus1fil</i>
</pre>
```

Font changes like italics and bold for emphasis will still also be honored within the preformatted block, and in a graphic display these would show up as slanted or bold typewriter type: in character browsers emphasis and italics may be shown otherwise:

```
\parindent=1em
\parskip=\baselineskip
\parfillskip=\parindent plus1fil
```

The elements which can appear in preformatted text blocks are the same as those for regular paragraphs, as shown in Figure 8.1. In the absence of elements to do tables in HTML 2.0, you can use this element to display columnar text in its preformatted form in fixed-width type (p. 208).

Inline code samples

Where you need to distinguish the specific usage of words because they are computer instructions of some kind, the `<code>` tag can be used:

```
You should never type <code>del *.*</code> unless you
really mean it.
```

This will display as typewriter type in a graphical browser:

> You should never type `del *.*` unless you really mean it.

This lets you identify commands or programming code separately from other uses of typewriter type.

Keyboard keys

For computing examples where you need to specify instructions which the reader is to type on the keyboard, there is a `<kbd>` element. Like the other elements which reflect computer material, this allows the author to keep specific usage separate from ordinary typewriter type:

```
When the menu appears again, press <kbd>X</kbd>
to stop the program.
```

If you are using a font-configurable browser, it might be better for it to appear in another typeface altogether:

> When the menu appears again, press X to stop the program.

Samples of literal characters

The `<samp>` element allows the separate specification of an inline sequence of literal characters such as samples of output from computer systems:

```
To display the file, type <code>more</code> followed
by the filename. This pauses with the word
<samp>--More--</samp> and the percentage through the
file at the end of each screenful.
```

and it could also be used for sample forms of words which are not part of the text itself in non-computing situations, such as incidental translations:

```
...as with the word 'telescope'
(Greek, <samp>see-afar</samp>)...
```

No specific font or typestyle is implied by this element, although typewriter type would seem to be a reasonable choice for browser implementors:

> To display the file, type more followed by the filename. This
> pauses with the word *--More--* and the percentage through
> the file at the end of each screenful.
>
> ...as with the word 'telescope' (Greek, *see-afar*)...

Computer variable names

A frequent occurrence in computer documentation is the indication of a variable
name or an item which requires user substitution. The **<var>** element is for this
kind of indication, where it is important to keep this usage separate from other
computing elements:

```
To increase paragraph indentation, set the value of
<var>\parindent</var> to a bigger dimension.
```

The content of this element would be expected to appear in typewriter type.

> To increase paragraph indentation, set the value of
> \parindent to a bigger dimension.

Exercise 8.12   Fixed-width type

Include your email address in your document, using the **<tt>** element.

Use the **<pre>** element to make a short block of text where the linebreaks and spacing are
significant.

Special characters

Because HTML uses the less-than and greater-than signs to identify markup, you
need to avoid confusion if you want to include the actual **less-than** and **greater-
than** characters themselves. To prevent them being misinterpreted as pieces of
markup, you need to use the symbolic names < for the less-than sign and

> for the greater-than sign. These names are called character entities, and there are many more of them to describe other symbols, especially accented characters (Table 8.2 on p. 170). The mnemonic name is preceded by an ampersand and followed by a semicolon, so the ampersand character itself has to be encoded this way: if you want to display one you need to type &. If you were documenting a program which said:

```
...using the condition if ((amount-paid<tax-paid) &
(tax-due>amount-owing)); we can check...
```

this would have to be typed as

```
...using the condition <code>if((amount-paid&lt;tax-paid)
&amp; (tax-due&gt;amount-owing));</code>
we can check...
```

If you simply typed it as it appears in a program, a browser might attempt to interpret `<tax-paid)&(tax-due>` as markup tags, because they would appear to be enclosed in angle brackets, and it might then also get confused over the apparent character entity `&(tax-due>amount-owing))` overlapping the middle of it, because it begins with an ampersand and ends with a semicolon. If you need to display the actual character entity name of the less-than symbol itself (`&lt;`), you would need to type `&amp;lt;`.

One other character occasionally needs to be treated this way: the double-quote mark (") when you need to use it in a place where the text is already in double quotes, such as within an attribute value. This is done with `&quot;` (but it is not in HTML 2.0 and not all browsers support it yet). These typewriter-style unidirectional double quotes are not used in normal text, where the open-quote and close-quote signs are used, 'like this'.

Exercise 8.13   Character entities

Use the less-than, greater-than and ampersand character entities to type into your file the paragraph above beginning 'If you simply typed it...', then display the result in your browser.

Marks of identification

When you want to indicate that there is something special about certain words or phrases, you may want to keep this information separate from the ordinary emphasis or typewriter elements. The visual effect for the user may be the same, or there may be none, but it makes HTML documents more useful for authors if categories of usage for special terms have their own elements, so that they can be indexed or referenced, or used in glossaries or databases.

Citations

Bibliographic references can be marked with the `<cite>` element:

```
See <cite>SGML: A User's Guide to Structured
Information</cite>, by Liora Alschuler (<cite>ISBN
1-85032-197-3</cite>).
```

which may typically display in italics:

> See *SGML: A User's Guide to Structured Information*, by Liora Alschuler (*ISBN 1-85032-197-3*).

Definitions

When writing text which introduces specialist terms such as jargon or technical words, you may want to highlight the first occurrence or definition of a word or phrase, so that it can be indexed or located as the place where the term is defined. The `<dfn>` element was introduced in an earlier version of HTML 2.0 to identify such defining instances, but was later removed and is now reappearing in HTML3.

```
This contrast in harmony and tonality between
soloists and orchestra, which became popular
towards the end of the 17th century, is known
as the <dfn>Concerto Grosso</dfn>.
```

The text does not even necessarily change typeface or appearance in the browser display, although those browsers which allow font configuration may be able to do so: the objective is to allow the author to keep track of the important occurrences of words. In the above example, if you needed to italicize the definition, an `<i>` element could surround the whole `<dfn>`. One obvious application is for a browser to build a list of these as it parses a document, and to display them

at the end as a glossary or index: if taken in conjunction with the use of the
<link> element from the header, which allows the specification of a link to an
external glossary or index, an annotational tool of considerable power could be
implemented.

Strikeout text

Texts which are sent for revision, especially manuscripts or legal documents,
sometimes need a way to indicate where text has been removed, while keeping
the old text visible for subsequent editors or authors, so that they can see what
used to be there, at least for the duration of the current edit cycle.

The original <strike> element in earlier versions of HTML provided this, and
could be rendered as letters with a slash or line through them. It is unclear if any
browser ever implemented this.

```
The premises may <strike>not</strike> at any time be
occupied by members.
```

It is being supplemented (as <s>) in HTML3 with <del>, and a new element
<ins> is being proposed to handle insertions (to replace material being deleted).
Details of HTML3 are in Appendix B.

Other typographic controls

There are two tags which are useful in controlling the formatting and layout of
your file: the forced line-break and the horizontal rule. These are empty elements:
they are just like start-tags on their own without matching end-tags. There are also
character entities which represent a non-breaking space and a soft hyphen.

Forced line-break

Although browsers usually do their own formatting correctly for normal paragraphs, if you find you have to force a line-break at a specific point in your text
(such as for poetry), there is the <br> tag:

```
On the next line, by itself, type the command<br>
<code>search italic in typo-1 since 13 feb</code>
<br>and press the <kbd>Enter</kbd> key.
```

which could be used to get:

On the next line, by itself, type the command
search italic in typo-1 since 13 feb
and press the Enter key.

See also the example of a poem on pp. 174–175.

■

Exercise 8.14   Identification elements

Use the elements discussed in this section to identify some examples in your text, and see how many of them take effect in your browser. Type in the following text:

```
<blockquote><p>Phonemes are the sounds or strictly the
distinctive sounds of language - cat consists of the phonemes
/k/, /&aelig;/ and /t/. (Palmer F, Grammar, Penguin
1971, p107)</p></blockquote>
<p>When using the phoneme analysis program, pressing P will
break the value of current_word into its phonemes.</p>
```

Mark the first occurrence of 'phonemes' as a defining instance; mark 'cat' in italics; the three phonemes in slashes as samples; and mark the whole citation in brackets (and within that, the title 'Grammar' in bold). Mark the words 'phoneme analysis' as a deletion and make the word 'PhonAl' after them an insertion (use typewriter type); then make the P a keyboard character and the term current_word a computer variable. Ideally, the display should look something like this:

> **Phonemes** are the sounds or strictly the distinctive sounds of language - *cat* consists of the phonemes /k/, /æ/ and /t/. (Palmer F, **Grammar**, Penguin 1971, p107)

When using the ~~phoneme analysis~~ PhonAl program, pressing P will break the value of current_word into its phonemes.

This kind of markup is very useful for typesetting and indexing routines.

■

Horizontal rule

You can get a horizontal rule across the screen by using the <hr> tag:

```
...and telephone the department when you have
finished.</p><hr>
<h2>Authorization for expenses</h2>
<p>Staff of Grade 3 and above are permitted to claim...
```

which makes a distinction between sections, or around important text:

> ...and telephone the department when you have finished.
> _____
>
> ## Authorization for expenses
>
> Staff of Grade 3 and above are permitted to claim...

Non-breaking spaces

A non-breaking space is useful to prevent a browser making an unwanted linebreak at a particular point, such as between someone's initials and their surname. You can do this by inserting the character entity   between the two words, leaving no other space:

```
It has been done at the specific request of the deceased,
Dr. A.B. See, whose express wish...
```

This avoids formatting routines in browsers making a break at that point if the words happen to fall where the end of a line would normally come, while keeping a printed space in the output:

> It has been done at the specific request of the deceased,
> Dr. A.B. See, whose express wish...

This entity has been proposed for early support in HTML but is not implemented in all browsers.

Soft hyphen

An opposite case to non-breaking spaces arises in long or technical words, where automated hyphenation systems may fail. To let authors mark the allowed breakpoints in a word, there is the ­ entity:

```
pneu&shy;mono&shy;ul&shy;tra&shy;mi&shy;cro&shy;scop&shy;
ic&shy;sil&shy;i&shy;co&shy;vol&shy;ca&shy;no&shy;co&shy;
nio&shy;sis
```

(pneumonoultramicroscopicsilicovolcanoconiosis [Liang 1983]: the display above has been deliberately broken to fit in the width of these pages—you would actually type it all on one line.). This entity is again a proposal for HTML and is not supported in all browsers.

Exercise 8.14   Rules and spacing

Insert horizontal rules above the section headings in your file, and use the forced linebreak tag to control the ends of lines in a paragraph. Separate any initials from surnames with the non-breaking space, and insert soft hyphens in any long words. Reload the file to see what your browser supports.

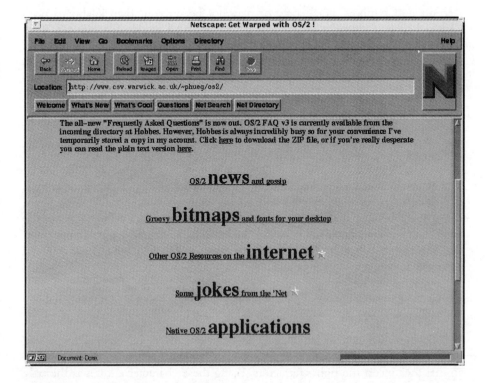

Figure 8.5   *Netscape* formatting in action

The additional elements proposed by *Netscape* for varying type size and for centering text are not part of HTML 2.0, although centering is implemented in HTML3 using an attribute. While there is unquestionably a demand for typographic controls like this, HTML elements are not always the place for them: the style sheet implementations in *Arena* and HTML3 will be much more effective. The benefit of the *Netscape* proposals was that it brought the discussion of visual appearance to the fore for consideration (Figure 8.5).

However, the same strictures apply to formatting in the Web as to handwriting, typewriting, wordprocessing, DTP, and other areas of graphic design: competent hands can do wonders with even limited resources, but the most powerful formatting system in the world can also be used to produce visual nonsense. Many Web information providers are now beginning to concentrate on content as well as appearance, because they know that it will be just as important to be able to retrieve information according to its sense or context (which can only be done if the text is marked up logically) as it is to be able to retrieve it in an attractive visual form.

Accents and symbols

Accents and symbols which may or may not be on your own keyboard need a special representation so that they will work on all kinds of computer. They have to be typed in a different form to do this, because hardware and software manufacturers have their own (sometimes idiosyncratic) ideas about how to handle accents. The Web is used internationally and HTML 2.0 provides direct support for accented letters in the Latin alphabet.

Accents

The standard way to represent letters with **accents** is to use character entities like those used for the less-than and greater-than symbols, non-breaking space and soft-hyphen (pp. 161–162). The entities are mnemonics for the names of the accents or symbols enclosed between the two characters '&' and ';' (ampersand and semicolon) as before. For example, to get an e with an acute accent, you type é as in the word 'Résumé':

```
R&eacute;sum&eacute;
```

HTML-compliant editors let you pick these from a menu, but to speed typing in other editors, you can usually use macros to redefine the accenting keys or menus so that they insert the right characters. Using these character entities is the only way to make sure your accents and symbols work in other browsers running on different computers to the ones you use. Don't be tempted to use your computer's own idea of accented letters or other special characters, because they may display completely differently on other users' computers.

HTML 2.0 supports the International Standards Organization's Latin-1 characters (see the full list in Table 8.1). There is much discussion over how or whether a future version of HTML should support extended character sets like Unicode or ISO 10646, which are capable of handling the increased number of characters in more complex writing systems such as Kanji (there's a mailing list to discuss this: see Appendix C). A separate but related issue is how such extended character sets should be encoded.

Table 8.1   International Standards Organization Latin–1 character entities

Copyright of the International Organization for Standardization 1986. Permission to copy in any form is granted for use with conforming SGML systems and applications as defined in ISO 8879, provided this notice is included in all copies

Name	Code	Char	Description	Name	Code	Char	Description
À	#192	À	capital A, grave accent	à	#224	à	small a, grave accent
Á	#193	Á	capital A, acute accent	á	#225	á	small a, acute accent
Â	#194	Â	capital A, circumflex	â	#226	â	small a, circumflex
Ã	#195	Ã	capital A, tilde	ã	#227	ã	small a, tilde
Ä	#196	Ä	capital A, dieresis/umlaut	ä	#228	ä	small a, dieresis/umlaut
Å	#197	Å	capital A, ring	å	#229	å	small a, ring
Æ	#198	Æ	capital AE ligature	æ	#230	æ	small ae ligature
Ç	#199	Ç	capital C, cedilla	ç	#231	ç	small c, cedilla
È	#200	È	capital E, grave accent	è	#232	è	small e, grave accent
É	#201	É	capital E, acute accent	é	#233	é	small e, acute accent
Ê	#202	Ê	capital E, circumflex	ê	#234	ê	small e, circumflex
Ë	#203	Ë	capital E, dieresis/umlaut	ë	#235	ë	small e, dieresis/umlaut
Ì	#204	Ì	capital I, grave accent	ì	#236	ì	small i, grave accent
Í	#205	Í	capital I, acute accent	í	#237	í	small i, acute accent
Î	#206	Î	capital I, circumflex	î	#238	î	small i, circumflex
Ï	#207	Ï	capital I, dieresis/umlaut	ï	#239	ï	small i, dieresis/umlaut
Ð	#208	Ð	capital Eth, Icelandic	ð	#240	ð	small eth, Icelandic
Ñ	#209	Ñ	capital N, tilde	ñ	#241	ñ	small n, tilde
Ò	#210	Ò	capital O, grave accent	ò	#242	ò	small o, grave accent
Ó	#211	Ó	capital O, acute accent	ó	#243	ó	small o, acute accent
Ô	#212	Ô	capital O, circumflex	ô	#244	ô	small o, circumflex
Õ	#213	Õ	capital O, tilde	õ	#245	õ	small o, tilde
Ö	#214	Ö	capital O, dieresis/umlaut	ö	#246	ö	small o, dieresis/umlaut
Ø	#216	Ø	capital O, slash	ø	#248	ø	small o, slash
Ù	#217	Ù	capital U, grave accent	ù	#249	ù	small u, grave accent
Ú	#218	Ú	capital U, acute accent	ú	#250	ú	small u, acute accent
Û	#219	Û	capital U, circumflex	û	#251	û	small u, circumflex
Ü	#220	Ü	capital U, dieresis/umlaut	ü	#252	ü	small u, dieresis/umlaut
Ý	#221	Ý	capital Y, acute accent	ý	#253	ý	small y, acute accent
Þ	#222	Þ	capital THORN, Icelandic	þ	#254	þ	small thorn, Icelandic
ß	#223	ß	small sharp s, German sz	ÿ	#255	ÿ	small y, dieresis/umlaut

Symbols

As you have seen, there are a some additional character entities for other symbols

Table 8.2 Numerical character references

This is derived from the ISO 8859–1 8–bit single-byte coded graphic character set

Name	Code	Char	Description
	#160		non-breaking space
¡	#161	¡	inverted exclamation mark
¢	#162	¢	cent sign
£	#163	£	pound sign
¤	#164	¤	general currency sign
¥	#165	¥	yen sign
¦	#166	¦	broken (vertical) bar
§	#167	§	section sign
¨	#168	¨	umlaut/dieresis
©	#169	©	copyright sign
ª	#170	ª	ordinal indicator, feminine
«	#171	«	angle quotation mark, left
¬	#172	¬	not sign
­	#173	-	soft hyphen
®	#174	®	registered sign
¯	#175	¯	macron
°	#176	°	degree sign
±	#177	±	plus-or-minus sign
²	#178	²	superscript two
³	#179	³	superscript three
´	#180	´	acute accent
µ	#181	µ	micro sign
¶	#182	¶	pilcrow (paragraph sign)
·	#183	·	middle dot
¸	#184	¸	cedilla
¹	#185	¹	superscript one
º	#186	º	ordinal indicator, masculine
»	#187	»	angle quotation mark, right
¼	#188	¼	fraction one-quarter
½	#189	½	fraction one-half
¾	#190	¾	fraction three-quarters
¿	#191	¿	inverted question mark
×	#215	×	Multiply sign
÷	#247	÷	Division sign

because using the regular characters for them in their raw state would conflict with HTML's own markup characters.

From Table 8.2 you can see that as well as the name of the character entity, each character has a numeric code. This is expressed in the same way as a character entity (starting with an ampersand and ending with a semicolon), but with a hash mark or number sign before the digits. These codes are intended for use instead of the name for those character entities which HTML does not yet support directly, such as £, because it allows individual browsers which *do* support them to display the right character.

There are many others defined in other ISO character sets, and a subset of the graphical characters is included in HTML 2.0 for use by reference to the character code number rather than the entity name (Table 8.2). This means that for a copyright sign © you need to type `&#169;` and for the pounds sterling sign £ you need to type `&#163;`. The complete set of all the character entities is in the entity files defining them, which can be downloaded from several sites on the Internet such as `ftp://sgml1.ex.ac.uk/pub/SGML/`.

The problems of using the Web for non-Latin-alphabet and multilingual documents are currently being discussed by the IETF Working Group. Many users around the world have adapted the software for local use, and have crested pages in a huge number of languages. François Yergeau of Alis Technologies (Montréal) maintains a list of some of these which I reproduce here (Table 8.3).

Table 8.3 Examples of non-Latin-alphabet and multilingual Web pages

Language	URL	Encoding
Russian	`http://www.free.net/Docs/cyrillic/alphabet_iso.txt`	ISO-8859-5
	`http://www.free.net/Docs/cyrillic/alphabet_koi.txt`	KOI-8
	`http://www.free.net/Docs/cyrillic/alphabet_alt.txt`	CP866, Cyr
	`http://www.free.net/Docs/cyrillic/alphabet_win.txt`	CP1251?, Cyr
	`http://www.elvis.msk.su/koi8/home.html`	KOI-8
	`http://www.ntt.jp/Mosaic-l10n/russian.html`	ISO-8859-5
Polish	`http://www.uci.agh.edu.pl/`	ISO-8859-2?
Greek	`http://www.ntt.jp/Mosaic-l10n/greek.html`	ISO-8859-7
Hebrew	`http://www1.huji.ac.il/www_teva/environment.html`	ISO-8859-8, unk
	`http://www.ntt.jp/Mosaic-l10n/hebrew-visual.html`	ISO-8859-8, Vis
	`http://www.ntt.jp/Mosaic-l10n/hebrew.html`	ISO-8859-8, Impl
Chinese	`http://www.ntt.jp/Mosaic-l10n/chinese.html`	GB 2312; GB
	`http://www.ntt.jp/Mosaic-l10n/chinese-hz.html`	GB2312; HZ
	`http://www.ntt.jp/Mosaic-l10n/chinese-big5.html`	Big5
Japanese	`http://www.etl.go.jp/Organization/welcome.html`	ISO-2022-JP
	`http://www.ntt.jp/Mosaic-l10n/japanese.html`	JIS X 208
Korean	`http://h20.kotel.co.kr/`	KSC 5601
	`http://www.ntt.jp/Mosaic-l10n/korean.html`	KSC 5601
Persian (Farsi)	`http://gpg.com/MERC/news/gpg.isi`	ISIRI 3342
German	`http://www.ntt.jp/Mosaic-l10n/german.html`	ISO-8859-1
Multi-lingual	`http://www.ntt.jp/japan/note-on-JP/multi-example.html`	ISO-2022

Comments

You can put comments in your file which you can see when editing it, but which won't get displayed to others who view the file using a Web browser. A comment looks like a tag but has no name: instead there's an exclamation mark and double-dash after the opening angle bracket and another double-dash before the closing one. The comment text inside the tag can go over more than one line:

```
<!--Here's a comment which I can see when I edit the file
but which is invisible to anyone reading the file via a
browser.-->
```

But be careful: most browsers can also display the raw HTML of any file they retrieve, so comments *can* be seen by users who use the *View source* function!

Several browsers implement comments wrongly, recognising `<!` on its own without the double dash. Although this avoids their authors having to code recognition of declarations like `<!doctype html...`, it also leads to some of them displaying pages wrongly, starting the display some way down the file instead of at the top.

■

Exercise 8.15   Accents and comments

Add a comment line to your file saying what editor you used to create it, e.g.

```
<!-- Edited with Emacs psgml-mode -->
```

Type the following sentence as a separate paragraph:

> My résumé says I made Münster cheese for the Mañana Cheese Co, but I was very naïve in those days.

Add a copyright statement to your file using the copyright symbol.

■

Block text

Block text is text that is set off from the surrounding or adjacent paragraph by being indented or separated by some space. It is frequently used for quotations of more than a line or so from other documents, and for addresses, warnings, and notes of various kinds.

We've seen indented text used in the items in a list, but block text elements can be used independently.

There are two elements in HTML 2.0 to let you indicate this: `<address>` and `<blockquote>`. Both of them go between paragraphs, not inside them, as they represent matter which is to be displayed as distinct blocks. An `<address>` element can occur within a `<blockquote>` element, but not the other way around.

The address element

Although its intention is clear from its name, the `<address>` element is not restricted to addresses. It typically causes a font change to italics, and may or may not be indented (in fact, *Arena* displays it right-aligned). As with most block-oriented elements, formatting is left to the browser, so if you need to split an address up into separate lines, use the **
** element (p. 164). The code

```
...If you would like to apply for this position, please
forward your r&eacute;sum&eacute; to:</p>
<address>Personnel Office<br>
ACME Widget Enterprises<br>
Nowheresville, KY</address>
<p>Applicants will be notified by postal mail of receipt
of their application...
```

would display something like:

> If you would like to apply for this position, please forward your résumé to:
>
> *Personnel Office*
> *ACME Widget Enterprises*
> *Nowheresville, KY*
>
> Applicants will be notified by postal mail of receipt of their application.

It is common practice to include an address block at the bottom of major files you write, so that your authorship is evident and readers can see who to contact.

Block quotations

As with the address element, this name suggests the use for quotations, but it can easily be employed for other block material such as warnings or exercises. Browsers usually indent this element, but there is no typeface change suggested. Because block quotation is an environment in its own right, it can contain other block-oriented elements like paragraphs and lists, so the text inside **<blockquote>...</blockquote>** must be at least within its own **<p>** element.

```
...as Peter Collinson says:</p>
<blockquote><p>It's good practice to sign each page and
place a date when the page was last changed.</p>
</blockquote>
<p>This lets the user identify...
```

> ...as Peter Collinson says:
>
>> It's good practice to sign each page and place a date
>> when the page was last changed.
>
> This lets the user identify...

Exercise 8.16   Blocks of text

Use the `<address>` element to add your name and address at the top or bottom of your file, using `<br>` to break the lines.

Complete the following limerick and display it using the `<blockquote>` element:

An HTML hacker called Tom...

Poetry

A special case of block text is poems, because they need fixed linebreaks, and are frequently divided into stanzas. One way of doing this is of course to use regular paragraphs and force the linebreaks with the `<br>` tag:

```
<p><i>Zerbrochen ist das Steuer und es kracht<br>
Das Schiff an allen Seiten. Berstend rei&szlig;t<br>
Der Boden unter meinen F&uuml;ssen auf!<br>
Ich fasse Dich mit beiden Armen an!<br>
So klammert sich der Schiffer endlich noch<br>
Am Felsen fest, an dem er scheitern sollte!<br>
</i><br>
<b>Johann Wolfgang von Goethe</b>, <i>Torquato
Tasso</i>.</p>
```

If the poem or extract is very long, you can avoid having to insert the linebreaks manually by using the `<pre>` element, but the result appears in typewriter type, which is less satisfactory.

However, poetry often consists of lines much narrower than the width of the page or screen, so a more balanced visual effect can be achieved by making use of the fact that the `<blockquote>` element is usually indented. The formatting within the block quotation is the same as within a paragraph, but if you have a heading or other text preceding the poem, the result is better-spaced:

Storm imagery in drama

The metaphor of the storm-tossed soul on the seas of life is extended by the irony of the sailor saving his life by clinging to the very rocks that wrecked his ship:

> *Zerbrochen ist das Steuer und es kracht*
> *Das Schiff an allen Seiten. Berstend reißt*
> *Der Boden unter meinen Füssen auf!*
> *Ich fasse Dich mit beiden Armen an!*
> *So klammert sich der Schiffer endlich noch*
> *Am Felsen fest, an dem er scheitern sollte!*

Johann Wolfgang von Goethe, *Torquato Tasso*.

Here the attribution has been moved into a separate paragraph.

Chapter 9

Hypertext links and graphics

- O About hypertext
- O The Uniform Resource Locator
- O Linking files for hypertext
- O Graphics, image maps, and multimedia
- O Documenting your files

The hypertext link is the facility that attracts many people's attention to the WorldWideWeb. From the users' point of view, all they do is click on a highlighted word or phrase, or on an image or icon, and Web magically retrieves further information related to it.

But in order to make it work, you as the author have to give the right information in the file about what to retrieve or what service to access. This process of adding to your text the information which is of value to your readers can take a some time, as it involves making decisions about how to phrase things, what information to point at, and the most effective sequence in which you want the reader to absorb the information.

As we saw earlier, **hypertext** has been defined as text which is 'not linear'. This means we need to assume that people will not read your documents through from start to finish in one go (unless they are very short), but they may go off at a tangent, taking what has become known as the 'scenic route' through cyberspace in a process of investigation.

This technique (called 'learning by serendipity', or the 'happy discovery' method) is frowned on by some educationalists, who feel that providing unstructured text encourages wandering at random, with a loss of effectiveness in the communication process between author and reader. The opposing view is taken by many Web users, who positively enjoy the process of discovery; but many will admit there is a lot of time wasted trying to locate information which is somewhere there but is not evident. Part of the skill in writing for hypertext systems lies in the choice of words and the direction in which they can influence the readers. Hypertext documents are not just files with links; a hypertext document is supposed to be a part of a greater whole, with the links providing the navigational aid.

Before we look in detail at how hypertext links are done, we need to know what can be done with them: what resources you can point at and how you refer to them. On pp. 95–103 we looked briefly at the Uniform Resource Locator as the way you address a resource on the network. The next section explains URLs in more detail.

The Uniform Resource Locator (URL)

A **URL** is composed of up to six pieces of information joined together with specific punctuation:

1   the **scheme** (protocol or access method) by which this link is to be retrieved;
2   the address of the **server** where the file is to be found;
3   the TCP/IP port number of the service;
4   a **directory** or path;
5   a **filename**;
6   an optional target label or **search term** where applicable.

The basic rules are:

- There is always a colon after the protocol, and the name of the protocol defines how the remainder of the URL is composed.
- In most cases there is a double slash between the colon and the server address.
- If the port number is given, it follows the server name, separated by a colon.
- The directory and filename are always given in Unix format, with a forward slash between directories, even if the server is not a Unix machine (servers on PCs and VMS computers translate these to their own format automatically).
- A target label is preceded by a hash mark(#).
- A search term is preceded by a question mark (?).
- The URL is always given in double quotes (these must be the regular typewriter unidirectional double-quote sign, *not* the apostrophe, grave accent, or the left- and right-hand typographic open-quotes and close-quotes that you would use for normal quotation of text).

The syntax of each element in full is:

The protocol

- `http:` for files available from an HTTP server;
- `ftp:` for files from FTP servers;
- `gopher:` for information from Gopher servers;
- `mailto:` for sending email from within a browser;
- `news:` for Usenet newsgroups;
- `telnet:`, `rlogin:` and `tn3270:` for login to interactive services;
- `urn:` (reserved for IETF Uniform Resource Names);
- `wais:` for access to Wide-Area Information Servers;
- `file:` for local files on your own computer disk which are not part of a server;
- `mid:` for access to repositories of mail by Message-ID;
- `cid:` for access to repositories of mail by Content-ID.

The protocol name is followed by a double slash (`//`), except for `news:`, which is followed directly by the name of the newsgroup; and `mailto:`, which is followed directly by the email address, for example:

```
<a href="news:biz.sales.closing-techniques">
<a href="mailto:listserv@irlearn.ucd.ie">
```

Browsers may pick up the name of the news server from the configuration file, or from an environment variable called **NNTPSERVER** specified when you set up your Internet software (or which will have been set up by the systems administrator if you are on an indirect connection). If you use the `file:` protocol for a local (non-server) filename on a PC running DOS or *MS-Windows*, you may need to replace the colon normally used after the disk letter with a vertical bar character. Browsers don't seem to be consistent about this—NCSA *Mosaic* for *MS-Windows* certainly seems to prefer it this way:

```
<a href="file://c|/mike/personal/resume.html">
```

If you use `file:` on a Unix machine, and the filename begins with a slash, you do need to include it, so that makes three slashes (looks odd but it's right):

```
<a href="file:///usr/mike/personal/resume.html">
```

The `ftp:` URL assumes that the connection will be made using regular anonymous FTP, but it is possible to specify a username and password in the form `ftp://username:password@server/directory...` although clearly you would want to keep files containing a URL like this out of the public view unless public access to the account is permitted.

The `telnet:` URL also allows you to specify the username and password in the same way as for FTP (but no directory or filename, as this is not meaningful for an interactive task). This should only be considered subject to the same security constraints.

Universal Resource Names (**URN**s) are a proposed development to describe 'persistent' objects: resources may be addressed in such a way that will make them available no matter what happens to the person, organization or machine they were originally on, so that duplication of existing copies or the tracking of multiple versions can be enabled. This is a piece of future-proofing and is not currently implemented: the future of Universal Resource Identifiers (**URI**s, including both URLs and URNs) is discussed in an Internet Draft, *Universal Resource Identifiers in WWW* [Berners-Lee 1994] by Tim Berners-Lee. The term Uniform Resource Citation (or 'Characteristic') (**URC**) is now being used to describe information that can be retrieved by reference to a URL (including names, titles, URNs, URLs, and URIs).

The Message-ID or Content-ID schemes are proposed methods of access to systems which transfer and store information in email form. Neither has yet been implemented.

The server address

The server address is a regular Internet hostname, the network name which identifies the computer where the server runs. The hostname is usually in the form *machine.site.country* or *machine.dept.site.network*, for example `www0.cern.ch` or `hoohoo.ncsa.uiuc.edu`. If you do not have the name, you can give the numeric IP address, like `143.239.991.288` (in cases where the machine is unnamed, or where your local nameserver is unable to resolve the name to a numeric address correctly).

If the service you want runs on a port other than the standard one (for example, 80 is the HTTP standard), you must follow the hostname with a colon and the correct port number, for example `telnet://lambda.parc.xerox.com:8888`. Each service has a standard port number allocated, which you can see on Unix machines with the command `more /etc/services`.

The directory and filename

The file specification must be given in the form *dir/subdir/filename.type*. There must be a single slash separating the directory/file specification from the server name, and a single slash between directory, subdirectory, and filenames. Take care with the file specification: some systems like Unix and Macs use case-sensitive filenames, where it is important if the letters are capitalized or not.

You can omit some of the items, depending on where the file is in relation to the current document, what kind of file it is, how you want to retrieve it, and what you want to do with it once it has been received:

- The protocol name and the server name go together in all cases (except `news:`, which never has a server name) so if you must either include both or omit both.
- If you omit the protocol name and server name, browsers will assume that a filename in the URL is to be fetched from the same server and by the same method as the current file. For example, if you just retrieved `http://www.acme.org/sales/blurb.html` and it contained a link to URL `orders/orderform.html`, then the browser would try to fetch that file from the `sales/orders` directory of `www.acme.org` using HTTP.
- If you omit all or part of the file specification, and follow the server name or partial file specification with a single slash, the server at the address given should respond by sending either its default index file or a directory listing. For example, `ftp://rtfm.mit.edu/pub` will result in a list of the contents of the `/pub` directory on the FTP server at MIT.

To ensure trouble-free interchange of URLs, only alphabetic and numeric characters should be used in the server names, directory names, and filename of a URL (apart from the slash, period, hash mark (#), and question mark. The asterisk and exclamation mark are reserved as they have a special meaning in some schemes. To escape from this restriction when you need to include some other non-alphabetic, non-numeric character you must encode them in hexadecimal and precede them with a percent sign (this is called 'escaping' such characters). In general, it is fairly safe to use a hyphen or a tilde (~), but in some circumstances even these can become mangled in email, for example, so you should substitute them with `%2D` for the hyphen and `%7E` for the tilde. The tilde is used by some servers (following Unix conventions) to allow individuals to maintain their own HTML files in their personal directories, outside the normal server directories, and have them addressed by their username preceded by the tilde (e.g. `http://www.acme.org/~mark/`: there are details of how to set this up on p. 247).

The anchor element

The hypertext link element is called an anchor and is done with the `<a>` element. This surrounds the text you want highlighted as the link phrase which the user can click on or whose number they can type in. You give the location of the document you want the link to point at as a URL (see the previous section) in the `href` attribute:

```
<h3>At last!</h3>
<p>Mark has written his
<a href="http://www.acme.org/~mark/markspage.html">home
page</a>!</p>
```

This makes it highlight the text:

```
Weekly Newssheet


   At last!

   Mark has written his home page!
```

The reader does not see the URL itself in the text, although some browsers display it at the bottom of the screen when the mouse cursor or arrow-key highlight passes through or is brought to rest on the phrase. Any word or phrase in the file can be made into a hypertext link in this way, but if the phrase you want to mark is a whole section heading, you have to put the link markup *inside* the heading element:

```
<h2><a href="http://www.acme.org/helpdesk.html">Customer
service desk</a></h2>
```

and *not* outside it like this:

```
<a href="http://www.acme.org/helpdesk.html">
<h2>Customer service desk</h2></a>
```

because what you're highlighting are the words 'Customer service desk', not the fact that it is a heading.

Although on most occasions the actual URL remains hidden from the user, there are times when you may need to be more explicit, such as with the `mailto:` URL: until this is supported in all browsers, it is a good idea to include the email address in the text as well as in the URL, for example

```
Please <a href="mailto:helpdesk@abc.def.org">mail our
Customer Service desk</a> at
<tt>helpdesk@abc.def.org</tt>.
```

The anchor tag is not restricted to surrounding text: you can make an image into a hypertext link, so that clicking anywhere on the image will make the link operate. We will look at this in more detail in pp. 187–201.

Targets and labels

When a user clicks on a hypertext link to a HTML file, the browser retrieves it and displays it starting at the beginning of the file. However, sometimes you might want to make the hypertext link a reference to a point further down the file, perhaps at the start of a specific subsection, or at the point where an important statement is made, and have the file start displaying at this point, rather than at the beginning.

To do this, you can use a form of the `<a>` element called a target in that file to mark the place you want to start at. This uses the `name` attribute instead of `href`. You set the value for `name` to a short label which you make up. Any letters or digits can be used, but it must begin with a letter. For example, suppose the file `prices.html` contained the following text:

```
There are <a name="discounts">reductions in unit price</a>
for volume purchases - the following list gives details
for domestic customers:
```

Here `discounts` is a label that the author made up, so it can be referred to as the target of a hypertext link in another file by adding the label name to the end of the URL, separated by a hash mark (#):

```
These prices are the best on offer for one-time purchase,
but larger volumes benefit from our
<a href="prices.html#discounts">discount arrangements</a>.
```

This means that when the reader of this text:

> These prices are the best on offer for one-time purchase, but larger volumes benefit from our discount arrangements.

clicks on the highlighted phrase 'discount arrangements', the file `prices.html` will be retrieved and the browser will search through it for an `<a>` element with the `name` labeled `discounts`, then position the line containing it at the top of the screen:

> There are reductions in unit price for volume purchases - the following list gives details for domestic customers:

The content of an `<a>` element which just has a `name` attribute does not get highlighted: only elements containing an `href` get highlighted. This labeled version of the `<a>` element has to have some text content: you can't use `<a name="dodo"></a>` without surrounding some text.

A label can be a target within the same file: if you write

```
See the <a href="#orders">ordering information</a>
for more detail.
```

with no file information at all, the browser will assume that the label `orders` occurs somewhere in the *current* file, and will search for it, then redisplay the document with the line containing the label at the top of the screen.

You can also combine both attributes in the same element:

```
The <a href="orderform.html" name="orders">online
order form</a>...
```

which makes that text both a link *to* the file `orderform.html` and also labels the same text as `orders` if you want to refer to it *from* elsewhere. In this case, it *will* display highlighted because there is a `href` attribute present.

Search terms

This is a slightly misleading phrase, because it implies that all documents can be searched, which is not the case. What it means is that this is a way of sending index or search keywords of some kind to a program accessible through the Web which will do some processing and send back a response in HTML format. This involves the target 'document' actually being a script or program which will accept input values, rather than a static HTML file. We will look in more detail at how you set one up in pp. 250–257 .

However, you can use many existing Web services like this by using a question mark after the URL, followed by the keyword or search term you want to use. The acronym and abbreviation server already mentioned (p. 68) is one example: if your file contains the text

```
The WorldWideWeb uses a protocol called
<a href="http://www.ucc.ie/cgi-bin/acronym?http">HTTP</a>
to request and send files.
```

this will result in the content of the `<a>` tag being highlighted in the normal way, and a click on the link will send a request to the acronym server to look up 'HTTP' and send back the output as a HTML file. The file **acronym** is a program that searches a database and then surrounds the results with HTML coding, so that the browser is wholly unaware that the results have come from a program: as far as it is concerned, it's just another HTML file.

This kind of facility can't be used with any static HTML file: it depends on the URL concerned being set up specially as an entry-point to a program which gets executed, rather than as a simple file to be retrieved, but the end-user need not be aware of this. Sending a search term in this way to a plain HTML file will of not achieve anything. Equally, the script or program must produce only valid HTML output, so that the results it generates can be displayed in the browser screen without the browser knowing that the text has come from a program. The program should also be able to cope graciously with being fed either garbage as a keyword or search term, as well as with being sent no term at all. There are examples of scripts on pp. 250–257.

Other attributes

There are five other attributes defined for the anchor element:

rel and rev

These attributes are to allow the relationship described by the hypertext link to be specified in either forward or reverse direction, for example:

```
<a href="chap4.html" rel="part">...
<a href="mybook.html" rev="master">...
```

This could be used to allow software to identify the relationships between files. The `rel` attribute shows the relationship of the target document to the current document: in the example above, the target document is a 'part' which 'belongs' to the current document.

The `rev` attribute describes exactly the reverse: it describes how the current document is related to the target one: in effect it 'points back' at the other document.

The use of these attributes in the `<link>` element is intended to enable browsers to implement facilities like tailor-made navigation bars. There is a proposed list of suitable relationship keywords being developed (listed in Appendix D). The topic of link relationships is discussed at `http://www.w3.org/hypertext/WWW/MarkUp/Relationships.html`.

urn

The nature and format of Uniform Resource Names are still under discussion by the IETF, so this attribute is not currently in use.

title

The title is for information purposes, to allow browsers which display the URL while the cursor is over the highlighted link to display instead a more meaningful description of the document, especially for files like graphic images or plain text documents, or menus retrieved from Gopher or Usenet News, which do not have an inherent title of their own, for example:

```
<a href="news:comp.fonts" title="Discussion of fonts
and typography">
```

methods

Although an HTTP server sends information about the method of use of a file when it sends it (the MIME Content-type), it is sometimes useful to be able to tell a browser in advance what functions it may perform on something, before it is retrieved, which may affect its rendering.

If used, the value of the `method` attribute must be a comma-separated list of allowed HTTP methods (see list in Appendix D).

Graphics

Graphics play a large part in WorldWideWeb documents because they are very easy to include. Used carefully, they not only brighten up your documents and make them more interesting to read, but they can make them easier to understand, and can be used to show things that would take many words to describe. But used carelessly, **graphics** can clutter the screen and infuriate the reader: more of this later.

There are two kinds of graphic you can use in HTML, inlined and external. Inlined graphics, as their name suggests, occur within the flow of text. External graphics are displayed outside the browser window as a separate image. Figure 2.2 on p. 9 showed a screen displaying a browser with inlined graphics in the browser window as well as in an external graphic displayed separately.

In theory, any format of graphics file can be used, provided you can be sure your readers have a suitable viewer that can be used with their browser. However, the three common formats used for images are:

●   GIF, Graphics Interchange Format (`.gif` files)
●   XBM, The X Windows BitMap format (`.xbm`)
●   JPEG, Joint Photographic Experts' Group (`.jpeg` or `.jpg` files)

In most browsers, the JPEG format can only be used for external images, not inlined ones (*Netscape* is one exception). It is possible to configure many browsers to accept other kinds of graphical formats (pp. 92–95) if you provide users with the right display program. System-specific graphics formats like *MS-Windows* BitMaps (`.bmp` files) or Apple Macintosh Picture format (`Pict` files) can easily be converted to GIF or JPEG format (pp. 196–197).

Use of the GIF file format compression techniques was licensed to CompuServe, Inc. (a large commercial email and discussion-group service which has recently connected directly to the Internet) by Unisys, the owners of the patent on LZW compression, a mathematical method of encoding a file to take less space. The use of such files is free, but software authors and distributors who wish to use LZW code in their programs have to license the technique from CompuServe.

Some unease was created when it was rumored that this involved plain users, but the licensing appears to apply only to those writing the compression techniques into a program. Details of the current status of this will be notified in `http://www.cis.ohio-state.edu/hypertext/faq/usenet/graphics/fileformats-faq/part1/faq-doc-39.html`, the relevant part of the Graphics File Formats FAQ maintained by James Murray.

An entirely new, portable, format for graphics files, the Portable Network Graphic Format [Crocker 1995] (PNG) has been written by a consortium of contributors to replace GIF. This is entirely free of legal restrictions, compresses better than

GIF, and offers more facilities, and will possibly take over from GIF as it becomes more widely used.

The character browsers, of course, can't display graphics, so if you are writing for the whole Web audience, you need to make certain that your pages will at least make sense for users of non-graphical systems, and we'll look at several ways of doing this.

Inlined graphics: the image element

Inlined graphics can be included at any point in the file where normal text occurs, including inside blocks of preformatted text. You insert an image with the `<img>` element (defined empty, so there's no end-tag involved) using the following attributes:

src

Contains the URL of the graphics image file you want displayed, in the same way as the `href` attribute is used for hypertext links.

align

Specifies how the image is to align with the adjacent text. Values are `top`, `bottom` or `middle`. Omitting this attribute means the bottom of the image will be aligned with the text. Note that it is the image, not the text, which gets moved to fulfil the alignment requirement. HTML 2.0 does not define a means for flowing the text around an image, but this is available in HTML3 and implemented in *Arena* (see example in Figure B.2, p. 300).

alt

Lets you supply alternate identifying replacement text which non-graphical browsers can display instead of the image. Without this, character browsers may display a marker like `[IMAGE]` where the graphic would normally come. Setting this attribute to null (`alt=""`) is a way of making character browsers display nothing at all in place of the image.

Although the `alt` attribute is only compulsory in Level 0 documents, its use is very strongly recommended, to make your document make more sense to users of character browsers. The text you give for this attribute cannot contain any element markup, and is treated as fixed-format text, so multiple spaces or linebreaks may be retained in the display, depending on the implementation of the browser being used. If you want to use double quotes in this attribute, specify them as `&quot;` to avoid confusion with the quotes which surround the attribute value.

Inlined images are retrieved along with the document and displayed as part of the text, so a simple example of an image in a heading might look like this:

```
<h1>Improved RINSO <img src="rinso.gif"
align="bottom" alt="Pack shot"></h1>
```

which would display like this in a graphical browser:

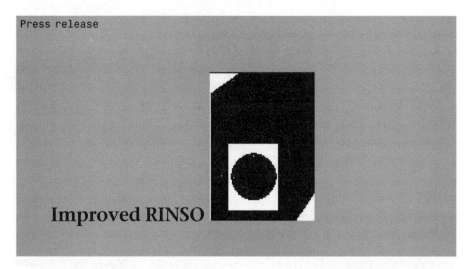

and like this in a character browser:

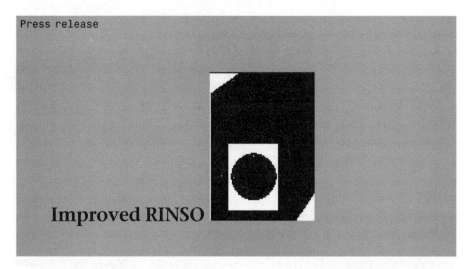

Inlined graphics are often in the form of icons: small symbols or pictograms representing an action or concept which symbolises or is explained in the adjacent text. You could use an icon to highlight certain paragraphs, for example:

```
<p><img src="warning.gif" align="middle"
alt="!!"> Paragraphs beginning with this warning are
intended for the more technical reader.</p>
```

which would display graphically as:

◈ Paragraphs beginning with this warning are intended
for the more technical reader.

and in a character browser as:

```
!! Paragraphs beginning with this warning are
intended for the more technical reader.
```

In HTML 2.0, any bulleting which is displayed for unordered lists (pp. 147–148) is determined by the browser, as there is no way to specify it in the markup. This means you can't use your own icons directly in the <li> markup, and inserting it with an <img> tag would only add it to the existing bullet. However, the definition list structure <dl> is not usually implemented with bulleting, so you can use a <dt> element with no content (or omit it entirely), and then use multiple <dd> elements for the list items, with an <img> embedded at the start of each:

```
<dl>
<dt></dt>
<dd><img src="star.gif" align="middle" alt="*">
Select the products of your choice from these pages</dd>
<dd><img src="star.gif" align="middle" alt="*">
Fill out the order form</dd>
<dd><img src="star.gif" align="middle" alt="*">
Add your credit card number and expiry date</dd>
<dd><img src="star.gif" align="middle" alt="*">
Send the form to us for processing</dd>
</dl>
```

Because the <dl> element indents the <dd>s in most browsers, the effect is something like this:

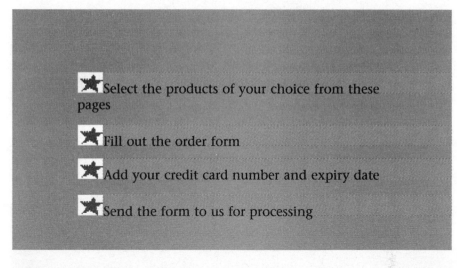

and in character browsers like this:

```
* Select the products of your choice from
these pages

* Fill out the order form

* Add your credit card number and expiry
date

* Send the form to us for processing
```

HTML3 provides for an attribute in the list elements where you can specify an icon image to be used as the bullet for that list.

Graphical browsers usually have a *Delay images* function to let you specify that you don't want graphics included when a page is retrieved. When this is activated, none of the images in a page are downloaded when the page is retrieved, but their position on the screen is occupied by a dummy image of some kind to indicate where they would occur. Figure 9.1 shows a page containing graphics that has been loaded using this feature. This speeds up the display of the *text* of the page unless this is already optimized by **asynchronous graphics retrieval** (see below). If you have activated this function, and want to start seeing graphics

Panel 9.1   Style guide

- Be careful about the quantity and size of inlined images: the many users who are on slow lines or congested networks do not appreciate a long wait while their browser downloads megabytes of pretty but non-essential pictures.
- Keep to fairly small images, perhaps up to a few square inches, unless they are really essential, like image maps (pp. 198–201).
- You can make a small preview of a bigger picture into a hypertext link to the full image (p. 194), so that users have the choice of downloading the bigger file or not.
- Try to avoid including lots of images on a single page, as the delay in loading them all may be nearly as bad as loading a single larger image (but see Figure 9.1).

again, deactivate it first, and then use the *Reload* function to make the browser fetch the current page again.

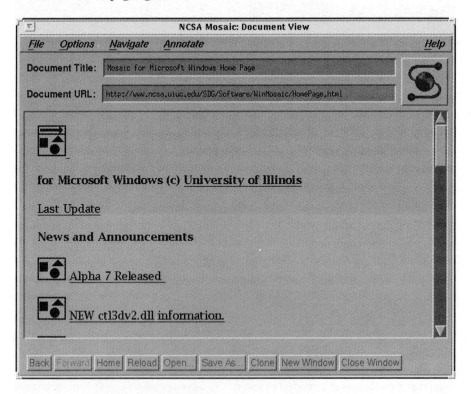

Figure 9.1   The delayed loading of graphics

Asynchronous graphics retrieval

Some browsers like *Arena, Netscape,* and Booklink Technologies' *InternetWorks* try to minimise the impact of large numbers of inlined graphics on slower connections like SLIP and PPP by desynchronizing the retrieval of images from the display of the text. This means the document text appears on-screen very quickly, and the images then appear one by one as they arrive. Two things happen to make this work:

1   when a page is retrieved, all the required images are requested simultaneously (or at least, as many of them as your system can handle at one time);
2   the text display is not held up until they arrive, but put on-screen immediately, with the position of the images occupied by an icon (in *Netscape*'s case, a fractured picture).

Figure 9.2 shows an example of this: the text of the page has been loaded and is on display, but some of the graphics are still in the process of transfer, using the interlaced nature of some GIFs to draw the image as a series of layers, a technique called 'venetian-blinding'. In the meantime, the page can be read and further links followed. The number of such simultaneous transfers is limited by the capacity of your network connection and the limit specified in your TCP/IP software.

External graphics

External graphics are activated by the user following a hypertext link which you have inserted in the text, which points at a graphics file rather than another text document. The browser keeps the main document on the screen, and retrieves the graphic file from the server, then runs a separate graphic display program to put the image on-screen in a separate window. The format of the link is identical to the normal hypertext link, using the `<a>` tag with the URL of the graphics file as the `href` attribute:

```
Visitors can <a href="citymap.gif">retrieve a map</a>
to show  how to get from the airport to our plant.
```

When the user clicks on the highlighted link, the graphics file is retrieved, but the server which sends it will spot the filetype (here `.gif`) and prefix the transmission with the correct MIME type (in this case `image/gif`). The browser will react to this by running whatever program is specified in its configuration for that type of file, and the image will pop up in a separate window.

External graphics are not restricted to GIF or JPEG formats, as there are many external display programs to handle different types of file where there is no requirement to embed the image inside the browser's display window. *PostScript*

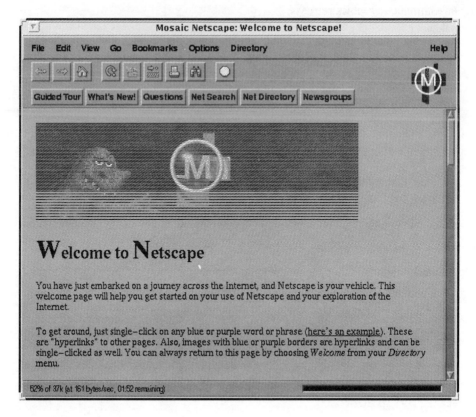

Figure 9.2   Asynchronous retrieval of graphics in *Netscape*
You can see how the graphical image is part-formed, being built up of horizontal slices

files are one possible format, using a *PostScript* display program such as *GhostView*; `.dvi` files output from *TᴇX* are another, using `xdvi` or similar. The external graphics mechanism, using the `<a>` tag, is also the means by which video and sound can be retrieved (p. 197). *Netscape*'s default is to retrieve external graphics inline (this can be changed in the configuration options by giving the name of an external viewer program) because it has the ability to display inlined JPEGs.

Referencing one graphic from another

A good way of allowing users to choose whether to retrieve large graphic files or not is to provide a **thumbnail** version of the picture (a postage-stamp size image) in the body of the text, as an icon, but make it a link to the full-size image:

```
<p>Visitors can use our <a href="campus-map-big.gif">
<img src="campus-map-tiny.gif" align="bottom"
alt="[full image]"></a>  map of the campus</p>
```

Surrounding the `<img>` tag (which includes the small icon) with the `<a>` tag makes it a link to the big picture. In this case, character browsers can also retrieve the bigger image, because they can download the file and save it to disk for later viewing or re-use on another machine, even though they cannot display it directly on the screen at the time.

The thumbnail image is shown with a highlight around it, so that it can be seen to be a link. It is essential here to use the `alt` attribute, so that users of character browsers can see a word or two to click on for the full image to be downloaded as a file for later use. You could of course also extend the scope of the `<a>` tag to include the adjacent descriptive text so that it was highlighted as well.

Creating and managing graphics files

The images you provide may be existing ones you want to use, or you may have to create new ones. There are several ways of getting the graphics files you want:

Using existing images

You can obviously use any graphics files you have available, but there are several archives on the Internet of icons and small pictures which people have made available for public re-use: one of the biggest lists is from the Yahoo directory, in `http://www.yahoo.com/Computers/World_Wide_Web/Programming/Icons/`.

Scanning new images

Pictures and diagrams can be scanned using any regular scanner and image-processing package, and converted to GIF or JPEG format. If you don't have a scanner of your own, or access to one, many printshops and graphic design studios will scan artwork or photographs for you, but make sure that their software can produce a file in a format and size that you can handle (pp. 196–197) and that it can be transferred to your server on diskette or tape (or over a network). Most scanners come with software to handle graphics, but if you have a large quantity, or require subsequent manipulation, a package such as Adobe *PhotoShop* may be needed.

Creating your own artwork

Small icons and simple illustrations can be done using programs like *MS-Windows Paint* or Macintosh *MacDraw*, and saved in a format that you can convert with a downloadable package such as *LView* or *WinECJ*. Photographs or more complex drawings need more sophisticated software such as *Corel Draw* or Adobe *PhotoShop*. Doing good illustrations in these packages is something of an acquired skill, so you may need advice from a professional graphic artist if you want high quality material.

Using other people's images

You can also download or capture images from existing Web pages, but you should ask permission from the owner to avoid copyright problems (Chapter 16).

Re-using external images

If you want to keep an external graphic for re-use, click on the application which is displaying it while it is on the screen, and use that application to save the file under some suitable name.

Re-using inlined images

To get hold of inlined images, use the ***View source*** function of your browser to display the HTML source file with the markup, and identify the reference to the image by inspecting the contents. Then use the ***Open URL*** function and copy-and-paste the URL from the source code display into the dialog box (or just retype it) so that it gets retrieved as a separate external graphic which you can save as described in the previous item.

Computer screens have nowhere near the fineness of resolution that a laser printer has, so there may be little point in providing ultra-high resolution images if the file size causes unnecessary delay in transmission. The sizing of images can also cause problems between different browsers and different screen resolutions. Additional attributes to the `<img>` element in HTML3 will allow you to specify the height and/or width that the image is to be displayed at.

Converting graphics files

There are several packages which offer conversion from one graphics format to another, and most graphics packages themselves offer a variety of file formats. The most widespread public domain converter is *Pbmplus* (**pbm**: *Portable BitMap*), which is a collection of programs to go between some dozen or more common file formats and its own `.ppm`, `.pnm`, or `.pbm` formats. Conversion from, say, GIF to *PostScript* (`.ps`) files therefore means running `giftopbm` first and then `pnmtops`.

There is no *PostScript* to GIF included, but the GNU *GhostScript* interpreter can convert from *PostScript* to many graphics file formats, including GIF and JPEG (see `http://www.cs.wisc.edu/~ghost/` for details).

You can of course use regular graphical viewers/editors like Adobe *PhotoShop* and many others, but it involves displaying the image on the screen first, and then picking the **Save As**..., so it is often faster to use a commandline program if there is no need for you to see the picture while you convert it, or if you have many files to process in a batch. The popular shareware viewers like Leonardo Loureiro's *LView* (see `http://mirror.wwa.com/mirror/busdir/lview/lview.htm`) or John Bradley's *xv* can also do this kind of conversion.

There is also a useful program by Andreas Ley called `giftrans`, which makes a selected color, usually the background, into a transparent 'color', so that it appears invisible over the background of whatever browser it is displayed in. You can download this from `ftp.rz.uni-karlsruhe.de` in `pub/net/www/tools/giftrans`. There is a similar facility in the program for the Mac called *GIFconverter*. The FAQs of the Usenet `comp.graphics.*` newsgroups are a good resource for finding conversion software for a wide variety of platforms and formats.

The choice between GIF or JPEG depends on the use to which you want to put the images. Most browsers support only GIFs for inline display, so JPEGs are best kept for external graphics. A JPEG file is usually smaller than a GIF file of the same image, because the JPEG algorithm can compress the data better (with a tradeoff in loss of quality), so JPEGs will be transmitted faster. However, because of the programming of the algorithm, interpreting JPEGs for display is slower than interpreting GIFs, so there is a tradeoff between speed of transmission and speed of display. It is impossible to give a hard and fast rule for how to choose between them, as a lot will depend on the quality of connection and sophistication of equipment that your likely readers will have. Because of the way in which they handle graphical data, GIFs tend to be better for sharply delineated pictures such as graphical drawings, bullets, and diagrams, whereas JPEGs are better at handling continuous tone material like photographs.

Sound and motion

As mentioned above, you can use the `<a>` element to give your users access to a sound or video file. In the case of sound, the file should be in RIFF WAVE (`.wav`) or Unix (Sun/NeXT) Audio (`.au`) format. For video, the Motion Picture Expert Group (`.mpeg` or `.mpg`) or QuickTime (`.mov`) formats are used.

Sound and video files, like external graphics, can be very large. It is not possible to use the `<img>` element to make the sound or video play automatically: they have to be referenced as external objects with the `<a>` element, like hypertext links, but you should try to warn your readers in any document you create with pointers to such files, because the download time can be substantial.

To play back these formats you need the relevant audio or video software, which can usually be found either through *Archie* or from the sites where you download Web browsers. Although the built-in loudspeakers of PCs can be used with public-domain sound programs like *wplany*, a sound card is essential for anything other than trivial use. Macintoshes have adequate sound facilities built in, as do most modern Unix workstations (you may need to provide the loudspeakers, though). Playing video can be a little jerky (depending on the speed and load of your computer), and gives only a very small image: for more frequent use a dedicated video card is needed.

To create sound and video, you need 'capture' software which will record sound from a microphone or video from a VCR. This is often supplied 'free' with the sound card or video processor card when you buy it (or comes bundled with the machine if you buy a 'multimedia' computer). Apart from quality and ease of use, the important thing is that it must be capable of creating files in the right format for use in the Web (see above).

Image maps

Image mapping is a way of letting you turn portions of an inlined image into separate hypertext links. This way, users can retrieve different files depending upon whereabouts inside the displayed image they click their mouse (this is clearly not a viable option for users of character browsers). You may need access to the server software to set up and install your own image-mapped graphics, although anyone with a graphical browser can use them without special facilities.

To display the image and make it 'clickable', you have to include the `ismap` attribute in the `<img>` tag: this indicates to your browser that mapping should be enabled for this image, so that it knows what to do with a mouse-click in the image area. You then enclose the image element in an anchor element which gives a symbolic name for the **mapping file** as its `href` attribute. The concept is similar to the one used on p. 194 to make a small icon (thumbnail) reference a larger image:

```
<a href="http://www.acme.org/cgi-bin/imagemap/factory">
<img src="factory.gif" ismap alt=""></a>
```

To make the image map work at the server end, you need to divide up the area of the image into circles, polygons or rectangles, each of which will bring about a different hypertext link. Software such as *xv* on Unix machines shows the (x, y)

```
default /examples/none.html
# Top fish eye
circle /examples/ow.html 313,28 313,44
# Bottom fish eye
circle /examples/ow.html 382,193 383,200
# Top fish
poly /examples/fish.html 298,93 251,26 300,0 453,0 511,48 511,101
474,65 420,55 358,88
# Bottom fish
poly /examples/fish.html 349,196 350,233 406,221 444,195 455,214
470,181 418,150
# Plant
poly /examples/plant.html 117,96 116,267 172,283 192,299 247,254
242,101
# Pillar
poly http://hoohoo.ncsa.uiuc.edu/examples/pillar.html 11,0 26,225
18,261 83,270 109,264 110,97 105,0
# Gold handrail
poly /examples/gold.html 307,199 245,177 239,115 511,91 511,121
292,144 346,166
```

Figure 9.3 Example image map data
This shows part of the result of mapping a picture of some fish in an aquarium (example from the NCSA's documentation)

coordinates of your mouse pointer when you display an image. By moving the mouse to trace the outline of each area you want activated, you can get the coordinates and store them in a mapping file.

Edit this file to add the URL to which each set of coordinates should point, or use one of the mapping management programs available to do the coordinate recording for you (Figure 9.3). A good document describing the procedure for the NCSA server is http://hoohoo.ncsa.uiuc.edu/docs/tutorials/ imagemapping.html. The NCSA and CERN servers supply an *imagemap* or *HTImage* program which does the lookup of coordinates into the image map file. You need to add a line to your server's image map configuration file, describing the map with a symbolic name and the real filename. This provides the link which tells the server that the response from the user's browser is to be interpreted as map coordinates into the relevant mapping file, rather than as a normal file lookup. Figure 9.4 shows the image of the fish whose map data is shown in Figure 9.3.

The internal mapping mechanism varies slightly between servers but they react in the same way to the image mapping requests from clients: for example the NCSA server used to use an `imagemap.conf` file to tell the server which URLs are image maps but now lets users create mapfiles anywhere in the document root, whereas the CERN server uses a combination of `map` and `exec` commands to tell the server where to find the map.

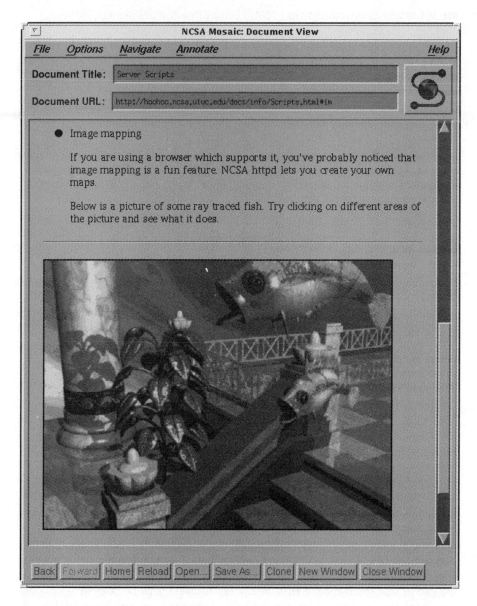

Figure 9.4   Some image-mapped fish

Mapping software

MapMarker is a tool for *X Windows* for generating clickable image maps, written by Gudge Chandramohan. It requires tcl7.3/tk3.6 (see `http://www.dl.ac.uk/ CBMT/tcl/HOME.html` for details) and loads `.xbm` or `.rppm` files (or GIFs) plus your image map file to create and edit the polygons and attach the URLs. Details are at `http://www.dl.ac.uk/CBMT/mapmarker/HOME.html`.

Mapedit by Thomas Boutell is a program for *MS-Windows* and *X Windows* which loads GIFs directly and lets you draw polygons, rectangles, and circles, specifying a URL for each. Further details are at `http://sunsite.unc.edu/boutell/mapedit/mapedit.html`.

WebMap for the Macintosh reads GIF and PICT files, and allows you to draw out the various graphic primitives (rectangle, circle, and polygon) that represent the hot areas on an image map. *WebMap* supports both the CERN and NCSA image map formats. Details and prices are available at `http://www.city.net/cnx/software/webmap.html`.

Documenting your files

Documentation is something everyone in the software business knows is essential, but which often gets neglected in the rush to get something working. Although it sounds trite to say 'do your documentation', it is a real necessity when you are setting up a service with potentially many dozens, hundreds, or even thousands of files. HTML provides facilities in the file header for documenting what the file is, where it's come from, who owns it, who wrote it, and how it can be accessed.

When we looked at the HTML header, we used the `<title>` element, as it is the only compulsory one. There are some others which can add functionality to your documents, although they may have no effect on the display. These elements are all empty: they do not enclose any text. An example of a header using them is in Figure 9.5.

The file link

The `<link>` element is used to indicate a connection between the file *as a whole* and something or someone external to HTML or the Web. It differs in this way from the hypertext 'anchor' link (the `<a>` element), which provides a link between a fixed point in your text and another file or service. The most common use is to identify an author or owner: someone to send email to if problems are encountered with processing the file:

```
<link rev="made" title="Mail author"
href="mailto:merlin@www.wizard.gov">
```

Some browsers (*Lynx* is a common example) can use this to send an automated email message if problems occur retrieving links from the document (this is useful if you are running a system where files are written by many different authors, as a way of notifying them to check or update a reference).

This element can occur as many times as needed. For example, you might want to indicate that the current file is a part of a series, so you could have <link> elements pointing at the first document of the series, at the one immediately preceding it and at the one following it; or you can point at indexes or glossaries.

The objective is to provide information for browsers to use in order to construct a customized navigation menu when the file is viewed. Surprisingly, given the obvious use and appeal of this treatment, no browsers currently implement it. It differs from the anchor element in that it does not link one phrase to a file, but is intended to act as a pointer for the whole document. It would be nice to see browsers making more use of this kind of link, given the demand for access to greater facilities for customisation. There is a list of some proposed attribute values for for the <link> element in Appendix D.

The href attribute is compulsory, and is used exactly as for the <a> element with a URL which points to the location on the Internet of the person, file, service, or other object being referred to.

Other header elements

The <title> is not the only element available in the header. The remaining ones documented here are for the control of the file in its environment in an information base and are all optional. An example of a full header using all of them is in Figure 9.5.

The file base

This element is used to identify the absolute (base) address for any relative addresses of hypertext references later in the file. Normally, when a browser is asked to activate a link (by the users clicking on it), it parses the URL and adds any missing parts, such as the protocol name, server address, and any parts of the directory structure which might have been omitted. As we saw on p. 181, this means that the browser uses the details from the URL of the current page to supply any missing parts for any URL it retrieves from *within* that page.

The <base> element can be used to specify that a different set of defaults is to be used for any partial references encountered in this document. This is useful way of pointing all requests for documents from the current page to a specific server or directory which is different from the one which sourced the current page. For example, if the base was set to http://www.abc.def.com/marketing/ then a hypertext link later in the document which said href="adverts.html" should be retrieved from the directory specified in the base, even if the current copy of the file on display came from somewhere else. This lets an organization distribute local copies of important documents to local servers but still have them point to fixed locations for their links.

The only attribute is **href**, which you set to the URL containing the default specification, for example:

```
<base href="http://www.acme.org/public/info/>
```

Index or search specification

An HTML file does not have to be a static text file: as far as the server and the user are concerned, the 'file' could be generated 'on the fly' from a shell script or program. This makes it possible to run a search in a database, and reformat the results as a HTML file to send back to the user. By making a URL in a hypertext link refer to a script rather than a file, clicking on it makes the server execute the script.

To let the reader enter a keyword and have it acted on by the script, the **<isindex>** has to be included in the header to indicate to the browser that the current 'document' is capable of handling this input. The browser pops up a dialog box or data-entry region where the user can type a keyword or search term, and this is sent back to the server appended to the end of the URL. The program then receives it and uses it in its processing. Details of how to do the implementation of such scripts are on pp. 250–257. The **<isindex>** element can also occur in the text body of a document, as a structural element between paragraphs or lists.

Metainformation

The **<meta>** element was originally defined as a means for embedding metainformation in existing HTML documents without having any impact on the presentation of those documents (browsers ignore it as just an unknown element). It fulfils an important goal of allowing user-extensible information to be embedded in documents and be accessible to maintenance tools and indexing engines [Fielding 1994]. The **<meta>** element is thus available to bear information which the author would like the document to carry as if it had been present in the response headers sent by the server. The **http-equiv** attribute lets HTTP servers provide this information separately, without sending the whole file, in response to a HTTP 'HEAD' request. Examples of use:

```
<meta http-equiv="Keywords" content="chocolate, mousse">
<meta http-equiv="Expires" content="Tue, 05 Sep 1995">
```

■

Exercise 9.1   Writing a fuller header

Add a `<link>` element to your file header to identify yourself as the author, giving your email address as the `href` value using the `mailto:` form of the URL.

If you have included a lot of hypertext links by now, you could specify a base address to retrieve them from with the `<base>` element.

Mail the authors of your favorite browsers, asking if they intend to implement the `<link>` element as described.

■

Editor sequencing

The `<nextid>` element is intended for use by hypertext editing software to identify the next unique identifier to allocate when keeping track of files and crossreferences. It takes a single attribute `n` with a value in the form of a letter followed by digits, for example

```
<nextid n="a123">
```

This is intended to allow SGML editors to ensure that files making up a database retain their referential integrity, but the author is unaware of any product which currently makes use of this element.

```
<!doctype html system "/web/doc/html2.dtd">
<head>
<title>Minutes of AG/37/1294 Safety Committee</title>
<isindex>
<base href="http://mgt.acme.org/services/secretariat/minutes">
<nextid n="ag38">
<link rev="made" title="Mail corrections to author"
href="mailto:mike@mgt">
<link rel="part" title="Index to all minutes"
href="http://mgt.acme.org/mgt/rev/1994.html">
<link rel="owner" title="Company safety policy"
href="ftp://mgt.acme.org/policy/safety.html">
<meta http-equiv="Keywords" content="safety policy">
</head>
```

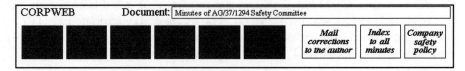

Figure 9.5   Example of a fully-documented header

Other attributes

The other attributes are optional, and are the same as for the anchor element <a>, and are explained on pp. 185–186: rel, rev, urn, title, and methods.

Figure 9.5 shows (hypothetically) how a more complete documentation of a file might be obtained for use with a browser which supports all the header elements. The <isindex> element implies that this 'file' has been generated by a script, probably from a corporate documentation database, and that the user can search for other documents (pp. 250–257); the <base> element fixes the directory in which any subsequent incomplete hypertext references should be sought; the <nextid> element specifies to the file owner's editing software that the next file in sequence should be labeled 'ag38'; and the <link> elements give the author's email address, the location of the index and a reference to another document related to the subject matter. The <meta> element lets search routines pick up on (in this example) keywords pertaining to the document as if they had been present in a real MIME header called Keywords.

The usefulness of this approach cannot be overstated, as it can provide a much more context-sensitive approach to navigation than is currently the case with most browsers and HTML pages.

Chapter 10

Tables, mathematics, and forms

O Tables using fixed-width characters

O Mathematics using $\LaTeX$

O Forms for collecting information

HTML 2.0 does not define any tags for tables or mathematics, so you can't directly enter into an HTML file equations which use non-alphabetic symbols, fractions, or subscripts, and superscripts, and there are some restrictions on how tabular information can be presented. Both math and tables tags are a part of HTML3, and are being implemented by some browsers already (*Arena*, *Mosaic* of various forms). Details of both are in Appendix B, but in the meantime, there are several other ways to provide these facilities. Data-collection forms were originally specified for the old HTML+, but were so useful they were implemented almost immediately by many browsers, and have become an integral part of HTML 2.0.

Tables

There are some simple options available in HTML 2.0 for the display of tables. The quick way out is to prepare the tabular part of your file as preformatted text in fixed-width (typewriter-style) characters and enclose it in the **<pre>** element:

```
<pre>
<b>Countries, currencies, and codes</b>
-------------- ISO two-  -------------------- Currency
Country        letter code  Currency             Code
-------        -----------  --------             --------
USA            US           US Dollar            USD
Canada         CA           Canadian Dollar      CAD
Germany        DE           German Mark          DEM
France         FR           French Franc         FRF
Belgium        BE           Belgian Franc        BEF/BFF
Luxembourg     LU           Lux Franc            LUF
Netherlands    NL           Guilder/Florin       NLG
Ireland        IE           Irish Pound          IEP
Great Britain  GB           Pound Sterling       GBP
Italy          IT           Italian Lire         ITL
Denmark        DK           Danish Crown         DKK
Spain          ES           Spanish Peseta       ESP
Portugal       PT           Portuguese Escudo    PTE
Greece         GR           Greek Drachma        GRD
Austria        AT           Austrian Schilling   ATS
Norway         NO           Norwegian Crown      NOK
Sweden         SE           Swedish Crown        SEK
Finland        FI           Finnish Mark         FIM
</pre>
```

The effect of this in a character browser, being based on fixed-width characters, is identical to the input format (apart from the limited highlighting), and its effect in a graphical browser is not markedly different. Markup affecting appearance is allowed even inside the preformatted element, so text can use any of the inline tags, including images, to make it stand out.

```
Countries, currencies, and codes
-------------  ISO two-   ----------------- Currency
Country       letter code Currency             Code
-------       ----------- --------          --------
USA           US          US Dollar          USD
Canada        CA          Canadian Dollar    CAD
Germany       DE          German Mark        DEM
France        FR          French Franc       FRF
Belgium       BE          Belgian Franc      BEF/BFF
Luxembourg    LU          Lux Franc          LUF
Netherlands   NL          Guilder/Florin     NLG
Ireland       IE          Irish Pound        IEP
Great Britain GB          Pound Sterling     GBP
Italy         IT          Italian Lire       ITL
Denmark       DK          Danish Crown       DKK
Spain         ES          Spanish Peseta     ESP
Portugal      PT          Portuguese Escudo  PTE
Greece        GR          Greek Drachma      GRD
Austria       AT          Austrian Schilling ATS
Norway        NO          Norwegian Crown    NOK
Sweden        SE          Swedish Crown      SEK
Finland       FI          Finnish Mark       FIM
```

If a variable-width typeface is essential, an alternative worth considering is to compile the table in some other system and create an inlined image which can be included with the `<img>` element in your HTML file. TEX has some powerful routines for formatting tables and could be used to good effect in this case.

Making the table a graphical image may actually have a positive advantage in cases where the tabular matter may change content or form over time but the surrounding text does not: if they are kept separate, it is easier to update the image file as required, without having to edit the HTML file.

On the other hand, if you need to use an anchor name label as a target for hypertext referencing in the middle of the table, this is obviously not possible using an image. The use of an image in this way would also prevents character browsers from displaying the file properly, as the `alt` attribute cannot easily hold tabular information.

Mathematics

Mathematics conventionally uses italic characters, so it is quite possible to enter simple alphabetic equations like $L = a + x - q$ as

```
<i>L</i>=<i>a</i>+<i>x</i>-<i>q</i>
```

Bear in mind that mathematics italicises only the letters, not the operators; that the spacing of mathematics is quite different from normal text; and that a hyphen makes a poor minus sign:

$L=a+x-q$

This method is suitable for very small or simple single-line equations using only alphabetic letters, and will even display in a character browser, although if the browser displays underscores to delimit italics, the effect may be less than readable.

$L=a+x-q$

There are no provisions for subscripting and superscripting in HTML 2.0, but these are being implemented in HTML3.

Because HTML 2.0 does not define any elements specifically for mathematics, one solution is to use some other system for the equations only, and convert them manually to inlined images which can be incorporated in your HTML file (pp. 188–193). The other is to use $\LaTeX$, for which a conversion routine exists to automate the whole process. HTML3 includes proposals for elements specifically for mathematics, but these are still under discussion.

$\LaTeX$-to-HTML

$\LaTeX$ is a document preparation system based on the $\TeX$ typesetting program, which among other features has the most comprehensive mathematical facilities of any text-handling program. $\LaTeX$ has the advantages that it uses a structured system of markup, not dissimilar in concept to HTML; it is in common use as the *lingua franca* of mathematicians worldwide; and it is available in both free and commercial versions for almost every computer system in common use.

In $\LaTeX$, equations are entered using a symbolic notation rather like the character entities used in HTML for accents, so a equation such as

$$b_4 i \sqrt{u} \frac{ru}{16} qt\pi$$

is typed as

```
$$b_4i\sqrt{u}{ru\over{16}}qt\pi$$
```

There's a short guide to getting started with *LaTeX* at `http://asis01.cern.ch/cn/CNASDOC/WWW/essential/essential.html`.

Nikos Drakos' *LaTeX2HTML* program takes a *LaTeX* file and processes the equations, creating a separate X bitmap graphic image file for each one, then converts the remaining text to a HTML file which includes references to the inlined images in the right places (Figure 10.1). The result can be displayed in a graphical browser, reproducing a legible representation of the equations embedded in the text. *LaTeX* works happily with all three of the common typefaces used for mathematics (Computer Modern, Times, and Lucida), two of which (Times and Lucida) are also available in the NCSA X Windows *Mosaic* display.

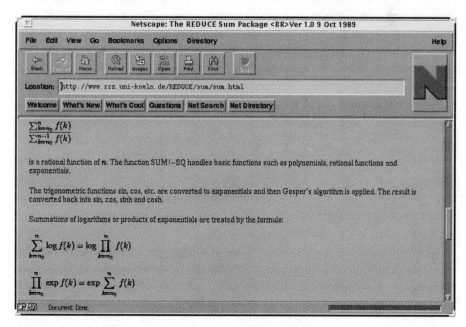

Figure 10.1   *LaTeX2HTML* used to create mathematical displays

The program is written in *Perl* and is available from any of the Comprehensive *TeX* Archive Network (CTAN) servers (`ftp.shsu.edu`, `ftp.tex.ac.uk` and `ftp.dante.de`) in the `tex-archive/support/` directory. The only disadvantage to this method is that the `<img>` tags used to hold the references to the equation images cannot make use of the `alt` attribute to hold the *TeX* symbolic notation for each equation, because it might contain characters such as less-than and greater-than which would upset browsers, so users with character systems have no means of seeing even this restricted view. However, the advantages of being able to use a system which handles mathematics correctly and converts the surrounding text to HTML far outweigh this small drawback.

You need a copy of *TEX* with the *LATEX* macros to handle the processing: this can be downloaded from any of the CTAN servers mentioned above, in versions for most operating systems and architectures. Commercial implementations are also available from many vendors: details of all systems can be had from the *TEX* Users Group (email `tug@tug.org` or see `http://www.ucc.ie/info/tex/ tug/tug.html`).

A different approach is taken by the *HyperTEX* project, which proposes the use of hypertext `\specials` in *TEX* files which can be interpreted by `dvi` viewers to implement links using standard URLs. There are already two products which work this way, *Xhdvi* and *HyperTEXview*. *An article* [Smith 1994] describing the project is available at `ftp://snorri.chem.washington.edu/hypertex` and there is a mailing list to discuss it: `hypertex@snorri.chem.washington.edu`.

Forms

The form-fill feature was an early enhancement to HTML proposed by the NCSA team, now supported in almost all browsers, to allow the user to fill in a form and submit it for processing by a server script or program. Forms have proved to be one of the most popular and useful features of HTML, and are used for gathering data in all sorts of circumstances, from the anonymous St. Valentine's Day greeting (Figure 10.2) to business order **forms**, survey questionnaires, and database queries.

A form is usually made up of text interspersed with a series of input areas which the user can fill in. When the user submits the completed form, it is sent to a destination which you (the author) specify. In most cases this destination is a URL which is a script or program which parses the input data and then stores or processes it or sends it to an email address. Some browsers have started to implement the sending of the form direct to an email address by using the `mailto:` URL form, and this is likely to become more widespread.

Details of how to do the processing using a script or a program are documented in the online material from the server suppliers (chiefly CERN and the NCSA), for example at `http://hoohoo.ncsa.uiuc.edu/cgi/`. If you want to use forms-processing scripts or programs, you do need to have access to a server where you can place the executable which you want to process the data until use of `mailto:` becomes more common. More details of forms-handling are on pp. 223–224.

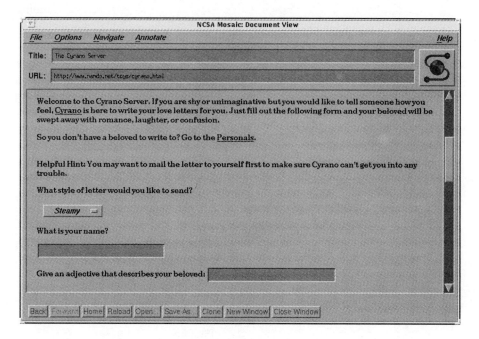

Figure 10.2   Forms application: the St. Valentine's greeting
You can find this gem at `http://www.nando.net/toys/cyrano.html`

The form element

A form must be entirely defined within the `<form>...</form>` tags. This element is block-oriented and its element contents are shown in the diagram in Figure 10.3. Note that while forms can contain other block-oriented elements such as paragraphs and lists (included in the `%body.content` entity), it cannot contain another form: the ⊘ operator precludes that, while the ◯ operator adds the three classes of field (data-entry area). The attributes for the element are:

Method of submission

The `method` attribute can be either `GET` or `POST`. The exact detail is explained below, but `GET` means that the data will be sent to a server shell script as a delimited stream attached to the end of the URL, and made available to a script in an environment variable, whereas `POST` means that the data is sent on the next record, and the server will make the data available at the standard input (logically equivalent to where you would type in data if you were actually running the script from a terminal).

Action to be taken

The `action` attribute specifies the URL for the server script or program which

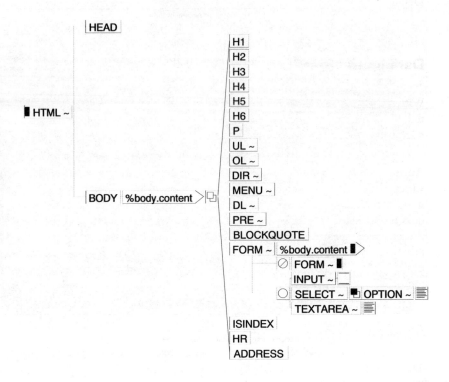

Figure 10.3   Element contents of a form within the HTML scheme

is to do the processing. Server authors have established the conventions of the Common Gateway Interface (**CGI**) which provide for scripts to reside in a separate directory (e.g. `cgi-bin`) on the server host. The CGI specifications specify a number of environment variables which the server can pass to the script or program to enable it to detect what manner of data it is handling. Scripts are discussed further on pp. 250–257.

Encoding type

The `enctype` attribute currently has only one possible value, so it is optional and need not be specified. This is taken as the default for the MIME Content-type: `application/x-www-form-urlencoded`.

An example of the `<form>` start-tag might be

```
<form method="GET"
action="http://abc.edu/cgi-bin/registration">
```

Details of how the data are passed to the server are explained on pp. 223–224.

Data input types

Within the form, explanatory text can be in headings, paragraphs, lists, preformatted, block quote, and address elements, mixed with the three data-input elements: `<input>`, `<select>` and `<textarea>`.

An input area (or 'field') is defined with one of these three elements, using a variety of attributes which specify the name of the field, what type of input it is, the maximum length (in the case of text) or a restricted range of values (in the case of radio or checkbox buttons). An example of a form using these input types is shown in Figure 10.4. You can see the effect of single-line text input for the name, radio buttons and check boxes for single- and multiple-choice questions, a menu for months, and free-format text for recording comments.

Free-format text areas

The `<textarea>` element is used when you want the reader to be able to type multiline text such as a comment or message. There are three attributes, all compulsory:

- **name** to give the field its name;
- **rows** to specify how many rows or lines of text are required;
- **cols** to specify how may characters wide the text area should be.

The text content inside the `<textarea>...</textarea>` tags can be used to give the panel its initial value. For example, the panel in the example in Figure 10.4 was produced with

```
<p><textarea name="comment" rows="5" cols="40">
Please use this space for any comments
</textarea></p>
```

The nature of the input area depends on the browser: some provide only simple text input, others provide more sophisticated scrolling regions with some limited wordprocessor capability.

The text in the field is returned as the fieldname followed by the entire text in lines. A blank line is returned if the user entered no input.

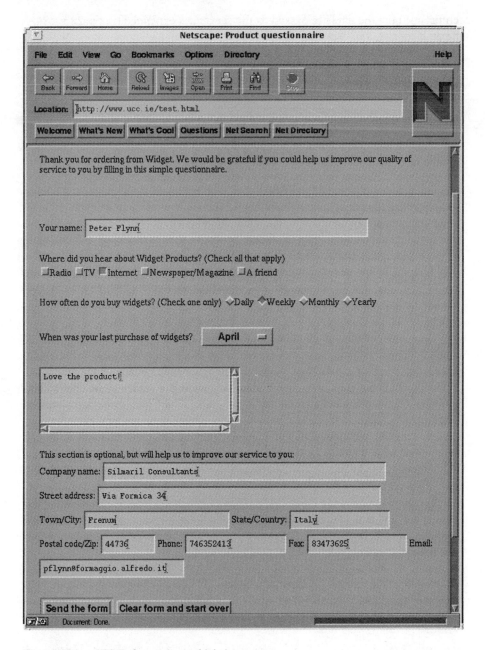

Figure 10.4 HTML form using multiple input types

Selectable or single-line input

The <input> element is for checkboxes and radio buttons, and for single-line text such as names, address lines, numbers, or other short values. This is an empty element, so there is no closing `</input>` tag. Each field must have the `name` attribute, and the type of field is defined with the `type` attribute, which determines both the appearance and the response to selection. The other attributes used depend on the type of field. Valid types are:

Text

Use `type="text"` for single-line fields to hold text or numeric data. You specify the size of the displayed data-entry box with the `size` attribute and the maximum allowed length of input with the `maxlength` attribute. The reason for having the two separate values is that browsers should be able to scroll single-line text entry horizontally within the field, so that even a short data-entry box can hold a long text value for submission.

```
Company Name:
<input type="text" name="company" size=60 maxlength=80>
<br>
Street address:
<input type="text" name="address" size=60 maxlength=80>
<br>
Town/City:
<input type="text" name="town.city" size=30 maxlength=40>
State/Country:
<br>
<input type="text" name="state.country" size=20 maxlength=40>
Postal code/Zip:
<input type="text" name="postcode.zip" size=10><br>
Phone: <input type="text" name="phone" size=20>
Fax: <input type="text" name="fax" size=20><br>
Email:
<input type="text" name="email" size=30 maxlength=60>
```

Figure 10.5   HTML code and display of text fields
See Figure 10.4 for a display of this form

The `value` attribute can be used to predisplay a default value which the user can leave if it is correct, or delete or edit if another value is required:

```
Which browser do you normally use?
<input type="text" name="browser" size=20 value="Mosaic">
```

Password

The `type="password"` is a special case of the text field which you can use for an application where you want the user to type in a password. The user's input is not displayed (or displays as asterisks), which is normal for password entry. Otherwise it functions exactly the same as the text type.

Check boxes

In cases where you want the user to be able to select more than one value for the same field, you can use several `<input>` elements, each with the same name and `type="checkbox"`. This is the 'check all that apply' kind of question. The browser will display a box or symbol for each occurrence of this type of `<input>` element, which will change color, darken, or otherwise highlight when selected. Each item you present for a group of such choices must have the same field name, so that they can be identified as belonging to the same question when the data is received by whatever program or script is to process it:

```
<p>Where did you hear about Widget Products? (Check all
that apply)<br>
<input type="checkbox" name="source" value="radio">Radio
<input type="checkbox" name="source" value="tv">TV
<input type="checkbox" name="source" value="internet"
checked>Internet
<input type="checkbox" name="source" value="paper">
Newspaper/Magazine
<input type="checkbox" name="source" value="friend">
A friend</p>
```

The choices are presented as unchecked, but one or more can be forced to display as checked by default if you use the **checked** attribute, as done with the entry for 'Internet'.

Radio buttons

The opposite form of choice question to the checkbox is the 'check one only' format, which is done with `type="radio"` (radio buttons are those where any button selected makes the others all switch off). The same principles apply as for checkboxes, in that the name of the field must be the same for all `<input>` elements in the items making up a single question.

```
<p>How often do you buy widgets? (Check one only)
<input type="radio" name="freq" value="daily">Daily
<input type="radio" name="freq" value="weekly">Weekly
<input type="radio" name="freq" value="monthly"
checked>Monthly
<input type="radio" name="freq" value="yearly">Yearly</p>
```

Only one can be selected: if the user changes the selection, the previous choice is automatically deselected. The **checked** attribute can also be used here to preselect one (but only one) item.

Hidden data

If you have information you want to transmit with the form, but you don't want it to be part of a question, you can use the attribute value `type="hidden"`. This is useful if you have several similar forms which will transmit data layouts looking the same, but you want to identify them separately. For example, order forms aimed at different segments of the market could have a different value:

```
<input type="hidden" name="market" value="youth">
```

Nothing about this element will appear on the user's screen, but the data transmitted will contain `market=youth` . Don't forget, though, that as with comments, a user who clicks the *View source* function of the browser can still see your original HTML code.

Resetting the form

It is common to have a button labeled Reset which lets users clear the data from the fields and start over with the form displayed as it was before data entry began. This is done with the `type="reset"` attribute value, to allow for those occasions when data entry has been muddled or there's been a change of mind on many questions.

```
<input type="reset" value="Clear form and start over">
```

This useage does not need a field name, but you can use the `value` attribute to give wording of your own on the button, otherwise you just get the word 'Reset'.

Submitting the form

The `<input>` element is also used to submit the whole form when it is completed. `type="submit"` is used like the `reset` value:

```
<input type="submit" value="Send the form">
```

The wording for the value is what appears on the submission button on the user's screen: if you don't supply a value, the button is labeled 'Submit'. A side-effect of this is that you can have multiple Submit buttons, any one of which will submit the form but include a different value depending on which one was pressed, by using the `name` attribute:

```
Press your party's key to submit your completed
questionnaire:<br>
<input type="submit" name="party" value="Republican">
<input type="submit" name="party" value="Democrat">
<input type="submit" name="party" value="Labor">
```

```
<input type="submit" name="party" value="Communist">
<input type="submit" name="party" value="Undecided">
```

An alternative method of submitting the form is to use an image map, similar to the way in which they are used in regular inlined images (pp. 188–193). Using `type="image"` you include a `src` attribute giving the URL of the image you want displayed, the same as for the `<img>` element, and there is an `align` attribute for alignment which takes the same values as for inlined images.

```
Click your mouse on your favorite breakfast food to submit
this form: <input type="image" name="sentfrom"
src="http://muesli.cereal.org/forms/breakfast.gif">
```

The x and y coordinates of the mouse pointer where the click was made are sent as part of the form data, each preceded by the field name of the image:

```
sentfrom.x=226
sentfrom.y=317
```

The coordinates are taken from the top lefthand corner of the image being $(0, 0)$. This method of submission is obviously only any use if all your readers have graphical browsers.

Menu selections

If the choices for a question would be better represented by a menu, you can use the `<select>` element. This implements an alternative method of selecting the value, using a menu, and is convenient if the number of choices is large, or needs compacter presentation. The `<select>` element must contain an `<option>` element for each option on the menu:

```
<p>When was your last purchase of widgets?
<select name="month">
<option>January</option>
<option>February</option>
<option>March</option>
<option>April</option>
<option>May</option>
<option>June</option>
<option>July</option>
<option>August</option>
<option>September</option>
<option>October</option>
<option>November</option>
```

```
<option>December</option>
</select>
</p>
```

In this case, only one choice will be allowed, and the *content* of the `<option>` element will be returned in the completed form as the value of `month`. You can change this so that predefined values of your own are returned instead, by using the `value` attribute:

```
<select name="month">
<option value="1">January</option>
<option value="2">February</option>
<option value="3">March</option>
<option value="4">April</option>
<option value="5">May</option>
<option value="6">June</option>
<option value="7">July</option>
<option value="8">August</option>
<option value="9">September</option>
<option value="10">October</option>
<option value="11">November</option>
<option value="12">December</option>
</select>
```

You can specify that one of the options is initially selected, by adding the `selected` attribute to the required `<option>` element.

Users can select options several times if the `multiple` attribute is added to the `<select>` element. Each choice will then be transmitted as an additional occurrence of the field name. For instantiations where the menu is presented as a scrollable region, the `size` attribute can be set in the `<option>` element to a value to specify how many of the options should be visible at a time.

The entire form shown in Figure 10.4 looks like this:

```
<html>
<head>
<title>Product questionnaire</title>
</head>
<body>
<h1>Product questionnaire</h1>
<p>Thank you for ordering from Widget. We would be grateful
if you could help us improve our quality of service to you by fill-
ing
in this simple questionnaire.</p>
<hr>
<form action="http://www.ucc.ie/cgi-bin/test-cgi"
method="get">
<p>Your name: <input type="text" name="name"
```

```
size="60"></p>
<p>Where did you hear about Widget Products? (Check all
that apply)<br>
<input type="checkbox" name="source" value="radio">Radio
<input type="checkbox" name="source" value="tv">TV
<input type="checkbox" name="source" value="internet"
checked>Internet
<input type="checkbox" name="source"
value="paper">Newspaper/Magazine
<input type="checkbox" name="source"
value="friend">A friend</p>
<p>How often do you buy widgets? (Check one only)
<input type="radio" name="freq" value="daily">Daily
<input type="radio" name="freq" value="weekly">Weekly
<input type="radio" name="freq" value="monthly"
checked>Monthly
<input type="radio" name="freq" value="yearly">Yearly</p>
<p>When was your last purchase of widgets?
<select name="month">
<option>January</option>
<option>February</option>
<option>March</option>
<option>April</option>
<option>May</option>
<option>June</option>
<option>July</option>
<option>August</option>
<option>September</option>
<option>October</option>
<option>November</option>
<option>December</option>
</select>
</p>
<p><textarea name="comment" rows="5" cols="40">
Please use this space for any comments</textarea></p>
<p>This section is optional, but will help us to improve
our service to you:<br>
Company name: <input type="text" name="company" size="60"
maxlength="80"><br>
Street address: <input type="text" name="address" size="60"
maxlength="80"><br>
Town/City: <input type="text" name="town.city" size="30"
maxlength="40">
State/Country: <input type="text" name="state.country" size="20"
maxlength="40"><br>
Postal code/Zip: <input type="text" name="postcode.zip"
size="10">
Phone: <input type="text" name="phone" size="20">
Fax: <input type="text" name="fax" size="20"><br>
Email: <input type="text" name="email" size="30"
maxlength="60"></p>
<p><input type="submit" value="Send the form">
<input type="reset" value="Clear form and start
over"></p>
</form></body></html>
```

Forms processing

When a form is filled out and submitted, the responses are sent to the server defined in the URL in the `action` attribute, and the server hands them to the script or program named in that URL. The method of passing the data depends on the value of the `method` attribute:

GET

In the `GET` method, data from each field in the form is passed as a *name=value* pair, with the pairs separated by an ampersand. These are attached to the end of the URL, separated by a question mark. In text, plus signs replace spaces and non-alphanumeric characters are converted to hexadecimal preceded by a percent sign. As an example, suppose a form has two fields **name** and **age**, which the user fills in as 'Brendan O'Reilly' and '37'. In the example above, the URL passed back to the server would be

```
http://abc.edu/cgi-
bin/registration?name=Brendan+O%27Reilly&age=37
```

These values (`name=Brendan+O%27Reilly&age=37`) are passed by the server at `abc.edu` to the shell script `registration` in an environment variable `QUERY_STRING`. It is then the responsibility of the shell programmer to split the string up into usable values for processing. Some examples of how to do this are on pp. 250–257.

The advantage of having the data passed as an environment variable is that it is very easy to write simple shell scripts to use it. The drawback is that some systems limit the length of data that can be passed this way. Limits vary according the operating system and manufacturer's flavor: on Unix systems it can be anywhere between 1Kb and 10Mb. If you are passing data this way to a C program, you retrieve the data from `argv()`.

There is an exception to this: if the data does not contain an equals sign, it is passed into the command line for a script as well as into `QUERY_STRING`. This would be the case for data gathered from `<isindex>`.

POST

In the case of `POST`, the values are passed from the browser to the server on a separate line, and made available in the place where a script would look for its default input (`std.in` in Unix terms).

The big advantage is that this method is not subject to the length limit of `GET`, but sending data this way is broken in some browsers. If you are using a script, you have to get the data by making a fixed-length `read` to `std.in` (the number of bytes to read is in the environment variable `CONTENT_LENGTH`).

A template C program for adapting to handle form data is available with the NCSA's server and is reproduced in Figure 13.1, p. 258, but what your own script or program does with the data once it has been received and identified is entirely up to you. In a very simple case, it might just reformat the values onto one line each by writing them into a temporary file, and then mail the file to some specified email address or append it to a database. At a more complex level, it might perform some processing on each value, checking it for validity, and creating some output.

The `mailto:` URL can be used in a form's `action` attribute to cause a browser to mail the contents of a filled-in form directly to a specified address. This is not widely implemented in browsers yet, so it is probably not wise to use it extensively unless you are certain that all your readers are using a browser that does, for example (perhaps on an in-house corporate Web where you can exercise this kind of control).

Whatever the processing involved, the script or program must usually generate some response, because the server will be expecting something to send back to the user's browser, and this must be generated as HTML. It could be a short thank-you message or a more complex analysis of results based on the form data: the section on scripts (pp. 250–257) explains the processing environment in more detail.

If you don't have the expertise to write a script from scratch, Steven Grimm of Hyperion has created `uncgi`, which is available at `http://www.hyperion.com/~koreth/uncgi.html`. This is a short C program that handles the data decoding and gives you simpler access to the fields on a form, so you can generate a form-processing program as a shell script.

In choosing between `GET` and `POST`, there is a very useful distinction recommended by the HTML specification document (details of where to get this are on p. 115): `GET` is for actions which are transient, such as looking up a term in an index or dictionary; `POST` is for actions which have a measurable effect on stored data elsewhere, such as adding your name and address to a database.

Chapter 11

Controlling appearances

O   Users' expectations

O   Users' demands

O   What can be done about them

O   Alternatives to HTML

To most computer users it is a natural assumption, on first seeing a graphical Web browser, that the Web is some form of wordprocessor or desktop publishing system. The deceptive slickness with which you can surf from document to document, each one typographically displayed, gives the impression that there is a full-featured repertoire of hard-wired formatting behind the appearance of each page. However, as we have seen, this is not quite the case.

Looked at purely from a typographical point of view, HTML is a seriously deficient means for conveying visual information compared with conventional DTP software such as *QuarkXPress*, *TEX*, *FrameMaker*, *Ventura*, or *PageMaker*. Even *MS-Word* or *WordPerfect* has more in the way of formatting capabilities. And yet, as we have seen, none of these has the combination of the other facilities which have made the Web so popular, such as hypertext, multiplatform networking, or image maps, and (with the exception of *TEX*) they are all commercially-controlled proprietary solutions which concentrate on appearance rather than content.

It is precisely because the Web was *not* developed purely for typographical reasons that we now have the flexibility it offers. This is small consolation to the many users who, while they appreciate the networking flexibility, still want to exert more typographic control over their documents. Publishers, advertisers, and marketing users in particular have been accustomed for some 550 years to having 100% control over the single-platform, single-medium material of printing, so naturally they find in some cases the transition to multi-platform, multi-media productions frustrating and disappointing, especially as the Web in particular has been presented to the non-networked world with considerable hype. It may take some time for us to relearn the concept that information is not now something static which we print on paper, but something fluid and dynamic which can change from one occasion to the next.

User requirements

From discussions, queries and complaints in the newsgroups and mailing lists associated with the Web, it is obvious that there are some core demands from new and existing providers for greater control over the display of their pages, while at the same time there is an equal demand from the users for the continued ability to control the display themselves.

To see to what extent these demands can be reconciled, we need to look in more detail at what is being demanded. From the large volume of email I received as a result of the original documents I wrote on how to use HTML (now superseded, but to some extent the progenitor of this book) I kept a log of the topics queried, and I have added to this the results of a quantity of other mail and newsgroup posts about the facilities of HTML which were sent to the IETF Working Group mailing list. The distribution of the queries raised is shown in Figure 11.1.

What is noticeable about these requests is that they are almost all about visual appearance: there were very few asking how the structure of an HTML file could be used to best effect. As these topics are clearly of serious concern to anyone wanting their organization to look its best in public, I have summarized below

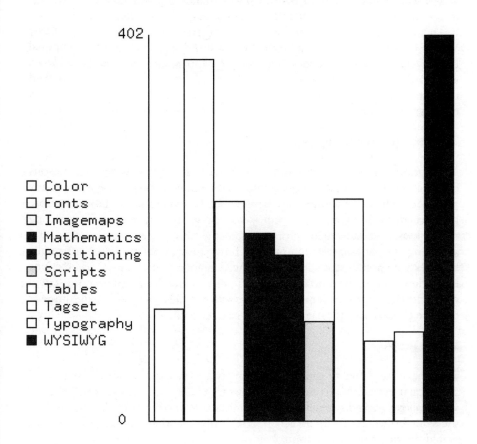

Figure 11.1   Summary of requests for clarification of HTML facilities

my responses to the individual queries raised, omitting those which do not relate directly to the adjustment of appearance (scripts, comments, image maps...)

Color

While it would be nice to able to dictate the background and foreground colors of the user's display, the users have in general more control over this themselves, and have become accustomed to configuring the colors for their own satisfaction. Custom rendering like color, font style, size, and spacing could in fact all be made attributes of elements without significant difficulty, so that the DTD could be modified to let people specify

```
<em color="red" size="36" font="Medway-Bold">
```

but this could in any case only ever be a recommendation. Another alternative would be to allow a form of backdrop to be painted with a GIF with an option to ignore the reference point and bounding box, so that subsequent text would not restart below it, but overwrite it. One suggestion reported from the Chicago WWW Conference was to allow the browser to display a slide-bar which would let the user set the browser's sensitivity to appearance on a scale from total user control to total publisher control. The style sheet proposals (pp. 310–312) currently under discussion by the Working Group may go some way towards meeting these demands.

Typeface (font) and type size

Most graphical browsers let you specify what fonts you want used for each element in HTML, but this runs counter to the requirements of some information providers to be able to control the typography. Commercial suppliers of graphical browsers have been asked to find a way of giving this level of control, and the proposed enhancements implemented by *Netscape* are one possible way of achieving this, although it is not clear how you can get the same effects in a browser which does not support enhanced typography, nor how you do it in a typewriter-style environment like a character browser. You can of course achieve nearly 100% control by supplying only *PostScript* files (or Acrobat files) but this cuts the character-mode user out of the market entirely.

Image maps

The image map facility (pp. 198–201) gives a very easy, attractive interface for graphical users, although it seems unnecessary to use it for a simple row of buttons when a close-packed series of button images made into hypertext links would have the same effect. As I said earlier (p. 201), implementing the use of the `<link>` would provide even better control.

Mathematics

Subscripts and superscripts are the two most sought-after items, both in plain text and in the mathematical field. They form part of HTML3 but may be introduced earlier in a revision of HTML 2.0. More complex math is also proposed in HTML3, and implemented in the *Arena* browser (pp. 85–86). To some extent the jury is still out on the implementation of large-scale math in SGML, and HTML cannot hope to match the descriptive or formatting power of a specially-designed language such as $T_{E}X$, or the larger-scale DTDs like Euromath or ISO 12083, but I would hope to see more browsers implementing HTML3 math in the near future.

Centering and positioning

This one topic seems to have become the *cause célèbre* of appearance control *vs* descriptive markup. As with arbitrary fonts, there is nothing inherent in centering some text which makes it mean anything in particular, but it is one of the most useful tools in the designer's box, and its proposed implementation in *Netscape* and in HTML3 is described in Appendix B.

Fixed spacing, tables, and indentation

People have had to resort to a variety of ingenious contrivances to forced fixed amounts of spacing into their pages. One way of getting vertical space is to add extra redundant `<p>` elements between paragraphs; another is to use an entirely blank transparent GIF file. A tiny one of these can also be used at the start of paragraphs to force some indentation. Doubtless the ` ` entity will also be used to force multiple spaces in a similar way until tabular alignment becomes common.

Tables are a special case of spacing because while the columns are usually at fixed points across the page, the spacing needed to achieve this using a non-fixed-width typeface has to be variable. The solution using `<pre>` is the only viable method until HTML3 tables become implemented.

Printing

It's at this stage that professional typographers get nervous, as the idea of the user being able to affect display impermanently on the screen is a transitory matter, but committing something to print which has come off the network without proper typographic control is rather more permanent. The only way this can be satisfied with any degree of confidence is for designers to check their work carefully using several browsers of varying capabilities, and to work within the restrictions needed to ensure that what the user prints will look satisfactory.

Forms design

A similar restriction has to operate when designing forms, because the widths of fixed-character data input fields will appear radically different between browsers, and the instantiation of checkbox and radio-button widgets also varies considerably. Although it uses more space vertically, leaving the page looking rather empty, it is sometimes better to use the list structure elements of HTML to control the placement of options or choices underneath one another, rather than trust to luck by having them all on one line, when you have no control over the width of the user's window or the size of the font.

Hyphenation and justification, margins

The typesetting of text with two vertically-aligned margins, which is normal in books and common in wordprocessing and DTP, can look out of place in a character browser, as fixed-width type loses a lot of readability when the spacing between words is allowed to vary. HTML3 proposals allow for the specification of justification, but there are rendering problems like what to do about hyphenation, and how to handle spacing algorithms in narrow windows or with long words. Most serious designers will want to avoid the appalling possibility of varying the interletter spacing, as is so often done in WP and DTP documents where hyphenation has been turned off. H&J routines in most systems still use the clumsy and ineffectual line-by-line approach, rather than the whole-paragraph method, and there are some substantial problems involved when you change language in a document.

Page division

HTML is essentially a pageless model of text, as the reader's flow can be interrupted at any time by their clicking on a link to another page, so having fixed-point pagebreaks does not carry much meaning. However, when a page is printed, there is no way to control the division into pages, and in certain circumstances on-screen, when you might want to prevent display of the next section until ready, there is no stop-point. If HTML becomes more permissive of intent, rather than descriptive of practise, it would be possible to argue for the introduction of a forced pagebreak `<pb>` along the lines of the existing forced linebreak `<br>` or even allow a specification like `<br type="page">`.

Bulleting

Under HTML 2.0, bullets get inserted in most browsers for itemized lists, menus, and directory lists. There is no way to include them in other lists, and no way to substitute your own symbol, other than inserting a GIF image at the start of each element. HTML3 proposals provide for the automated inclusion of a user's GIF image or one of a selection of bullets provided by the browser authors.

Special effects

The effects available in DTP systems such as boxing and shading, distortion, and realignment, can only be achieved in the Web by using images prepared in some other system. While some extension of HTML could ultimately allow for constructions such as `<p format="boxed">`, this would not appear to be high on the agenda.

WYSIWYG editing

There are some editors listed on pp. 116–125 which fit the bill for what most people would describe as 'What You See Is What You Get'. But as we have seen, what you see on your own screen is not necessarily what the user sees, because of the huge variation in people's computing environments and the facilities of the browsers.

In general, what this demand means is 'is there a way of hiding and revealing the markup so I can see roughly what to expect?' and indeed all the conformant editors do this. The problem with the non-conformant ones is that the markup in HTML does actually *mean* something, whereas using a DTP system to put a phrase in 24pt Prumyslava Oldstyle in bright green doesn't actually *mean* anything apart from 'I want this phrase to stand out'. There is an ongoing discussion in the HTML development field of the use of style sheets (pp. 310–312) for helping users control the typography, but at the moment control is not possible to the full extent that it is in wordprocessors or DTP systems.

Alternatives to HTML

HTML was designed because it was important to pick a language which could describe a file regardless of the nature of the computer it was being sent from or received onto, and regardless of the complexity or simplicity of the software the user or owner had at their disposal. Having proved over the years that this was a wise choice, in that it has enabled the Web to spread around the world no matter what equipment is being used, questions are raised about its continuance as the bearer structure for Web files.

Obviously this could not be changed overnight, as the legacy of HTML files is by now too vast, but some serious consideration has been given to using other forms (or indeed, *any* form of SGML, as with SoftQuad's *Panorama* browser), and to the use of combined descriptive/display languages such as Adobe's *Acrobat*.

The advantage of using SGML is that it is the globally accepted international standard, it has a logically parseable structure, and its development is in public hands. This last point is important, as several systems can claim to be 'standard' (either *de facto* like T_EX or *PostScript*, or *de jure* like SGML), and several systems have structures testable by logic, but only a publicly-maintained standard can be considered sufficiently open for publicly-available text. In an interview in *Personal Computer World* [Akass 1994], Tim Berners-Lee put it succinctly: 'The ideal thing is that [standards controllers] allow any changes that have to be made to the standard to be done in the light of public discussion, in an open process.' At the moment there is no other candidate that fulfils this requirement, but if one emerges as an obvious contender, it would have to be considered.

Part Three

Running a service

- O Setting up a server
- O Running URL scripts
- O Data integrity
- O Rights and responsibilities
- O Copyright and intellectual property
- O Authentication and encryption
- O Future developments

Chapter 12

Server software

- O   How to choose a server platform
- O   Details of servers available
- O   Installation and announcement
- O   Management and maintenance

The first Web server was written on a NeXT computer, a desktop machine running a Unix operating system. Both client and server software were written so that they could be compiled for any mainstream Unix system, and they were soon ported to a wide range of other platforms. Because the original program code was made publicly available, other people around the world adapted it to run on non-Unix machines, so servers are now available for almost any kind of computer.

A Web server is more properly described as an HTTP server, as it operates specifically the HyperText Transfer Protocol, rather than any of the many other forms of Internet communication that browsers can handle. A **server** is a program which runs silently, sitting in the background, waiting for a request to come in. Because browsers can handle multiple protocols, you can in fact run a service providing HTML files from an FTP or Gopher server, and this is not uncommon in environments where running extra servers is not encouraged, although the response is slower.

In the case of HTTP, incoming requests normally arrive on port 80, the port officially assigned to HTTP servers. Although it is possible to run a server on any port, port numbers below 512 are reserved for official assignment to existing protocols, so where an alternate port is used, it is a higher number (8080 is a typical choice). The server program itself is usually called `httpd`, following the traditional Unix practice of ending server program names with a `d` for 'daemon', the term used to describe a server program.

A 'port' is a TCP/IP concept, being an equivalent in computer logic to a physical socket through which information is transmitted and received. Computers don't actually have 80 or more sockets on the back, they just have one Internet connection, but information is coded so that it can be addressed to the right server, as each one has a port number assigned to it. Above the 512 limit, however, users without systems privileges (authorization to make modifications to the system setup) can run a service provided they use a port number that no-one else on that machine is using.

When a request arrives on port 80, the system routes it to the server program, which reads it and responds accordingly. Requests for HTTP service are formatted according to the HTTP specification by the browser which sends them, and the server sends back the results in a form which is also prescribed by HTTP. You can find the draft specification for HTTP at `ftp://ds.internic.net/internet-drafts/draft-fielding-http-spec-01.ps`. Setting up a server on a PC or Mac can be a very simple and straightforward operation: doing so on Unix or VMS takes a little more knowledge of the operating system because these machines are generally multi-user and more complex in their design.

If an error occurs, such as a file not being found, the server will return an error code and possibly some explanatory text. There is a list of HTTP return codes in Appendix D.

Picking a platform

In many cases, HTTP servers are run on existing computers, especially while a service is in an experimental phase, or where it is run as an unofficial service on an individual's desktop machine. While there will always be a place for small-scale (or even medium-scale) services like this, an organizational decision to run a public service such as a company server will usually mean a more formal approach, both to the choice of computer and to the content of the information.

From a technical point of view, Unix must remain the dominant choice because most of the software development is done on such machines, so the latest releases are available for them first. However, as development has progressed, other platforms are beginning to offer differing facilities, so it may be important to compare your plans for the information content with the availability of special features.

With this in mind, it is possible to categorise the information content of a server into three groups, although there are some areas of overlap:

Static information

Static means that the information does not change significantly over time. Company presentations, product blurbs, descriptions of research, bulk text of one form or another, even price lists and order forms are all relatively static. Being held in HTML form, they are easy to edit and keep up to date. All servers handle these files, and there are extensive facilities for maintaining them and ensuring link validity (pp. 262–263). Static information can also include a certain amount of graphics where this too does not change very much or is in the nature of illustrations such as embedded images: company logos, product pack shots, staff mug shots, maps, and diagrams.

Graphics

Images which are held separately as an archive are a separate category. Here we would place bigger or more numerous graphics which form part of a collection or library: art reproductions, research photographs, samples of clip art, and historical or other images of value. Such collections may be dynamic or static (that is, they may be added to, changed, or deleted at any rate from frequently to never). Their most measurable aspect is that they tend to be either large files or large groups of smaller files, so there are considerations of retrieval speed and/or frequency to take into account.

Dynamic information

Dynamic means that the information either changes frequently or is generated on-the-fly using a script from a source other than the HTTP server. Stock market share price data is the classic example of fast-changing information, but anything which is either retrieved through manipulation of other data, or has its origins in data which may change from one access to the next may be considered dynamic. Dynamic information may be either graphical or textual: the Hubble telescope pictures, or weather satellite photos are both dynamic and graphical.

The most notable feature of serving dynamic information is that it consumes more processing time than serving static information.

The essential points to consider when choosing a platform are availability, reliability, speed, capacity, and ease of use (not necessarily in that order). Price is a more sensitive issue, and may be subject to organizational constraints which have nothing to do with the technology.

Availability

Clearly you want a machine that can be supplied on time and in the right configuration. Few suppliers of desktop computers will fully understand what is implied by running a Web server or service, so beware those who try to modify your requirements in favor of equipment which they can supply off the shelf unless you are certain that it will do what you want.

Reliability

Once you start providing a service, people will expect it to be available 24 hours a day, 365 days a year, regardless of how that affects your business. If you are undertaking to provide this level of service, you may need a backup machine to provide the service if the main one needs taking down for maintenance. Pick a computer that you know can be serviced locally: although modern desktop machines are relatively reliable compared with a few years ago, you don't want to be stuck with a return-to-base maintenance arrangement if customers are relying on your service.

Speed

Estimating demand (number of times people access your server and what files they request from it) is probably the most difficult aspect of sizing. The way in which a particular server responds to requests is an important consideration, as servers which originated under Unix tend to be multi-threaded (they can respond to multiple requests simultaneously by creating new images of themselves to handle them) which can be a heavy overhead on non-Unix machines. If you are beginning a new service, there is probably no easy way to estimate demand apart from starting it and seeing. If you are offering a service which proves so popular that the world is beating down the door of your server to use it, that's great in the popularity stakes but a killer for a small, slow machine.

Capacity

Disk space requirements are a little easier to calculate than the need or speed, because you presumably know roughly what kind of information you are going to serve up. As a rule of thumb, HTML markup increases file size by about 10% for short (2–3 page) documents and much less for longer ones, if they are end-nodes (that is, they have no links to elsewhere in the Web). But as URLs can be long, adding even two or three per paragraph can double the size of a short file. If you intend keeping local copies of popularly-requested information (to make things faster for your users), you need to make a decision on how much of a particular side-branch of information you want to carry on your own disks before users' requests start to need files from elsewhere.

Memory requirements are more tricky, and are closely related to the demands of the server software and the number of simultaneous requests which will be served. Amigas have the reputation of doing a lot of work with minimal resources, whereas PCs and Macs tend to need at least 8Mb just to handle a few common office packages. While it is physically possible to run a Unix or VMS HTTP server on an 8Mb machine, most workstations would tend to have at least double that to start with.

Network capacity (bandwidth) requirements for an HTTP server are dependent almost entirely upon the volume of material you estimate you will send out, as the incoming traffic is just a single line per request, but the response may be files of arbitrary size. If you are planning to run your service on a machine which also acts as FTP server and more (e.g. Usenet News, Telnet access to databases, etc.), you should consult with local systems experts at the planning stage.

Ease of use

Who is going to be running the service? Although once a service is established, it can run unattended for long periods, a check needs to be kept on the log files to monitor the level of usage, and someone needs to be responsible for maintaining the files. In case of serious problems, you need to have access to someone with a good depth of operating system and Web familiarity. The availability of local skills in your organization may therefore play a large part in determining the platform you choose.

Servers available

The common platforms all have at least one server available: Unix, Mac, PC (MS-Windows), Amiga, VMS, and VM. As with browsers, the initial software is free, and can be downloaded using anonymous FTP. Commercial versions are also available, including some 'secure' versions of HTTP (pp. 283–284). As with the browsers, the sites given below are the canonical ones, usually the author's home machine: always check with *Archie* to see if there is a closer copy you can use.

Apple Macintosh

MacHTTP by Chuck Shotton from `www.uth.tmc.edu` in `public/mac/`
`MacHTTP`. This provides regular HTTP service plus scripts using *AppleScript*
and *AppleEvent* support, and allows multi-threaded transfers. Details are at `http:`
`//www.uth.tmc.edu/mac_info/machttp_info.html` and the software can
be downloaded from any of the *Info-Mac* archives (e.g. `ftp://sumex-aim.`
`stanford.edu/info-mac/comm/tcp`). MacHTTP has the reputation of being
one of the easiest servers to install and maintain.

The CERN server

The CERN `httpd` is a generic hypertext server which can be used as a regular
HTTP server to serve hypertext and other documents, and also as a proxy—a
server on a firewall machine—that provides access for people inside a firewall to
the outside world (pp. 263–265). When running as proxy, it may be configured to
do caching of documents resulting in faster response times and lower impact on
the network traffic to the outside world.

You can get the source code from `www0.cern.ch` in `pub/www/src/`
`WWWDaemon.tar.Z`. Note that this package does not contain the CERN Library of Web server subroutines, which is needed to compile the server. This
must be downloaded from the same site in `pub/www/src/WWWLibrary.tar.`
`Z`. Precompiled binaries are available for Sun4, Solaris 2, HP Snake, NeXT,
NeXT-386, Decstation Ultrix, DEC OSF/1, SGI, and AIX in `pub/www/bin` and
there's a list of other platforms supported at `http://www.w3.org/hypertext/`
`WWW/Library/User/Platform/Platform.html`. Precompiled binaries with
direct WAIS access are available for both Sun4 and Solaris: more details are
at `http://www.w3.org/hypertext/WWW/Daemon/WAISGate.html`. The binaries for utility programs (`htadm`, `htimagem cgiparse`, and `cgiutils`) are
distributed in a separate `httpd_utils` file in the relevant platform directory
below `pub/www/bin`. Online documentation, including full installation instructions, is at `http://www.w3.org/httpd/` and the email address for queries is
`httpd@www.w3.org`. Also available for VMS: see `http://delonline.cern.`
`ch/disk$user/duns/doc/vms/distribution.html`.

NCSA HTTPD

Along with the CERN server, the most popular of the Unix HTTPDs. Source
code and binaries for Unix and PCs are available at `ftp.ncsa.uiuc.edu` in `Web/`
`ncsa_httpd`, with extensive step-by-step installation instructions and examples
held at `http://hoohoo.ncsa.uiuc.edu/`. If you are getting the precompiled
binary, you still need to download the `.tar.Z` file containing the system setup
files as well, so that you have the latest copies of sample scripts and the proposed
directory structure. This is the only server available in both Unix and MS-Windows
versions, with most of the features preserved, including scripts.

Region6

This is a threaded VMS server which avoids the heavy overhead of Unix-style operation by using DECthreads to manage its multi-threading. Details are available from `http://kcgll.eng.ohio-state.edu/www/doc/serverinfo.html`.

WebSite

WebSite from O'Reilly & Associates is a server for Microsoft *Windows NT* 3.5, using the graphical interface to provide server management features like a display of all your documents and links, as well as access authentication and the ability to run applications like *Excel* or *Visual Basic* from within a Web document, using the standard CGI interface. Product details, pricing and availability can be obtained by sending email to `website@ora.com`.

Purveyor

Purveyor is another server for *Windows NT* comes from Process Software Corporation, and will support *Windows 95* when available. The package includes sample HTML templates and basic authentication using IP addresses as well as NT File Manager access control, with all the documentation online. Details are available at `http://www.process.com`.

GN Gopher/WWW

This is an unusual package in that it is a Gopher and HTTP server in one. It lacks some facilities of the CERN and NCSA software like scripting, but allows the two protocols to share the same information base, giving the advantage of Gopher-style indexed access to serving Web files. Details from `http://hopf.math.nwu.edu/`.

Plexus

A server written in *Perl*. *Perl* is rapidly becoming one of the languages of choice for Web programming. Details on `http://bsdi.com/server/doc/plexus.html`.

Webmaster

A server from EIT which simplifies downloading, installing, and customizing a Web service. The *Webmaster's Starter Kit* uses forms to get basic configuration information, and writes your configuration files for you as you download the software, in a similar way to the installation for the *InternetWorks* browser (p. 84). Once the basic server is running, it serves up virtual documents for you to use in your browser that can automatically download and install server extensions. The package includes a simple form-based home page generator, the `verify_links` tool for finding broken links, the `libCGI` library for virtual document programming, the *Hypermail* engine for 'webifying' mail archives (plus a form interface for defining archives) and the *GetStats* http log analyzer (plus a form interface). There are versions for SunOS, Solaris, IRIX, OSF/1 AIX, SCO, and HP/UX. Details are on http://wsk.eit.com/wsk/doc/.

HTTPS

A server for Microsoft Windows NT available from emwac.ed.ac.uk in pub/https. Details on ftp://emwac.ed.ac.uk/pub/https/https.txt.

SerWeb

The smallest and easiest server for *MS-Windows* 3 as well as NT, an ideal starting point for the nascent service. Limited facilities (no scripts, terse logging) but a robust and simple piece of design. Download the Windows 3 version from winftp.cica.indiana.edu in pub/pc/win3/winsock/serweb03.zip or the NT version from emwac.ed.ac.uk in pub/serweb/serweb_i.zip.

Web4Ham

A fairly comprehensive server for *MS-Windows* from the University of Hamburg, Germany. Download from ftp.informatik.uni-hamburg.de in pub/net/winsock/web4ham.zip.

OS2HTTPD

A server for IBM's OS/2 available from ftp.netcom.com in pub/kfan. Details at ftp://ftp.netcom.com/pub/kfan/overview.

NOS11C

The public-domain KA9Q TCP/IP package for MS-DOS includes an HTTP server from inorganic5.chem.ufl.edu in pub/nos.

Amiga HTTPD

The *AMosaic* package for the Amiga includes its own HTTPD server. Details from http://insti.physics.sunysb.edu/AMosaic/home.html

RickVM

A server for IBM VM/CMS, details at http://ualvm.ua.edu/~troth/rickvmsw/rickvmsw.html.

Netsite

Netsite is Netscape Communications Corporation's server, which partners their *Netscape* browser. This is one of the few servers to offer some form of security (pp. 283–284). Details from `http://www.netscape.com/`.

SGI WebFORCE

Silicon Graphics, Inc. makes a specialised high-performance commercial server based on the *Indigo* workstation, using Netscape Communications Corporation's *Netsite* server software. It comes bundled with their *WebMagic* editing and authoring software. Details from `http://www.sgi.com/`.

BASIS

BASIS Webserver is a server acting as part of an electronic publishing database from Information Dimensions. This provides searching and indexing as built-in functions of the server aimed at corporate use, and it can handle support for other SGML applications as well as HTML. Details are at `http://www.oclc.org/oclc/idi/idihome.html`.

WN

WN is based on the philosophy that an HTTP server should do more than just serve files: it should play an active role in both navigation and presentation issues. It runs on a wide variety of UNIX platforms and is available at no cost for any use under the terms of the GNU public license. It has a variety of built-in searches including title searches, keyword searches, or fielded searches for user defined fields. There is an overview at `http://hopf.math.nwu.edu/docs/overview.html` and the software can be downloaded from `ftp://ftp.acns.nwu.edu/pub/wn/wn.tar.gz`.

Installation

As with browsers, server software comes with very explicit instructions on how to install it, which there is little point in reproducing here. There are, however, several principles which are much the same in almost all cases, and it is worth taking a little time to read through the documentation carefully and plan the installation before you start.

A server program and the files it serves usually live in different directories, so that the internal details of your server setup and operation are kept away from the actual HTML and other files. The server program can reside in whatever convenient directory or folder you wish, but this and the directory for your Web files need to be specified as part of the setup. The terms used by the NCSA's server, `ServerRoot` and `DocumentRoot` are usefully descriptive of these two areas of disk (terms used by other servers vary). In the server root lives the server program itself, configuration files, script directory, log files, security and authentication files, and other files relating to the administration of the server. In the document root live all the HTML and other files for public consumption. The server root has a directory structure suggested by the authors of the server (and created when you unpack the distribution files): the document root can have whatever subdirectory structure you wish to use. When you download the software, the documentation will suggest a location or structure for the server root.

Having downloaded the software (and compiled it, if needed), you edit the configuration files according to the installation instructions. Both CERN's and the NCSA's are online in the Web, which makes it easy to use them on-screen while you set up the server.

You need to establish the name of your principal entry-point file, known as your **welcome page**. This is sometimes wrongly called a **home page**: a home page is in fact the the page someone's browser starts up with, which may well be the welcome page of their or someone else's organization; or it may be their personal page, because the term 'home page' is also misleadingly used to refer to someone's personal page (p. 247).

In a lot of URLs you will see the welcome page named `welcome.html` or something similar (like `home.html`!), but the exact name is not important: what you are specifying here is that when a user connects with the URL ending just with your server name (plus perhaps a trailing slash), this is the file that should be returned. By default, if no such file is specified, a server will return a directory list of all files in your document root, which you may not want. To prevent users browsing like this, the CERN server lets you put a file called `NOBROWSE` in any directory for which you want to prevent browsing. The NCSA default is to look for a file called `index.html`.

Before starting to add files to the document root, you may need to create directories with access control files if you need to restrict certain portions of the disk to access from specific machines. The server documentation explains how to (if it supports access control) and there is a tutorial on security with the NCSA server at `http://wintermute.ncsa.uiuc.edu:8080/auth-tutorial/tutorial.html`. Access control files can be created in each directory under the document root, with instructions in them about which machines on the network may or may not retrieve files from that directory. It is not possible to limit access on a per-user basis with this method, only on the basis of the IP address or network name or domain.

For the final stage you will need root access (systems administrator's privileges). First, you need to add the specification line to the system's `services` file (called `/etc/services` on a Unix machine) which tells the system that you are running a HTTP server on port 80:

```
http       80/tcp      www       # WorldWideWeb server
```

You don't have to use 80, but if you use another number, it must be over 512, and you must remember to tell everyone to use it after your server name in all requests, separated by a colon, e.g. `http://www.acme.org:8825`. The last thing is to run the server program: for Macs and PCs, just double click on it in the normal way and then put it in the `Startup` program group or `System` folder so that it will start automatically when you next reboot. Under Unix, you type the program name (`httpd`) to start it running: you then have the choice of setting it to run at reboot from the initialisation daemon `inetd` or from a line in `rc.local`: the NCSA documentation warns strongly against using `inetd` because of the heavy overhead in cloning images for each request that comes in. Depending on your machine, you may need to take advice from a local expert in your type of system.

If there are error message files supplied with the server software, you may want to edit these to reflect the name of your server or to reword the messages in them. The response codes that can be generated by a HTTP server are defined in the draft HTTP standard [Berners-Lee, Fielding and Frystyk 1994] and listed in Appendix D.

Announcing the birth

When you've finally got everything installed and working, and have started filling up your server space with files, you can announce it to the world. The two principal places are the **www-announce** mailing list and the **comp.infosystems.www.announce** newsgroup. It is not a good idea to 'spam' the network with announcements to every mailing list and newsgroup in existence (see the section on network etiquette, pp. 268–272).

The other places are the maintainers of various 'what's new' pages, such as the CERN Virtual Library at `http://www.w3.org/hypertext/DataSources/bySubject/Overview.html` and the NCSA's What's New page at `http://www.ncsa.uiuc.edu/SDG/Software/Mosaic/Docs/whats-new.html`; the indexers of resources such as ALIWEB (`http://web.nexor.co.uk/aliweb/doc/aliweb.html`) and the EInet Galaxy: mail `galaxy@einet.net`. If you reckon it's cool enough, several authors run a 'cool pages' collection which they ship with their software (such as Netscape's), and there's WIRED Magazine's NetSurf pages, but if you're that cool, they'll find you!

Management and maintenance

Taking on the responsibility of running a server means undertaking to keep the information correct, up-to-date and available. Most of this has to do with the content and correctness of your HTML files, and the best person to do this is the author of each file. This may of course be *you*, but if you are running a service for others, they will need login or FTP access to manage their files (and encouragement or hassling to do so).

In an ideal world, each department or section of an organization would be wholly responsible for the creation and maintenance of its own portion of the organization's Web service, doing the editing and updating themselves, and thus freeing the people who install and run the server from the necessity of writing all the files themselves. There is a large training task involved in doing this, but the benefits of closer involvement of the people at the sharp end with the provision of information are that they will become much more aware of their part in the organization's external profile. A good document for new providers to read is *Making the most of the WorldWideWeb for your organization* [Gass 1994] by James Gass of Hughes STX Corp, and they can find it at `http://www.gsfc.nasa.gov/documents/making_most_www.html`.

One useful practice is to maintain tables of contents: `htmltoc` is a *Perl* program to generate a table of contents for HTML documents. You can get more information at `http://www.uci.edu/indiv/ehood/`, where there is also a list of *Perl* tools for the Web maintained by Earl Hood which do hierarchy trees, file documentation, navigation paths, and various forms of conversion, including email to HTML, which is a useful way of maintaining a database of email on various topics.

Although a HTTP server manager may not be concerned with the *content* of the files in the document root, as this may be the responsibility of their various authors, there is usually a need to identify an expiry date for files, so that authors can be prompted to check them for correctness. HTML and HTTP have no direct method of handling this, but if authors are encouraged (or forced!) to use the `<link>` element with their email address, then a simple check on file creation date can be used to identify files over a certain age, and the email address extracted. There are details of more facilities in Chapter 14.

Log files

Servers keep logs of who has accessed the system and what file has been requested. On a busy server the log files can grow fast, so you may need to analyse them before you dump them off to tape or backup disk. Most logs record date, time, the name of the machine requesting a file, and the name of the file itself, and in some cases it is possible for the server to try to determine the username as well. There are several packages you can use to keep track of who is requesting what (or you can write your own, of course).

Thomas Boutell's *Wusage* creates reports directly in HTML, with graphics to show the geographic origin of requests and the trend in volume. Details are at `http://siva/cshl.org/wusage.html` and the software can be got by anonymous FTP from `isis.cshl.org` in `pub/wusage`.

GetStats, by Kevin Hughes, does an analysis by month, week, day, or hour, and there are extensions which also produce graphical summaries and HTML reports. The software comes from `ftp.eit.com` in `pub/web.software/getstats` and their pages are at `http://www.eit.com/software/getstats/getstats.html`.

WWWstat is a *Perl* script by Roy Fielding to process NCSA log files and output HTML reports. Qiegang Long has provided an add-on called `gwstat` which produces graphs from `WWWstat` output. `WWWstat` comes from `liege.ics.uci.edu` in `pub/arcadia/wwwstat` (information at `http://www.ics.uci.edu/WebSoft/wwwstat`) and `gwstat` is at `dis.cs.umass.edu` in `pub/gwstat.tar.gz` (information at `http://dis.cs.umass.edu/stats/gwstat.html`).

WebStat is a log-analysis program which can also generate HTML reports with a longer listing sent to a maintainer. For more information see `http://www.pegasus.esprit.ec.org/people/sijben/statistics/advertisment.html` (*sic*) or FTP the software from `ftp.pegasus.esprit.ec.org` in `pub/misc/webstat.tar.gz`. You will need a copy of the Python language interpreter to run *WebStat*, and you can download this from `ftp.cwi.nl` in `pub/python`.

Users' personal pages

Most servers seem to have adopted the convention of supporting access to a specific subdirectory within each user's home directory on the server host, so that users can have their own personal files served to the world, without requiring privileged access to the document root.

A directory such as `public_html` in any user's home directory can be made 'public' by enabling this facility in the server configuration. Files within this one directory can then be addressed by a URL containing the user's username preceded by a tilde character, for example `http://www.acme.org/~jill/projects.html`.

Only files in the directory and beneath can be accessed: the user's remaining directory tree remains inaccessible. It is becoming conventional to advertise your personal page(s) in this form by quoting the URL on your business card or letterhead, in addition to your organization's normal welcome page.

Unattended and offline operation

Standalone mode was one of the earliest requests from the user community when *Mosaic* was first announced. This means the ability to use the program on an isolated machine with no network connection, just reading local files from the hard disk. To overcome the early limitations (where browsers automatically looked for a network connection, and would halt if one was not found), a special version of the PC *WinSock* program was written which faked a network response so that the programs would run. Most browsers nowadays can work happily with local files only, and the `file:` URL, which was often used for FTP, is more widely used for meaning 'look on my local disk'.

Provided the links between such files are correct (that is, they refer to each other and not to network resources), many of the graphical and character-mode browsers can be used as a local hypertext information system in standalone mode.

Kiosk mode is a special adaptation of a browser so that it can be run exclusively with the mouse, with the keyboard removed or locked away, so that the browser can be put on public display without the risk of casual users breaking out of the program and interfering with the system. Spry's *AIR Mosaic Express* is a good example, where the kiosk mode can be entered from the button bar, but requires a keypress (Esc or Ctrl K) to re-enter keyboard control.

Chapter 13

'Searchable' URLs

- ○ Passing values for processing
- ○ Shell scripts for the Web
- ○ Including processing without a script

We saw in Chapter 9 that a URL can end with a 'search term' separated from the filename with a question mark. The use of the word 'search' is unfortunate, as it implies that searching is all it can do, which is not the case. The words or values after the question mark are in fact 'arguments' which can be passed to a script as values to use in processing, in the same way as a command typed in a text interface can be followed by values to use. The use of the `<isindex>` element implies that the URL is not a static piece of text but something generated on the fly by a process running on the server computer, so it can accept the data after the question mark as input, do some processing by re-running the same script, and create some HTML code for transmission back to the browser.

In the case of HTML forms, a greater volume of data can be passed in a similar manner, but the result is the same: some processing occurs and the script must usually return some HTML code to the server.

Scripts

A script (a shell script in Unix terminology) is a file containing a sequence of computer commands similar to those typed at a terminal, which you want the operating system to read and perform without you having to retype them every time. In effect it is a program, although it is not compiled and saved in the internal binary form that a normal program uses, but re-read and interpreted afresh each time it is used.

The equivalent in MS-DOS terms is the **batch file** (a filename ending in `.bat`); and on VAX/VMS computers it would be a **command file** (a filename ending in `.com`). Apple Macintosh computers originally had no such facility in the operating system, but following the success of commercial scripting languages like *Userland Frontier*, one called *AppleScript* was introduced by Apple themselves in 1993.

From an early stage, the NCSA's HTTP server had the ability to treat certain kinds of URL as references to scripts, so that clicking on a hypertext reference to one of them would cause the server to run the script and transmit the output of whatever it did back to the client for display. It is immediately obvious that any script used in this way must only output HTML, and this is therefore the primary requirement of writing server scripts.

On a Unix server, a script can be in any of the interpreted languages supported by the operating system in use, most commonly the C and Bourne shells, and the *Perl* language. On Apple Macs, *AppleScript* is used; on *MS-Windows*, *Visual Basic* seems to be the language of choice so far.

Writing shell scripts

Before we look at what's involved, consider the example of a HTML file containing the following fragment:

```
...Using a script, it is possible to see <a
href="http://www.widget.org/cgi-bin/users">who is logged
in</a> to the machine at the moment...
```

This would display in the normal way, with the tagged phrase highlighted:

...Using a script, it is possible to see who is logged in to the
machine at the moment...

Clicking on the highlighted phrase causes the server to check the URL, and it will
recognise the file attributes when it locates the file **cgi-bin/users** as identifying
an executable file (i.e. a script), and therefore make it run, rather than transmitting
its contents. Suppose this file contained the following Unix commands:

```
#! /bin/sh
echo Content-type: text/html
echo
cat <<EOT
<html><head><title>Run the who command</title></head>
<body><h1>Users on
EOT
echo 'hostname'
echo \</h1\>\<pre\>
/usr/bin/who
echo \</pre\>\</body\>\</html\>
```

The **echo** command transmits anything that follows it: this forms the MIME
header (including the blank line sent by the second **echo** command) which is
a prerequisite of all files sent by HTTP. With regular (static) files this happens
automatically, using tables of filetypes held by the server, but for scripts you have
to include it explicitly.

The **cat** command used this way just outputs any text on subsequent lines: here
it is being told to do so until it finds a line containing **EOT**, so in both cases it will
output the HTML text given. This text ends part-way through the <h1> element
where the result of the Unix command **hostname** is inserted, which gives the
name of the computer.

The **echo** is used to finish the heading element and start a <pre> block, which
will contain the output of the **who** command, which lists the names of users
logged in. The final line contains the end-tag for the preformatted element, and
finishes the HTML 'file'. The effect of this would be for the browser to display
something like this:

Users on widget

```
brendan   ttyp4   lynx    00:54:42
angela    ttyp3   vi      00:17:22
tanaqui   ttyp7   emacs   01:32:17
```

As far as the browser is concerned, it requested an HTML file and it got an HTML file. The user is merely aware that by clicking on a phrase in the normal way, she got the response she expected. The fact that, behind the scenes, the server was running a miniature program to achieve this is entirely hidden from view.

Clearly there is scope for considerable power here. A script can be programmed to perform any command or run almost any program on the computer, the only restriction being that the output must be something digestible as HTML. Those with even a small knowledge of Unix and the extensive facilites offered by manipulation languages such as **sed**, **awk** and **perl** will readily appreciate that almost any data or text can be retrieved, torn apart and reassembled in the required form, and transmitted to the user, who will remain unaware of the activity being carried out to achieve the results. On PCs running the NCSA's Windows server, *Visual Basic* is used as the scripting language; on Macs, *AppleScript* is used; on *VMS* it would be *DCL*.

There is no space here to conduct a full-scale tutorial on command-language processing, but there are several programs which can help with functions like searching.

Oscar Nierstrasz's *Htgrep* is a *Perl* script to query any document accessible to your server on a paragraph-by-paragraph basis. *Htgrep* understands HTML documents, plain text, and 'refer' bibliography files, and supports various formatting options such as automatically generating hypertext links for URLs within plain text (details on `http://iamwww.unibe.ch/~scg/Src/Doc/htgrep.html`).

For the Mac running *MacHTTP* there isAdrian Vanzyl's *TR-WWW* which allows users to search and subsequently browse document collections using a forms based interface. You create document sets on your server, consisting of text, HTML or *MS-Word* files. Users can then search these using boolean terms, and view the results either as keyword in context lists, or WAIS-style relevance ranked results. More details are available at `http://www.monash.edu.au/informatics/tr-www.html`.

Many servers on several platforms now offer script handling, and most adhere to the standard introduced by the NCSA for writing scripts, known as **CGI**

(Common Gateway Interface). Details of the standard are available at `http://hoohoo.ncsa.uiuc.edu/cgi/overview.html`

The following examples of scripts show a few of the uses that this facility has been put to.

The first is a simple one to display the current date, using the same technique as before:

```
#! /bin/sh
echo Content-type: text/html
echo
echo \<html\>\<head\>\<title\>\</title\>\</head\>
echo \<body\>\<p\>Today is
date
echo \</p\>\</body\>\</html\>
```

The surrounding HTML code is static, so it is transmitted as it stands, with the output from the system's **date** command embedded in the paragraph.

The second script uses the single string passed from the browser as a value to search for in a file, and reformat the results. It formed the basis for the acronym server already referred to (p. 68). If this script is called with no argument, only the static portions of the HTML are returned, which include the `<isindex>` element, thus enabling the user to type in a search term.

```
#! /bin/sh
echo Content-type: text/html
echo
cat <<EOH
<html><head><title>Acronyms and
   abbreviations</title><isindex></head>
<body><h1>Acronym and abbreviation database</h1>
<p>Type your search term in the dialog box</p><hr>
EOH
if [ $* != 0 ]; then
echo \<h2\>Results of search for \'$1''\</h2\>\<dl\>
grep -i '$1    ' acro.dat | awk '$1 != last{print
   "<dt>",$1,"</dt>";last=$1} {print "<dd>";for(i=2;i<=NF;++i) print
   $i;print "</dd>"}'
echo \</dl\>
fi
cat <<EOT
</body></html>
EOT
```

(The **grep** and **awk** commands occupying three lines on this page are in fact one continuous line in the file.) The Unix **grep** command searches the file for the string and returns all matching lines. The file format uses an ASCII tab character to separate the acronym from the expansion, so the search is carried out for the string followed by a tab (not spaces). The output is piped through awk, which identifies multiple occurrences of the match field and adds the HTML code for definition list format. Note the use of static code reproduced by cat for those portions of output which are invariable. The first two lines of echo (Content-type) are compulsory for any HTML file generated this way, as the server needs to prefix the file with this MIME type for transmission back to the browser.

The third example is a more complex piece of reformatting. The structure is the same as the previous example, but in this case, data is taken from a form which is generated by the script itself. On the first time of access, only the form is produced: when it is filled in and submitted, the data is used to perform a search of the Archie file database, and the results sent back to the user with another copy of the form for a subsequent search.

Again, indentation shown here means that the indented line is a continuation of the previous line.

```
#!/bin/sh
ARCHIE=/usr/local/bin/archie
echo Content-type: text/html
echo
TYPE='echo "$QUERY_STRING" | awk 'BEGIN {FS="&"} {print $1}' | awk
    'BEGIN {FS="="} {print $2}''
TERM='echo "$QUERY_STRING" | awk 'BEGIN {FS="&"} {print $2}' | awk
    'BEGIN {FS="="} {print $2}''
MAX='echo "$QUERY_STRING" | awk 'BEGIN {FS="&"} {print $3}' | awk
    'BEGIN {FS="="} {print $2}''
SERVER='echo "$QUERY_STRING" | awk 'BEGIN {FS="&"} {print $4}' | awk
    'BEGIN {FS="="} {print $2}''
cat << EOH
<html>
<head>
<title>Archie</title>
</head>
<body>
<h1>Archie - the file archive</H1>
<p>This is a gateway to the <b>Archie</b> archive of files
available for
<a href="http://www.widget.org/howtoftp.html">anonymous
<tt>ftp</tt></a>.
Enter your search term and pick the server nearest you.</P>
<form method="get" action="http://www.widget.org/cgi-bin/archie">
<dl>
<dt><b>Search term:</b></dt>
<dd>Substring search: <input name="type" type="radio" value="c">Case
    sensitive or <input name="type" type="radio" value="s">case insen-
    sitive</dd>
<dd>Name search: <input name="type" type="radio" value="e"
    checked>Exact match or <input name="type" type="radio"
    value="r">regular expression</dd>
<dd>Search term: <input type="text" name="term" length="40"> Max hits
    to return: <input name="max" type="text" value="95" size="4"><dd>
```

```
<dt><b>Servers available:</b></dt>
<dd><input name="server" type="radio" value="archie.doc.ic.ac.uk"
  checked>United Kingdom (Imperial College)
or
<input name="server" type="radio" value="archie.funet.fi">Finland (FU-
  NET)
or
<input name="server" type="radio" value="archie.cs.mcgill.ca">Canada
  (McGill)
or
<input name="server" type="radio" value="archie.sura.net">USA (SURA,
  MD)
or
<input name="server" type="radio" value="archie.au">Australia
</dd>
<dt> <input type="submit" value="Search"> <input type="reset"
  value="Clear form"></dt>
</dl>
</form>
EOH
if [ $TERM != "" ]; then
echo \<hr\>\<h2\>Results for \'\<tt\>$TERM\</tt\>\'\'\</h2\>
cat <<EOB
<p>Results are grouped into <a href="#Directories">Directories</a>
  and
<a href="#Files">Files</a>, sorted by the location of the server
  with
most recent files first. </p>
EOB
$ARCHIE -$TYPE -m $MAX -h $SERVER $TERM | awk 'BEGIN {OFS="";dq
  = sprintf("%c", 34)} /Host/{hostname=$2; hlen=length(hostname)-
  2; domain=substr(hostname,hlen,3)} /Location:/{dirname=$2}
  {if(dirname=="/") dirname=""} /DIRECTORY/{print "Directo-
  ries;",domain,";<a
  href=",dq,"ftp://",hostname,dirname,"/",$7,"/",dq,">",hostname,
  dirname,"/",$7,"/","</a>;",$3,";",$4,";",$5,";",$6} /FILE/{print
  "Files;",domain,";<a
  href=",dq,"ftp://",hostname,dirname,"/",$7,dq,">",hostname,dirname,
  "/",$7,"</a>;",$3,";",$4,";",$5,";",$6} /No matches/{print "No
  matches;"} /timed/{print "Server timed out: too busy, please
  try later;"}' | sort -t\; -bd +0 -1 +1 -2 +6nr +4Mr -5 +5nr -
  6 | sed -f domains1 | sed -f domains2 | awk 'BEGIN {FS=";";dq
  = sprintf("%c", 34);OFS=""} $1 != type{print "</dl><h2><a
  name=",dq,$1,dq,">",$1,"</a></h2><dl>";type=$1} $2 != domain{print
  "<dt><b>",$2,"</b></dt>";domain=$2} {print "<dd><tt>",$3,"</tt>
  <b>",$4,"</b> <i>",$5," ",$6," ",$7," ",$8,"</i></dd>"}'
fi
cat <<EOT
</body></html>
EOT
```

The final example generates a control file for a third-party program, in this case the *PAT* text database product from Open Text Corporation, which is used here to search an SGML file for a keyword, and return the whole article in which it occurs. The script writes the control file to a temporary name, then runs PAT using it, and calls on *PAT*'s ability to understand the HTML encoding of the database of articles to write the results to another temporary file. This is then read, and the results returned to the user.

```
#! /bin/sh
echo Content-type: text/html
echo
if [ $# = 0 ]; then
cat <<EOM
<html><head><TITLE>INFOSYS database search</TITLE><isindex></head>
<body><H1>INFOSYS database</H1>
<p>This lets you search issues of INFOSYS for a keyword and returns
   the articles in which the word was found.</p>
<p>Please enter a keyword, or use your \'go-back' command or
   button to return to your previous screen, or display the <a
   href="http://www.ucc.ie/cgi-bin/infotoc">table of contents</a></p>
</body></html>
EOM
else
cd /research/textbase
if [ -f /tmp/infosys.request ]; then
/bin/rm -f /tmp/infosys.request
fi
if [ -f /tmp/infosys.result ]; then
/bin/rm -f /tmp/infosys.result
fi
if [ -f /tmp/infosys.log ]; then
/bin/rm -f /tmp/infosys.log
fi
echo article = region \"\<h2\>\"..\(shift.-4\"\<h2\>\"\)
   >/tmp/infosys.request$$
echo *article including $1 >>/tmp/infosys.request$$
echo \{SaveFile \"/tmp/infosys.result$$\"\} >>/tmp/infosys.request$$
echo save.region.*article >>/tmp/infosys.request$$
echo quit >>/tmp/infosys.request$$
/usr/local/pat/bin/pat41 infosys.dd </tmp/infosys.request$$
   >/tmp/infosys.log$$
echo \<html\>\<head\>\<title\>Result of INFOSYS
   search\<\/title\>\<\/head\>\<body\>
echo \<h1\>INFOSYS article[s] containing \'$1\'\<\/h1\>
echo \<p\>Your search for \'$1\' returned the following article[s]
# echo \(Keywords located are in \<b\>bold type\<\/b\>\)
echo \<\/p\>\<hr\>
cat /tmp/infosys.result$$
/bin/rm -f /tmp/infosys.request$$ /tmp/infosys.log$$
   /tmp/infosys.result$$
fi
```

A similar technique is being used experimentally in the access to ancient Irish literature provided in the Thesaurus Linguarum Hiberniae of the CURIA project at `http://www.ucc.ie/curia/`, but in this case, some prior mapping has been used to create an HTML version of the texts. References like occupations are made as hypertext links to a script, with an argument of an attribute value known to exist in the original SGML file, which was encoded using the DTD of the Text Encoding Initiative. This allows the user to look up the exact encoded portions of a text where a name or other marked element occurs.

Executable programs

For forms generating large amounts of data, a C program offers better control of the data and environment than a shell language. The program shown in Figure 13.1 is a skeleton to handle data coming from forms using the **post** attribute.

Remote execution

One question often asked in the discussion groups and mailing lists for the Web is 'how can I get a command to execute on a server?' The stock answer is that you really don't want to allow this: no-one wants an (inherently anonymous) Web user to cause your server to execute unscreened commands which could wipe your disk or send copies of your files to anyone on the Internet.

To overcome this problem, a version of the Tool Control Language (**Tcl**) is being developed, called **Safe-Tcl**. This can be sent inside a MIME multipart message, so it can be received and understood by a HTTP server. The restrictions proposed for Safe-Tcl make it much less likely that a user can send destructive commands for remote execution. An implementation of Safe-Tcl can be found at `ftp://ftp.ics.uci.edu/pub/mrose/safe-tcl/safe-tcl-1.2.tar.Z`.

Including external data

Several servers, notably the NCSA and CERN ones, allow the in-line inclusion of external data by embedding processing commands in the HTML file. This is not a part of HTML and is dependent on server-specific support.

Earlier versions of the servers used a non-standard element `<inc srv "...">` but this has been replaced because it could not be parsed (because there was no equals sign defined between the **srv** attribute and the value).

The processing instruction provisions of SGML (`<?command>`), which could have been used, are deprecated in *The SGML Handbook* [Goldfarb 1990], and

```c
#include <stdio.h>
#include <stdlib.h>
#define MAX_ENTRIES 10000
typedef struct {
char *name;
char *val;
} entry;
char *makeword(char *line, char stop);
char *fmakeword(FILE *f, char stop, int *len);
char x2c(char *what);
void unescape_url(char *url);
void plustospace(char *str);
main(int argc, char *argv[]) {
entry entries[MAX_ENTRIES];
register int x,m=0;
int cl;
printf("Content-type: text/html%c%c",10,10);
if(strcmp(getenv("REQUEST_METHOD"),"POST")) {
printf("This script should be referenced with a METHOD of
  POST.\n");
printf("If you don't understand this, see this ");
printf("<A
  HREF=\"http://www.ncsa.uiuc.edu/SDG/Software/Mosaic/Docs/fill-out-
  forms/overview.html\">forms overview</A>.%c",10);
exit(1);
}
if(strcmp(getenv("CONTENT_TYPE"),"application/x-www-form-urlencoded"))
  {
printf("This script can only be used to decode form results. \n");
exit(1);
}
cl = atoi(getenv("CONTENT_LENGTH"));
for(x=0;cl && (!feof(stdin));x++) {
m=x;
entries[x].val = fmakeword(stdin,'&',&cl);
plustospace(entries[x].val);
unescape_url(entries[x].val);
entries[x].name = makeword(entries[x].val,'=');
}
printf("<H1>Query Results</H1>");
printf("You submitted the following name/value pairs:<p>%c",10);
printf("<ul>%c",10);
for(x=0; x <= m; x++)
printf("<li> <code>%s = %s</code>%c",entries[x].name,
entries[x].val,10);
printf("</ul>%c",10);
}
```

Figure 13.1 Skeleton C program to handle form data

The source code reproduced with permission from version 1.3 of the NCSA httpd server package distribution written at the National Center for Supercomputing Applications (NCSA) at the University of Illinois, Urbana-Champaign the normal syntax forbids the use of the greater-than sign, which would create problems for Unix and DOS commands which redirect output, so the current mechanism is to insert the details of such server-side inclusions in a regular HTML comment. This way they become transparent to editing software because they are simply ignored, but HTML files can be scanned for such usage by servers, and the embedded commands acted upon.

The recommendation of the NCSA server authors is that such files should bear the filetype `.shtml` to obviate the server having to scan all HTML files for possible server-side inclusions. When the server detects such a file containing embedded instructions, the command is processed and the output or contents inserted into the stream of data at that point, with the enclosing comment code eliminated. This means that the following file fragment:

```
<p>Thought for the day</p>
<blockquote><p>
<!--#exec cmd="/usr/games/fortune" -->
</p></blockquote>
```

would be transmitted to the browser as

```
<p>Thought for the day</p>
<blockquote><p>
[some witticism]
</p></blockquote>
```

The full details of this mechanism require some knowledge of the operating system and the writing of shell scripts. Documentation can be retrieved at `http://hoohoo.ncsa.uiuc.edu/docs/tutorials/includes.html`. On a Unix system it is possible to set a soft link (an alias) for the filename, so that you can refer people to a `.html` file which is a soft link to the real `.shtml` file.

Chapter 14

Keeping things straight

- O Maintaining hypertext links
- O Security and access
- O Firewalls and protection

As your server collection of files grows, some links will unavoidably get out of date as authors elsewhere revise and move them. As was mentioned earlier, *Lynx* will report on missing links that it encounters, if the author has included a `<link>` element in the file header containing a valid email address. There are also several tools to examine your pages and do the same checking.

Checking link integrity

Most HTML authors do try to keep files in the same place they were originally put, because other people may have made links to them from their own files, but if a file gets moved, there is no simple way to notify the rest of the world, and in general you don't know who has got links to your files, and who has got local copies of them.

If you do have to move files, it's a good idea to notify this to the relevant newsgroups and mailing lists so that other authors can pick up on it and modify their files accordingly. Not all authors do this, though, so you need a way of checking that the links you have created are still valid.

One way, of course, is to manually follow every highlighted link from each of your files, to see if it is still pointing at the right URL. The other way is to use software which does this for you.

Figure 14.1 *HTMLmapper* display of the links from a PC HTML file

HTMLmapper for *MS-Windows* will draw a map of all the links off a given (PC) HTML page and continue to map the links of those pages pointed to until all links are exhausted. Missing, circular, and offsite links are marked accordingly. Maps may be printed or saved as ASCII files. Download from `s850.mwc.edu` in `pub/pc/htmlmap.zip`. *X Windows* and Mac versions are under development (Figure 14.1).

Verify-Links is a similar tool with online documentation at `http://wsk.eit.com/wsk/dist/doc/admin/webtest/verify_links.html`.

James Pitkow has written an `html_analyzer` which performs analysis of HTML databases. Specifically, all `.html` files are processed to:

- validate the existence of anchors;
- check that all tags used have links associated with them throughout the database;
- check for a one-to-one relation between links and anchor contents.

The validation process checks only HTTP and relative addresses (links), but can be very valuable in maintaining large collections of files.

`W3new` is a program by Brooks Cutter that will extract a list of URLs from a *Mosaic* hotlist or a HTML document, retrieve the modification dates for each document listed, and output a HTML file with the URLs sorted by their last modification time. Details from `http://www.stuff.com/cgi-bin/bbcurn?user=bcutter&amp;pkg=w3new`, needs *Perl* v4.036.

Server security

There are two aspects to this, security from corruption and data loss, and security from damage or data theft caused by intruders on (or even users of) your systems. Regular backups and health checks guard against the first, but the second is a more complex problem.

Backups and health checks

It's so true it's almost laughable, except that it's simply not funny: people do lose their data and they don't do backups. It's bad enough when you lose personal material, and you have only yourself to worry about, but if corporate data has been entrusted to you, you have an obligation to prevent its accidental loss.

If you're running a server and making it available to other people to store their own files on, you will need some kind of backup storage. This can be simple disk-copying on a regular basis, using one of a number of backup or compression programs, or more complex automated systems using high-capacity tape or disk. Machines in computer centers run by professional operators will usually be backed up as a matter of course.

At the top end of the range, for mission-critical use, is an arrangement known as 'disk failover' or 'disk shadowing'. With this, you have twice as much disk storage as you plan for, in effect duplicating everything. If one disk goes bad on you, its twin immediately takes over: in fact with some systems you can hit the power-off switch right in the middle of working, and the users will never see a blip, and you can power right back on again and the disk which was offline will bring itself back up to date automatically. This costs major money, though.

For important but non-critical applications, daily backup is essential: twice daily if the rate of changes to the data is high. With many regular commercial computer applications which are only active from 9 a.m. to 5 p.m., the evening is traditionally used for backups. But the Web is global, so a Web server is likely to be used 24 hours a day unless it is an entirely private service. One common arrangement is a full backup each night with an incremental one at lunchtime: as these will have to be on-the-fly (while the application is running), users must be made aware that if they modify files while backup is in progress, their changes may or may not be backed up depending on whether or not the routine has gotten around to their files yet, something which is not usually possible to predict with much accuracy.

For less intensive use, or where the data is changed rarely, weekly or even monthly backup is possible. In all cases, however, a cycle of disks or tapes should be used, so that there are always multiple copies, going further back in time, with the oldest being recycled at each new backup.

Data on disks is stored in chunks of a fixed size, and when a file is deleted, the chunks freed up are made available for subsequent files to use. Because files are of different sizes, each one written to disk may require more or less space than the file which previously occupied the space now vacated, so some space will be required elsewhere on the disk, or some space may be left empty still. After prolonged usage, spare disk space tends to be in small quantities, scattered around the disk surface, and files occupy portions of the disk space essentially at random, leading to it taking longer to locate all the bits which go to make up a file. This effect is called fragmentation.

Many larger systems have inbuilt routines which periodically check for fragmentation, and rebuild the disk structure automatically. Desktop machines such as Macs and PCs, however, need manual attention, so if you are running such a system with a lot of file deletion and creation, you should use a defragmentation program each week or month depending on the volume of traffic on the disk.

Security of access

We will look later at the problems of authentication (checking that a user has a right to use your machine, Chapter 17), but there are also some problems inherent in running a service like Web access on a corporate or campus network where security requirements mean that an electronic barrier has been erected. This is known as a **firewall**, and it prevents or controls direct access to the Internet by machines on network segments within the firewall on a per-service basis. Firewalls are usually installed by systems administrators, as it is a complex task. Its effect, though, is to make it impossible to use a Web browser without additional software which can act as a gateway to prohibit or permit specific kinds of traffic.

One way to overcome the barrier safely is to use a **proxy** server. This is a server which runs on a machine which is a part of the firewall's defenses, and filters Web traffic to the inside and outside world. Requests from a browser go to the proxy, which then requests the files on the user's behalf from their server on the network outside. Because the server itself sits on the firewall, it remains accessible to external users as well as being available to internal ones. CERN's server will act as a proxy, and has the additional advantage that it caches frequently-requested files, so a local copy of such files is available on request, rather than having to be fetched from afar every time.

Another way of filtering requests is a facility called *Socks*, which fulfils a similar function for browsers but has no effect on servers. Using *Socks* means you have to modify the source code for the browsers, so this is a task for a network programmer. C&C Software Technology Center of NEC Systems Lab have done this for *Mosaic* to go with their version of *Socks*: details are available at `ftp://ftp.nec.com/pub/security/socks.cstc`.

Chapter 15

Rights and responsibilities

○   Behavior on the Internet

○   Etiquette and conduct

○   What to do when something goes wrong

Using a network like the Internet means that you are sharing resources with other people all the time. There are therefore rights and responsibilities—actions which are permitted and those which are not; and actions which you have to take and those which you ought to take—if you are to behave as a responsible 'net.citizen'. There is very little in the way of formal definition about what you can and cannot do, for reasons given below, although your organization or network provider may provide some guidance.

In general, subject to certain constraints, you have the right to retrieve any information which is made available for public use; to exchange messages with other users; and to make available any non-private information you wish for the use of others. The constraints are usually imposed by your local service provider, and are usually subject to (or a requirement of) the law of the territory in which you and others operate. These usually include a prohibition on defamatory, obscene, or otherwise illegal material, actions which would injure others, actions which would injure the performance or integrity of the network itself, and actions which entail a breach of confidentiality or an attempt to access restricted information.

You also have the responsibility to ensure that those who are under your guidance (superiors, employees, co-workers, students or clients) understand the 'rules', such as they are, and operate in accordance with them. You probably also have other responsibilities which are internal to your organization, if you are using the network other than as a private individual, such as abiding by company or institutional rules on privacy and confidentiality, access rights, password cracking, and so on. If you are an information provider, you have additional responsibilities to ensure that the information you provide does not entail in itself a breach of the guidelines applicable to those who access the information. To some extent there are also obligations which fall into the category of social or moral ones, such as ensuring that a service you claim to provide does in fact exist.

Conduct and etiquette

As I mentioned at the outset, the Internet is self-governing. The original intent of the Arpanet from which it evolved (being then a military-based operation) was to build a network from discrete pieces which would stay working even if some of the individual segments were disrupted due to nuclear attack, so a very high degree of autonomy was built into the way in which the network was designed and run.

To a large extent, this plan has succeeded admirably, in that the autonomy has persisted in such a way as to make it virtually impossible for individuals or 'authority' (that is, governmental authority) to impose their will on the network contrary to the will of the users. Individual portions of the Internet have from time to time been attacked, shut down, purged (in various ways) or otherwise persuaded to comply with a variety of well-meaning or ill-inspired directives, but the resilience of the network organism as a whole is very considerable.

The self-regulation of conduct is carried out according to a generally accepted and largely unwritten code, augmented in some places by a written **statement of acceptable use** which users must sign before being granted access. Unfortunately there is as yet no driver's license for the information highway, so the occasional influx of new users who are ill-informed or uninformed sometimes leads to skirmishes between them and the old hands who feel their ways are being upset, with the newcomers unable to understand what they have done wrong. A brief summary of the most important points is presented below.

Sensitivity to netiquette is even more important when publishing material through Web than it is when using electronic mail or Usenet newsgroups. When you post an article to a newsgroup or mail a message to a mailing list, you are publishing your views to a predefined set of people. They may be rather hazily defined, given that subscription to most mailing lists and access to most newsgroups is unmoderated, but the topic matter to some extent predefines the likely readership. On the Web, however, people can browse at random, coming across pointers to information that they might not ordinarily have discovered. Your potential readership (assuming you place no explicit access restrictions on your text) is therefore not necessarily limited by any topical boundaries: anyone can read what you provide.

Full connection to the Internet was originally designed for computers which would be connected permanently and never switched off. This means they would always be ready to receive incoming calls: electronic mail, for example. In the case of dial-up connections, whether SLIP/PPP or indirect, which terminate when you finish work and hang up the phone, service providers need to allow for their machines to remain able to receive incoming material for you such as email, or to be able to respond appropriately to other attempts at connection. For this reason, there is a responsibility on all users to connect regularly and not allow an unreasonable backlog of material to accumulate.

Generalized code of conduct

Overall

- Be polite: readers cannot see your facial expression, so they may not understand that you are joking, or being disapproving, or angry or whatever.
- Don't make racial, sexual, religious, or other social comments which might offend your readers.
- Be tolerant of apparent misconduct in others: it may often be due to a misunderstanding or lack of experience.
- Don't transmit or retrieve illegal or otherwise actionable material.

Electronic mail

- Reply promptly (read your incoming mail at least once a day if possible) even if only to say that you are working on the matter and that a fuller reply will follow.
- Don't quote any of a correspondent's personal messages to you in mail that you send to others, unless you have the original author's permission.
- Use a mail editor which prefixes cited text from others with some kind of symbol (the greater-than sign [>] or an indent is conventional), but only cite text which is relevant to your reply, not great chunks of it.
- Don't type lines longer than 79 characters, because some intervening systems between you and the reader may mangle them. Better, use an editor which wraps the text properly.

On mailing lists and Usenet newsgroups

- Don't post novice questions to a list or newsgroup until you have read the document on Frequently-Asked Questions (FAQ) for that list or newsgroup first. The FAQs are usually posted regularly, and can be retrieved at any time from `ftp://rtfm.mit.edu/`.
- Read the existing posts on a list or newsgroup for a little while to get the flavour of it, before you start posting.
- Don't cross-post your replies to other lists or newsgroups unless it is essential for the discussion.
- If you don't like what's being said, use the Delete or Next key: that's what they are there for.
- Don't waste bandwidth by posting trivial or inconsequential replies.
- The rules for private electronic mail apply here also.

Telnet

- Keep all passwords secret: never write them down and never lend them to others;
- Don't stay online to a service when you're not actually using it.
- Don't try to break into machines where you don't have authorised access.

FTP

- Check by using the `archie` command before you start, to find the best location of a file.
- Only download the files you want, not everything in sight.
- Use the file server where what you want is available nearest to you, not one half-way across the world.

WorldWideWeb and Gopher

- Don't include large graphics needlessly: some users may be on slower lines than you;
- Make sure your files are conformant, so that they display properly.
- Don't assume everyone has the latest, slickest software: phrase things so that they are universally meaningful.

Breaching the code

What do you do if you make a mistake, especially one which affects others? There are three golden rules:

1   Don't panic: everyone makes mistakes.
2   Apologise immediately: most users are very tolerant if you make it clear you know you have offended, and that you have learnt from your mistake.
3   If your actions have caused damage (file loss, corruption, disruption etc), do what you can to put it right: if you don't know how to, call in an expert who does.

If someone does something that causes you problems, put yourself in their shoes. There's an accepted sequence of events here too:

1   If it was a genuine mistake, they will probably apologise if you point out the error politely.
2   Be aware that the offending item may be a forgery, either from someone faking the address that the item purports to come from, or from someone using a person's account without permission (the infamous Unattended Terminal Syndrome, where another user takes the opportunity offered by a person's temporary absence from their seat to send spurious messages 'as a joke').
3   If the offence is more serious or is repeated despite your requests, you can take matters higher:

a   If it is in private email or a personal message, or on an unmoderated newsgroup, ask your systems administrator, postmaster, or news administrator to take it up with their opposite number on the offender's machine.
b   If it is on a mailing list, ask the list owner to perform this task.
c   If it is on a moderated newsgroup, ask the moderator.

4   If this brings no redress, you will have to take up the matter with the systems administrators at the next higher level: it then becomes an organizational matter. Other users of the same mailing list or newsgroup (if that's where it happened) may be prepared to support your case.

Remain calm at all times, and be factual: don't rant and rage at them. Keep copies of all the relevant messages: the message ID, date, time, and address are *very* important. Remember also that phrases or words which press your own panic-buttons may be perfectly innocuous to others: don't make the mistake of assuming everyone else thinks as you do.

In cases which involve more sensitive personal issues such as race, sex, or religion, exercise discretion. Most systems administrators, postmasters, and news administrators are more than happy to help where a serious offense has taken place. They do not, however, appreciate being approached on a regular basis over trivial matters. If the problem has a personal content which causes you embarrassment or other difficulties, bear in mind that they have probably seen it all before, and are not going to waste time standing in moral judgment on you. Having said that, there are of course a few with extreme personal views of their own which they misguidedly allow to spill over into their professional lives: in these cases you may want to take advice from friends or colleagues in the network environment where the problem occurred.

Chapter 16

Copyright and intellectual property

○ Development of copyright

○ Current legal position

○ Effect on Web traffic and publishing

○ Potential developments

The basis for the concept of **copyright** was the perceived need for the creators of original work to retain certain exclusive rights to enjoy the benefit of the created subject matter for a limited time [Laddie, Prescott and Vitoria 1980]. The present solutions to the problem are far from optimal, and the mixture of copyright and computing has formed a legal minefield for the last 30 years or so. The early arguments were over whether or not a computer program or an algorithm was copyrightable in the same way that a book, picture, or play was. These have still not yet been fully resolved, and there are now many more aspects to the problem because advances in the technology have meant that information is available in a greater variety of forms and can be transmitted and received in ways that were not allowed for when legislation was drafted.

To understand the problems as they relate to the WorldWideWeb, we need to look first at the development and meaning of copyright, and then at its application. We also need to distinguish between several associated fields such as patenting, the mechanisms for charging for usage, and the moral ownership of intellectual property.

The information presented here is only a summary, viewed from the standpoint of users and providers in the Web. As with any legal matter, professional advice is essential before making any decision or commitment about the provision of information or its use.

Panel 16.1   Copyright: how it used to be

'. . . the work being good, well paid, and type plentiful, I managed to earn nearly forty francs the first six days. . . After the novel of "Woodstock" was completed, came Cooper's "Last of the Mohicans," and then a pocket edition of the works of Lord Byron, which was followed by other popular works, pirated from English authors and proprietors as fast as they made their appearance. The want of an international law of copyright was the occasion of our prosperity; and the question of printer's piracy, though it was not very profoundly discussed amongst us, was, whenever alluded to, invariably settled on the principle that "whatever is, is right".'—Charles Manby Smith, in *A Working Man's Way in the World* [Smith 1857], writing about life as a compositor in Paris in the mid–19th century.

Development of copyright

Until the invention of printing from moveable type around 1450, if you wanted a copy of a text or a painting, you went to a copyist and had it made by hand. The expense was so great and the volume so low that little attention was paid to the concept of remunerating the original creators on a per-copy basis: it was assumed that they had had their rewards from their patrons in the first place, or that they had done it for the good of humanity. Acknowledgment of the original ownership of the intellectual content was a matter for the person who commissioned the copy.

As the new technology of printing spread across Europe, it became subject to the same restrictions that were placed on other craft skills: licensing and the apprenticeship system. In England the easy multiplication of copies was perceived as a threat to the establishment, and presses were restricted to London, Oxford, and Cambridge. In 1624 the Monopoly Act abolished the concept of carrying on a trade only by privilege, but the right (or more accurately, the power) to make copies of a work (by printing) remained in the hands of the printer/publisher until 1709, when authors were granted the sole rights to the property in their work. The Constitution of the United States vested in Congress the famous authority to 'promote the progress of science and useful arts by securing for limited times to authors and inventors the exclusive right to their respective writings and discoveries', and in 1791, France granted the first real patent rights to inventors, which became the pattern in the following century in most countries in the western world.

A fundamental difference remained between the Anglo-American concept of a restriction on the right to make copies, and the broader definitions of the rights of intellectual ownership common in most other countries [Dietz 1987]. Copyright in the first sense, *per se*, is not a right to do something, but to stop others from doing something [Laddie, Prescott and Vitoria 1980]. Specifically, for an infringment to have taken place, there has to have been the act of copying, and the material must be or have been derived from someone else's work.

What is a 'work'? In most copyright legislation, it used to be an original piece of literary, dramatic, artistic, or musical creation, and this was progressively extended to include the technological developments of telegraphy, sound recording, or transmission, film, and television. There is no presumption or judgment of artistic or æsthetic merit: a 'work' doesn't have to be 'good' to qualify for copyright protection, but the assumption was that it had to have a material existence, and this is what caused the original difficulties over whether or not a collection of positive and negative charges in an array of wire-wound ferrite loops (early computer core memory) could be said to 'exist' in the same way as a book or a piece of music.

It has been accepted for many years that a program can be copyrighted, and manufacturers can attempt to protect against breaches of this right with a variety of tools, from simple © signs to the forcible entry and removal of goods authorized by the UK's 'Anton Piller' orders. By the same token, the existence of an author's copyright in electronically-stored text, music, or pictures has not been generally disputed, and is explicit in some countries' legislation (e.g. the UK's *Copyright, Designs and Patents Act, 1988* [Cornish 1989]): the problems are much more associated with its enforcement. Whether or not you agree with the concept of restricting the use of electronic property (and there are some cogent arguments against such restrictions [Stallman 1986]), the present state of affairs has arisen because speed of change in computing and networking technology has long since outpaced the capacity of governments to legislate or delegislate.

As things currently stand, any text (or pictures, sounds or movies) which you make available through the WorldWideWeb in an unrestricted manner can immediately be read by anyone anywhere on the network. If you wrote, recorded, or photographed the material, and it was all original, devised and executed by you, then you are the owner of the copyright to it, and you can do whatever you like with it. If it was done as part of your work, your contract of employment may state otherwise, and your employer may own the copyright.

If, however, all or some of it was written, composed, or designed by someone else (so they own the intellectual property it), then the law of copyright in most countries says that you need their explicit permission before you can publish it. Exceptions are made for varying quantities of material which you may copy in the course of review, research, and criticism (and some other grounds). The exact limit on this is not usually explicit: most countries' laws use phrases like 'fair use' (USA), 'fair dealing' (UK), 'small parts' (Germany) or 'short articles' (Netherlands) to describe how much can be reproduced without permission before a breach of the law occurs [Dietz 1987]. 'Copying' in this sense refers principally to manual reproductive copying, as with a photocopier, and it is unclear if this is accepted as grounds for extending the same privilege to the copying of files or the use of a laser printer. In France, you may copy only for yourself, not for groups, and you have to do the copying yourself, personally; in Italy it is for individuals and libraries only; in Germany it is limited to seven copies, not for distribution, but someone else can make them for you; Denmark permits only one copy per person; Ireland makes no provision for library copying... and so on [Dietz 1987]. International networks make it relatively easy to circumvent copyright laws, especially in countries with few constraints on reproducing material downloaded from a network [Peltu Dec 1994].

Researchers, especially academics, are only too familiar with the problems which arise when copies of rare or out-of-print original works are needed but none is available. You cannot reasonably ask a publisher to print a handful of copies; or the owner of the copyright may not be ascertainable; or they may be unwilling to grant permission for copies to be made. The only alternative is to make illegal photocopies, or (equally illegally) to scan a copy and make a machine-readable version by optical character recognition. If such copies are then distributed to other people, which is very easy when the text exists in computerised form, a breach of the copyright legislation will probably have occurred.

Publishers are therefore understandably extremely uneasy about creating electronic editions which can be copied, and about giving permission for others to make such editions, even of works which are long out of print, as it creates the potential for the loss of a source of revenue.

Copyright law

The ultimate objective of copyright is to protect the creators of intellectual work from having their livelihood threatened. This is an unquestionably honorable intent, given the ease with which they can be deprived of their means of existence by those who do not scruple to profit by theft of the material.

When authors die, copyright in their works continues for a specific period, varying from country to country, and ranging from 25 to 80 years [Copinger and James n.d.], in order to provide their dependents or successors with income from sales or royalties. But if you create a new edition of someone else's work, perhaps by correcting mistakes, adding notes, bibliography, and other matter, providing illustrations or commentary, you thereby obtain a new copyright in the new publication, which in turn will subsist for another period after your death. UNESCO publish a table of comparative copyright legislation in *Copyright Laws and Treaties of the World*, and there is a summary of this in many of the standard books on the subject such as *Copinger & Skone James on Copyright (op. cit.)*. New European legislation proposed for mid-1995 is planned to extend copyright protection to 70 years after death in some cases, and this has caused consternation, as it appears that the proposals may result in some works going *back* into copyright.

To obtain the full protection of the law in some countries (notably the USA), you are required to affix a copyright notice to your work and register two copies of it with a Copyright Office [Cornish 1989]. Elsewhere, copyright is deemed to exist from the moment of creation, whether the work is published or not, but there may also be the requirement of a *dépôt légal*, the deposit of copies with the country's premier Library of Last Resort.

Intellectual property

Both programs and data (text) are literary works within the meaning of the Copyright Acts of most countries, as they are considered a product of the author's mind [Laddie, Prescott and Vitoria 1980] even though they may never have had a tangible physical existence like a book. It is this moral ownership of the intellectual labor of an author which was recognized by the Berne Convention on Copyright of 1886, which gave authors the right, even after assignment of the copyright, to 'claim authorship' and to object to distortion or mutilation 'prejudicial to [their] honor or reputation'. To this extent, intellectual property right is no different from any other kind of property right [Kruse 1939].

Statutory protection for these rights is, however, still national in scope, and in some cases is even further restricted by decisions taken pursuant to the effect of such protection on trade: although the European Court in Luxembourg has affirmed the continued existence of national intellectual property rights, it held that the exercise of those rights is circumscribed by European Community law [Guy and Leigh 1981].

Although this distinction between the existence of a right and its exercise may appear artifical, any attempt to harmonize the present jumble of legislation must require some give and take, and ultimately the existence of an intellectual right does have to be practicable if it is to be implemented in a workable fashion. The principle of 'territoriality' is also well-established in the European Union, where you may not restrict the distribution of your work abroad to a single channel even though your national legislation may grant you a monopoly over its distribution in your home country [Guy and Leigh 1981].

A further distinction is made in many jurisdictions between the 'performance' of a work and its 'distribution'. In the case of radio, film, and television, performance is seen as public in the sense that anyone and everyone can come and see it, but they pay for it on each occasion; whereas distribution implies eventual individual sale, and the work, once bought, can be used and re-used an infinite number of times without further fee. This has very major implications for the reproduction and transmission of electronic material, because it is clear (at least to users) that if you regard a file as a 'book-equivalent', then you should only be expected to pay for it once, but if you regard it as a 'play-equivalent', you would expect to pay for it each time you see it. This distinction has its possible realization in the difference between texts in Usenet newsgroups or public mailing lists, where material passes in front of your eyes unbidden as you scan the morning email or news, and texts in files made available by anonymous FTP, where you must explicitly go and fetch the material when you want it.

One area which is affected in a very positive way by the use of electronic media is the right of recall and the right of recognition, which are an integral part of some countries' copyright legislation (Germany, France, and Italy are notable cases). These concepts allow the author an explicit right to recall the work for revision (of a non-trivial nature) or the reimposition of acknowledgement even though the copyright itself may have been reassigned to another person (such as a publisher). Clearly it is substantially easier (and probably cheaper) to undertake this kind of revision when using electronic methods, particularly if the work is held in such a way that the components of it are accessible by computer logic (such as an HTML or other SGML file).

Prohibition and permission

If your text or images are covered by copyright, where's the problem? The law provides you in most cases with redress for a breach of the copyright legislation: you can sue. But that doesn't stop the breach taking place, and the ease with which such a breach can occur is at the base of the problem.

If I buy a book, or a picture, or a statue, or even a sound or video recording, it is of course possible for me to get copies made. But in general it's fairly expensive and time-consuming to make even one copy of a whole book. To copy a video you need two VCRs, and apart from individual private copies of music from disk to tape, multiple copies need specialist equipment which the average user couldn't be bothered with. But if I buy a program or data supplied on disk, CD-ROM, tape, or over the network, it can be copied in a few seconds or minutes at negligible cost. Making multiple disk copies of course needs equipment similar to that for bulk audio tape duplication, but sending multiple copies to people over the Internet requires hardly any effort at all. Even printing copies is easy, because unlike photocopying a book, it can be left to run unattended.

Using the network to publish material which hitherto would have been printed on paper therefore carries at the moment a serious risk of revenue loss. A lot of attention has been directed at the provision of secure transmission and the authentication of the recipient and the sender (see the next chapter), but this is to no avail if the document can arbitrarily be reproduced once it is in the hands of the customer. Many suggestions have been put forward to solve this, including levies on volume transmitted, levies on connections, and hidden codes which printers would detect to permit or deny further copies. None of them attack the fundamental problem that bulk reproduction or dissemination of electronic material is fast, easy, and cheap compared to its predecessors. All the laws in the world will not stop an activity if it is simple and untraceable.

In the end, we may have to accept that we need a new paradigm. The objective of copyright—to protect authors' revenue, as distinct from the right to be acknowledged as that author—may perhaps have had its day. Even in the last decade and a half we have seen the considerable success of the concept of shareware, where you can copy a program to other people as much as you like, but you only get the manual and support if you register with a small fee. It relies to a large extent on people's honesty, but the fees involved are usually within the reach of the average pocket in the western world. Although it does not easily scale up to operations like IBM or Microsoft, it indicates that there do exist other channels for distribution than the regular methods of purchase.

The classic example of the move away from using copyright to prohibit distribution is the *GNU Manifesto* [Stallman 1986]. **GNU** is a project started by Richard Stallman, formerly of the AI Labs at MIT. The original problem was that manufacturers of operating systems, especially Unix, were using copyright and proprietary measures to restrict customers to their own products, which went against the concept of openness which had grown up around Unix. Stallman felt this was unacceptable, and set out to write his own system, which is available free, and can be copied, but cannot subsequently be charged for by a redistributor (excepting the cost of media and copying). Over the years, this has contributed in a large way to the vast quantity of software available for Unix and other systems, much of it superior to anything produced by regular commercial companies. Many of the arguments against free distribution are competently answered in the manifesto, and Stallman's campaign for **copyleft** has attracted widespread support.

The result of these moves towards changing the way we think about revenue protection and charging has led to many practical benefits, both for the users and for the companies who have examined them. It has always been common for manufacturers to entice their prospects with freebies, but the practice is now firmly established on the Internet of making copies of software available free for personal use, while still conducting normal, chargeable sales at a corporate level and for users who want a more intense level of support. Companies involved in the development of Web software have been amongst those at the forefront of this, with SoftQuad making the *HoTMetaL* editor available, Netscape Communications Corp, EINet, and many others providing browsers, and information providers allowing Web access to data which would have been prohibitively expensive for the individual before. In many cases the product is a 'Lite' version, but the effect in terms of publicity and goodwill is clearly worth the effort.

There is equally no reason why traditional paper publishers could not provide sample chapters of books or extracts from manuals and directories on a similar basis, although while unauthorized reproduction of a work remains uncontrollable once in the hands of the user, there seems little prospect of being able to use the Web or Gopher to publish the full document and retain control of the future revenues. In any event, it is perfectly possible to restrict access to online information in the case of those documents where the user only wants to look at a small portion. Manuals and directories are the obvious examples, and there is potential for generating revenue from high-volume, low-unit-cost lookups if the ease of use makes it attractive for the user. A good example is the PC-Travel service, where Web or Telnet access is provided to the world's scheduled airline services, with the ability to make a booking, charge it to your credit card and have the tickets delivered the next day by courier. Doubtless many users will only access it to check on timing and availability without buying, but the company is clearly pinning its hopes on the revenue from bookings outweighing the small incremental (per-access) cost of providing the service.

Whether we end up permitting or restricting access to full copies, the ability of the Web to provide information *about* goods and services is not in doubt. It remains to be seen whether or not existing copyright legislation can hold its own in the face of increasing public demand for 'free' information.

Chapter 17

Authentication, encryption, and charging

- ○ Checking who you are
- ○ Controlling who uses what
- ○ Accounting for what's used

Every day, millions of users all over the world receive email purporting to come from certain addresses. In almost all cases, these messages are perfectly valid and are not a cause for concern. But there is no guarantee attached to most of them, nothing to certify that they do indeed come from who they say they do, or that they have not been tampered with *en route*. The matter is taken on trust, and in most cases it is not misplaced.

Authentication is the provision of proof at an acceptable level that a message is genuine. **Authorization** is the application of this proof to permit access to certain facilities (like a username and password to an account). Where the transaction of business involves the transmission of sensitive information, there is also a need for **encryption**.

Authentication

Proving that you are who you say you are, or that a message does come from the address it claims to come from, is not a simple business on a network designed originally for use by trusted groups of colleagues in a laboratory or office where there was no need for such proof. It is horribly easy on most Unix systems to fake the origins of mail and posts to newsgroups, as has been amply demonstrated over the years by various messages ranging from humorous spoofs to death threats. Fortunately it occurs rarely in comparison to the enormous bulk of regular everyday mail.

At the bottom level, a simple check can be done on the existence of the domain name and hostname of the purported originator. This in itself guarantees nothing except that the names exist in some tables maintained by the network administration, and that there is a machine out there somewhere responding to `ping, whois` or `nslookup` requests. An expert eye can often detect any likely irregularities in the headers of mail messages which retain a certain amount of routing information gathered along the way, but this is not a viable option for other protocols which use the IP address alone, or for those not expert in the composition of mail headers.

Information about the existence of a specific username can be gathered from the `identd` server if one is running at the site in question. This is a process which responds to requests by sending details of a username. It is intended for machine-to-machine communication, rather than person-to-machine, for which `finger` is the more normal choice. The use of `identd` is voluntary to the systems administrator at each site, but is becoming very common. As with the methods for checking site names, it offers no guarantees, and only provides a check on the existence of a specific username being valid for access, so it says nothing about whether any particular message was sent by that user. You can test if your system is running an `identd` server by using Telnet to connect to 130.236.254.1 114 (port 114).

In the case of non-mail, non-Usenet messages, such as requests to HTTP or

Gopher servers, most server software provides a log of accesses, and this may include the purported username and sitename where possible. However, as an increasing amount of traffic is coming from SLIP or PPP users, where the connection and identity are temporary and may change from one occasion to the next, this does not in itself provide proof.

The most specific way of controlling access is by username and password. These can be set up for CERN and NCSA servers as files stored in each directory you want to restrict which hold the username and password you decide on. These usernames and passwords are purely your invention: they have no connection with any user's (or your) real login username or password. A program (`htpasswd`) is provided with the server software for maintaining these password files.

The tutorial already mentioned at `http://wintermute.ncsa.uiuc.edu:8080/auth-tutorial/tutorial.html` explains the process in more detail, with live example you can click on and enter usernames and passwords to test and demonstrate it.

Secure transmission

There are several proposals being made for the establishment of secure communications using HTTP (or a secure equivalent) which would allow private transactions over the public networks. All propose some form of cryptography, with or without the need for prior public-key or private-key licensing. The proposals cover several classes of security, weak and strong authentication, signature, encryption, and attack prevention.

SHTTP (Secure HTTP) would enable the private transfer of data, so that private matters such as credit card numbers and regular business transactions could be exchanged over the Web. A copy of the proposals is at `http://www.commerce.net/information/standards/drafts/shttp.txt`. An implementation of SHTTP is available from Terisa Systems Inc. (*SecureWeb*) which allows security functions to be fully integrated and controlled by the application, and provides security information and management functions at the client and server: details are at `http://www.terisa.com/prod/prod.html`. Spry, Inc. are also developing a version of SHTTP.

SSL (Secure Sockets Layer) is a proposal from Netscape Communications Corp. for a security protocol that provides privacy over the Internet. The protocol allows client–server applications to communicate in a way that cannot be eavesdropped. Servers are always authenticated and clients are optionally authenticated. Details of the proposal are at `http://home.netscape.com/info/SSL.html`.

A reference implementation of SSL is available from Netscape, who are also marketing *Netsite*, an HTTP server which incorporates some security features based upon public key cryptographic technology, including encryption to ensure the privacy of client–server communications, and server authentication which uses a certificate and a digital signature to verify the identity of the server. Netsite installs as a regular HTTP server, but still makes it possible for a company to run two servers, one ordinary one for serving material which does not need security, and one secure one on another port for private transactions.

There has been some confusion over exactly which implementations are 'official', and the WorldWideWeb Consortium has issued a statement to clarify this (Panel 17.1).

Panel 17.1   WorldWideWeb Consortium statement on security

The last two meetings of the W3C Security Group had made clear that there is a great need for a W3C Security Standard that will be

1   rapidly and decisively generated;
2   that can meet multiple user requirements (security scenarios);
3   that will enable interoperability with existing Web products and
4   that will gracefully expand toward expected future security requirements.

In the last meeting of the W3C Security Group on February 22, 1995 a strong sentiment was expressed that development of the W3C security protocol could proceed from an existing commercial design through the addition of features of other competing designs. Unfortunately, this suggestion was interpreted by some as endorsement of the base design as the W3C security standard.

This is not the case: No current security protocol has been endorsed by W3C security standard. To ensure that the future W3C security standard is widely accepted in accordance with the above objectives, current development is proceeding both top-down and bottom-up along the sequence scenarios—requirements—design—implementation. It is a plan of the W3C team that transition to the W3C security protocol be enabled by software which will interoperate with existing Web products that provide security.

At the February 22 meeting, several W3C members offered development resources toward this standard. While a formal release date has not yet been set, we expect an initial release to be issued by the end of the year. Formal adoption of the protocol will proceed according to the W3C Consortium standard setting process.

Much more development is needed in this field, as both SHTTP and SSL are only proposals. There are useful pointers to the work being done at `http://galaxy.einet.net/galaxy/Engineering-and-Technology/ Computer-Technology/Security/security-links.html`, `http://www-ns.rutgers.edu/www-security/https-wg.html`, and `http://www-ns. rutgers.edu/www-security/www-security-list.html`.

Authorization

Once an address has been established as genuine, it can be validated against an information provider's own data to see if it is authorized to access it. Both the CERN and NCSA HTTP server software provides for a limited form of authorization checking, and this is increasingly being supported by browsers.

How you maintain your internal lists of authorized users is a matter for local policy and management, but HTML forms can be used to gather names and passwords, and further access can be permitted or denied on that basis.

One problem inherent to HTTP is a result of its statelessness. If I point my browser at your server at 2.14 p.m. and it's a slow day for communications, it might be a minute or so before your server receives the request. If it's a big file, I might not finish receiving it for several more minutes, and it might take me a while to read it, or I may go off following links from it to elsewhere on the network, and not come back to your server for a long while. During this period, there is no communication between my browser and your server, so your server has no idea if I'm finished for the day, or just taking my time, gone for coffee, or even if the network connection has fallen over. When I next contact your server, is this a new job, requiring the authorization process all over again, or is it a continuation of the previous request?

While the authorization itself is not a problem to perform, its repetition on every occasion is tedious and irksome to a user, so some judgment has to be made in setting the timeout delay if one is used, or to work in some kind of heuristic to help in determining if this is a continuation or a fresh task.

Encryption

This is a subject which has occupied the public mind in the computer field for several years, with the attempts by governments to claim, reclaim, or establish a hold on various methods of coding, to permit them a back door into all communications. While the public reaction varies from the bored to the politically active, there seems to be a general feeling that unrestricted official access to everyone's private messages is either unwise or simply unconstitutional in many countries.

Two spies can communicate by postal (paper) mail in the reasonable security of knowledge that no-one is going to open their mail and read the contents unless they are under active surveillance. The same cannot be said of email or other files in transit, which are best treated as if they were postcards. Although reading someone else's mail is just as much an affront to civil liberty as opening their letters would be, the operators whose job it is to keep the networks running do have to unclog the system from time to time, and the contents of email and other files can be open to their view when they do this. Generally they are far too busy to bother reading it, and are unlikely to be interested in any case, but the possibility nevertheless exists.

Of much more concern is the unauthorized and deliberate intrusion of the individual who is actively trying to see things which should be private. There are at least half a dozen programs available from the public archives which let a user on a corporate or campus Ethernet watch or record every packet that goes past. These might include usernames and passwords, credit card numbers, personal records, or private email, as well as the bulk of traffic like FTP, HTTP, Gopher, News, and others.

By agreement with individual correspondents, you can of course agree on a private coding scheme that will protect your text against unwanted intrusion, but the invention of Public Key Encryption by RSA has led to several further developments which enable anyone to encode their transmissions in such a way as to make them virtually uncrackable except to the intended recipient. The most popular in recent years on the Internet has been *PGP*, or Pretty Good Privacy, invented by Phil Zimmermann. *PGP* combines the use of Public Key techniques with those of conventional cryptography to enable encryption without the need for users to exchange keys first. *PGP* can also be used to authenticate the originator of a message. The US government's initial reaction was perhaps predictable, seeing that they would not have any way to break the code in times of perceived serious need or otherwise, and the early versions were prohibited from export, even to 'friendly' countries. Needless to say, the use of the network itself defeated this restriction, and copies were available on FTP servers around the world within minutes of its release (the restriction was partly relaxed on subsequent versions). The public version is now available from MIT for the USA, and from a variety of servers in many other countries, and a commercial version is marketed by ViaCrypt.

Many people who use *PGP* regularly have made their public key available using the `finger` service, so it is simple to retrieve the string and use it to encode a message for them. Its use in the Web is more limited, although if you provide your public key by `finger` in this way, a HTTP server could employ it to encrypt files sent to you. *PGP* is now being used by state and local government in the USA on occasions when they need to secure their own transaction.

Charging and accounting

Finally, when you have checked authenticity, validated the password and decoded the text, you can provide a service. If it's a commercial service, you then want to charge for it and keep accounts. Most HTTP servers provide log files (*SerWeb* seems to be an exception), and there are many analysis and extraction routines available to sort, summarize, and report on the contents of the logs (pp. 246–247).

Charging by credit card is the most immediate and direct way, provided you and each user have all installed sufficient protection against unwanted interception of the card number and other details by using some form of encryption. Regular account holders would normally expect a monthly invoice for usage instead, if it is at a level to warrant it, and this can easily be generated from the logs by any competent programmer using one of the logfile analysis programs mentioned earlier, or from other record-keeping done as part of the operation of scripts. In combination with the access control facilities of browsers, and the proposals under way for secure transfer of data, the move from an insecure, trust-based network to a privacy-enhanced one is under way.

Two recent developments have introduced the concept of digitized cash payment to the WorldWideWeb. The DigiCash project aims to test the concept of secure but untraceable cash-style payments: a sum of $1,000,000 'Cyberbucks' is being made available in slices of $100 to intending service providers and participants from `http://www.digicash.com/ecash/trial.html`, and they provide server and client software to handle the transactions. The CyberCash payment system facilitates the purchase of goods and services on the Internet by providing a secure environment for transactions between consumers, merchants, and their banks as well as between individuals. There are other non-cash projects under development which are being documented at `http://ganges.cs.tcd.ie/mepeirce/Project/oninternet.html`. An excellent article discussing the problems and benefits of moving to a network-based digital cash society appeared in the Economist recently, entitled *So much for the cashless society* [Anon. 1994]. Banks themselves are also getting into the act: the Bank of Ireland and WebNet Technologies came together to provide the first retail bank branch on the Internet. It is an extension of the Trinity Branch, which is located in Trinity College Dublin. The services on offer are on a trial basis at present. Users can browse for information about the bank, request additional information, and take part in a survey to ascertain what they would like to see from a virtual branch. These survey responses will be used to add important new services that users need. The branch is located at `http://www.webnet.ie/cust/boi/index.html`

Chapter 18

Future developments

○ Expansion of the Web

○ Software developments

○ The WorldWideWeb Consortium

The implications of what the Web is capable of have far-reaching consequences. No other information system has caused the White House to install a server, or encouraged companies to connect to the Internet in such volume, or encouraged the average user of a desktop computer to spend hours of personal time making a database of the local team's baseball or cricket statistics available to the world. It's not just the appeal of 'point-and-click' ease of use, although the Web, like the Gopher system, has an enviable reputation in ergonomics. As we have seen, it is a combination of hypertext, images, uniformity of interface, and the unrestricted nature of the Internet which make it so attractive... and time-consuming. Webwanderers are a growing problem in universities and companies alike: people who spend their waking hours navigating all over the Internet. One of the major barriers to retrieving information, the instructional learning curve, has disappeared.

Less obvious to the user, but equally important to information providers, is that the bulk of the textual information itself is stored in a portable form which is common to all platforms, so once created, there is no conversion to be done, and no barriers to the movement of information between systems. It also means that information is not subject to the restraints of proprietary formats, and although this is still regarded with scepticism in some quarters, there seems to be general acceptance that the use of open systems, or more correctly 'open data', is the direction in which the world is moving.

For business, the Web can provide public and private access to corporate publicity on a wide scale, especially to sales, marketing, and user support information. This can release valuable human resources from the field of information provision, particularly in answering phone calls, although we are still a long way from achieving the kind of universality which the phone has got.

A lot of software is being developed for the Web:

- The *Cyberleaf* converter (Appendix A) means the ability to use a familiar wordprocessor to create and maintain your document base, but have the files turned into HTML for you. This is the opposite direction from the argument commonly made of moving everything into SGML, and it is too early to predict which will predominate.
- SoftQuad's *Panorama* and EBT's *DynaWeb* SGML browsers mean that the Web need not be limited to HTML documents: any SGML DTD could be used, so a much richer language will become accessible to users and providers.
- The *Rainbow DTD* and its associated software from EBT at `ftp://ftp.ebt.com/pub/outgoing/rainbow/` allows the description in SGML (and thus the conversion) of files from various wordprocessors. The direction of moving 'legacy' text from non-SGML systems into SGML is one which will play an increasingly important part in the development of the Web, but see the comments earlier about the opposite direction.
- Virtual Reality Markup Language or **VRML** is an evolving specification for a platform-independent definition of three-dimensional spaces within the WorldWideWeb. It is designed to combine the best features of virtual reality, networked visualization, and the global hypermedia environment of the WorldWideWeb. Details are at `http://www.wired.com/vrml/`.
- There is a proposal in HTML3 to let browsers transmit a whole file back to a server—in effect a file-upload capability. Although this has security and performance implications, these are being addressed in a revised Internet Draft at `ftp://ds.internic.net/internet-drafts/draft-ietf-`

`html-fileupload-01.txt.`

● Another proposal is for the inclusion of *client-side* image maps, where the HTML code would include specifications of which areas of an image could be clicked on for specific files, thus devolving this function to the user's desktop rather than have it handled by a server as described earlier.

Overall development for the future of the Web is being monitored by a variety of organizations, principally the WorldWideWeb Consortium, which is a collaboration between **INRIA** (the *Institut National de Recherche en Informatique et en Automatique* in France, who have taken over the running from CERN), and the Laboratory for Computer Science at MIT. In collaboration with many other institutes and companies, its purpose is to support the stable evolution of the WorldWideWeb and its protocols by adopting a single standard (on the IETF model of a pilot implementation first and formalization after); by promulgating a reference implementation; and by disseminating information. Among the deliverables are the organization of the consortium itself; the production and maintenance of the protocol suite (for example, the CERN Common Code Library, which is at the heart of most browsers); to pilot exemplary use; to maintain public awareness of related technologies; and to help industry use the Web. Details of commercial participation can be got at `http://www.w3.org/hypertext/ WWW/Organization/Consortium/Prospectus/Overview.html`.

Appendix A

Converting existing text

On many occasions, instead of writing HTML files from scratch, you can re-use existing files written in some other system. Few other text-handling systems provide the sort of structural markup needed for direct conversion to HTML format, but many indirect methods exist, and it is usually not difficult to convert other files unless they are in a particularly uncommon format.

The popular wordprocessors and desktop publishing systems, with a few exceptions, are geared towards purely visual display, with little attention given to re-usability of text. On the contrary, until recently, manufacturers thought it was in their interests to trap their customers into a proprietary format with their choice of wordprocessor. Happily, most of them now provide sometimes quite extensive conversion utilities to allow files to be imported and exported using other file formats. However, because they deal mostly with visual markup, the file formats that they can create are often aimed at providing typographical detail which may not be relevant in a multi-platform environment. If possible, you need to make sure that fonts have been used in a regularised manner if you want to minimize the amount of manual tidying-up.

Some of the conversion software is not fully HTML-compliant, so this tidying-up may have to be done in a plain file editor before loading it in an HTML editor. If you have a lot of this conversion to do, it is probably worth investing some time in learning one of the more powerful text editors with programmable facilities such as *Emacs*, so that you reduce the amount of time spent on repetitive changes.

Conversion programs

At the time of writing, the following major programs are available for direct conversion to HTML format:

RTF and MS-Word

RTFtoHTML converts from Microsoft's RTF (Rich Text Format), which is a popular and highly descriptive file format used by Microsoft *Word*, and which is usable by *WordPerfect* and many other wordprocessors. To save a wordprocessor file in RTF, pick `Save As...` from the wordprocessor's `File` menu, and pick `RTF` as the format in which to save it (the filetype should be set to `.rtf`). The program is available for MS-DOS, Unix, and Macintosh and can be downloaded from the NCSA's FTP server (`ftp.ncsa.uiuc.edu`) and many others.

WordPerfect

WPtoHTML converts from *WordPerfect* 5.1 and 6 into HTML using macros. You can download it from the SimTel archive (at `oak.oakland.edu` and many mirrors) in the   directory. Another set of macros to handle 5.1 files is available from Southampton University at `ftp.soton.ac.uk` in `pub/www/sucs/wphtml.zip`.

LaTeX

The *LaTeX2HTML* program is discussed in the section on mathematics (Chapter 10). It converts files from *LaTeX*, a structured typesetting system, into HTML. Because *LaTeX* does real math formatting, it makes any formulae into graphical images and includes them in the HTML file. Details of availability are on p. 211.

FrameMaker

Frame2HTML converts frame files and books in *FrameMaker* and MIF format. It deals with figures and tables as well as text, and maps graphics and mathematics to external images. The source code can be downloaded from `ftp.nta.no` in `pub/fm2html/Frame2html-x.y.z.tar.Z`

WebMaker is a Converter for Frame files from CERN, now marketed by the Harlequin Group (`http://www.harlequin.co.uk/`) but is available free for personal academic, research, or internal business use. The system runs on Unix

(Sun, HP, IBM/RS and SGI) and is available from `ptsun00.cern.ch` in `pub/webmaker/wm14`.

QuarkXPress

The *qt2www* program is a *Perl* script to convert Quark-tagged plain text file to HTML, acting as a filter by mapping one set of tags to the other. It is available for Macs, PCs, and Unix from `the-tech.mit.edu` in `pub/WWW/`.

HTML to PostScript

Going in the other direction is the *html2ps* package by Jan Kåmann, which converts HTML files to *PostScript* for printing. This is a *Perl* program, available at `ftp://ftp.tdb.uu.se/pub/sources/html2ps/html2ps_0.1beta.tar` with facilities for scaling, styling and landscape printing, but images are not supported.

SGML2TₑX

Modesty compels me to include my own program, *SGML2TₑX*, which takes an arbitrary SGML file (including HTML) and converts all the tags to *TₑX*-like control sequences, so that `<head>...</head>` becomes `\STARThead...\FINISHhead`. It performs no parsing, so the onus is on the user to ensure that the input file contains validly-constructed, fully-normalized markup. The process creates a template `.sty` file with empty definitions for you to fill in with whatever formatting you wish (or you can provide a configuration file beforehand to force interpretation with specific *TₑX* code). The software (MS-DOS only at the moment) is in -test and can be downloaded from `ftp://www.ucc.ie/pub/tex/sgml2tex.zip`.

There are many dozens of other products which perform conversion of one kind or another, from simple macros to larger-scale specialist systems, and more are being written every month. The most popular are listed with links to the source code and documentation in CERN's HTML Tools pages at `http://www.w3.org/hypertext/WWW/Tools/Filters.html` and in the Yahoo database at `http://www.yahoo.com/Computers/World_Wide_Web/HTML_Converters/`. In particular, one new cross-platform product is *Cyberleaf* (from Interleaf), which aims to integrate HTML creation both with editing and conversion facilities from a wide range of other WP or DTP products. Details can be obtained from `http://www.ileaf.com/`. For large-scale conversion, including document and hypertext management, Exoterica Corporation produce *OmniMark*, a programmable system for converting in either direction between SGML applications like HTML and almost any other kind of text representation.

Appendix B

HTML3

The changes to HTML for version 3 are being made with a close eye on compatibility with HTML 2.0. There's still a head and a body, `<h1>` through `<h6>` for headings, and the familiar paragraphs, lists, and forms. The major additions are mathematics, tables, figures, client-side event-handling for figures, and a new container class of `<div>` to enable sectional material to be handled more effectively. There are also more descriptive elements for the markup of content, a proposed mechanism for uploading files to a server, and support for style sheets or stylefiles. The overall structure is shown on Figure B.1. Some of these additions have already been implemented on a pilot basis in *Arena*, *Netscape*, *Emacs* `w3-mode`, and some versions of *Mosaic*. The latest version of the HTML3 DTD can be found at `ftp://hplose.hpl.hp.com/pub/WWW/html3.dtd` and the descriptive text at `ftp://hplose.hpl.hp.com/pub/WWW/html3.txt`

The Document Type Declaration changes, of course, and to take full advantage of the added features you can enforce the stricter usage by starting your HTML3 files with

```
<!DOCTYPE HTML PUBLIC "-//IETF//DTD HTML 3.0//EN"
[<!ENTITY % HTML.Recommended "INCLUDE">]>
```

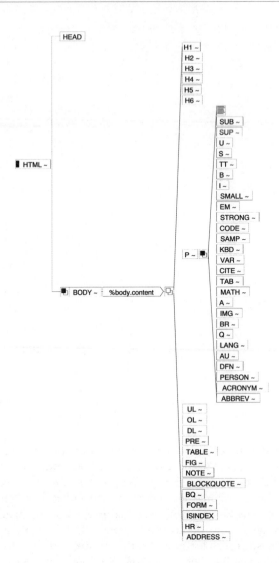

Figure B.1   General structure of HTML3

New header elements

In the header there are two new elements, `<range>` and `<style>`, for specifying subportions of the document and for implementing style sheets.

The `<range>` is intended to let you mark independently any portions of your document which may be subject to some external processing, such as searching or special typographic treatment. This element has `from` and `until` attributes to refer to the beginning and end of portions of the document which you define.

You mark these in the text body with the <spot> element, using the id attribute set to some label you make up. The value of from and until is then the value of the id attributes of the 'spots' which mark the start and end of those portions of the document you want to define. The class attribute lets you name what kind of portion this element refers to (e.g. search, annotate, etc.).

The <style> element surrounds style sheet information (pp. 310–312) and has an attribute of notation to let you define what kind of style sheet notation you are using.

Body content

All body (structural) elements can now have a class attribute to let you tie them to a style sheet class (pp. 310–312); a lang attribute to identify the language used (p. 319); a background attribute to specify a graphical background; and an id attribute as a target for hrefs (a change from the use of name in HTML 2.0 anchor elements). An additional attribute of clear with values of left, right, or all lets you suggest to the browser how to flow block-oriented elements around or past figures. The value clear=left means 'move down until the left margin is clear of pending figures'. Alternatively you can use values such as 20em to give the minimum text width required.

The <banner> element allows you to specify a portion of text which is to remain statically on display, regardless of whereabouts in the document the user has scrolled to.

As with HTML 2.0, sections of your document are usually marked by the use of headings like <h2>. A new element, <div>, lets you enclose or surround entire divisions and use the class attribute to specify what kind of division it is (chapter, section, subsection, etc.). Heading elements can now have an attribute of seqnum to specify a start value for numbered headings (if implemented); dingbat to let you pick standard names for icons to appear beside the heading (from a list in the HTML3 specification); src to let you use an image file instead; and nowrap to prevent the browser wrapping lines (you then have to wrap them in your markup with br).

Superscript and subscript are available in ordinary paragraphs without having to enclose them in a <math> element. The <sub> and <sup> elements can both contain text and descriptive (non-structural) elements, and can take the attribute align with a value of left, right or center to specify positioning.

Tabbing is implemented with the <tabstop> and <tab> tags (both empty). <tabstop> with an id attribute set to some label value means 'set a tab stop at the point on the screen where this tag happens to fall'. The <tab> tag can then

As you can see, HTML 3.0 supports text flow around floating figures. Other major additions include fill-out forms, tables and mathematical equations, and features for greater control of layout.

Fill-out forms may include a range of input controls including checkboxes, radio buttons, single and multiline text fields and selection menus. Client side handling of constraints is possible via simple scripts linked to the form. Tables are built up from header or data cells, and you

A pause after a hard spell of fishing   © Time-Life 1987

can merge cells for more complex layouts.

Figure B.2   Flowing text around a figure in HTML3

be used in a subsequent line (probably after a `<br>`) with the `to` attribute set to the label value to jump to that position.

As mentioned above, the `name` attribute of the anchor tag, for making a target for hypertext references, is being replaced by a more generalised `id` attribute, so any element can become the target of a reference. The `name` attribute will continue to be supported by browsers until HTML 2.0 files get converted to HTML3.

Notes (footnotes and others) have been introduced with the `<note>` element, with a `role` attribute to indicate what kind of note it is. Perhaps some browsers might instantiate them as sidenotes, or pop-ups, maybe even as yellow 'stickies'.

Character-level elements

The `<s>` element replaces `strike` for strikeout text, and is joined by `<del>` and its counterpart `<ins>` for marking deletions and insertions where they need to be retained for display, even though changed in the document (e.g. in legal uses).

There are two new display-oriented elements `<small>` and `<big>`, which leave the implementation of exactly what font sizes to offer up to the browser authors.

The `<q>` element lets you identify quoted speech *without* giving the quotation marks, so that browsers can be localised in different countries with varying ways of showing quotes. `<lang>` lets you enclose a different language to the one you are writing in. `<au>` (author) and `<person>`, `<acronym>`, `<dfn>`, and `<abbrev>` are there to provide the hooks on which indexing or database systems can run.

Lists

Menu and Directory lists have been dropped, and their functionality subsumed into ordered, unordered, and definition lists with an `<lh>` element to supply a list header before the first `<li>` and a `wrap` attribute to specify wrapping direction for the item texts. There is also support for user-supplied list item bullets, with a `dingbat` or `src` attribute to specify the icon or URL of a suitable image. The `label` attribute is for some text to allow 'bullet' rendering by a character-mode browser. This revised structure is shown in Figure B.3.

Tables, figures, and images

Two new structures appear, `<table>` and `<figure>`, which are shown in Figure B.4.

Figures supplement the HTML 2.0 images to allow for captions and associated text. The `<figure>` element can contain a `<caption>` followed by text for display with the image (this can be in any of the regular block-oriented elements like headings, paragraphs, preformatted blocks, lists, addresses, block quotations, tables, and notes). The figure can have an `align` attribute, and `height` and `width` attributes so that browsers can preallocate space on the screen.

```
<figure id="d69" src="http://abc.xyz.org/ pat/house.gif"
align="center">
<caption align="bottom">My house</caption>
<p>Picture of my mansion in the hills above
Naples, note the <a href="fire.html" shape="rect
```

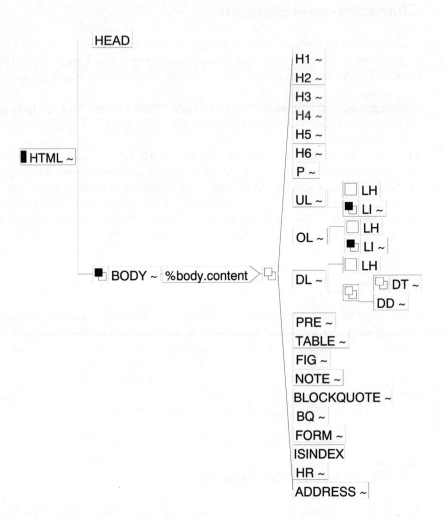

Figure B.3   Additions to the lists in HTML3

```
20,120,50,140">hole in the roof</a> where the
lightning struck.</p>
<credit>The local paper took this shot.</credit>
</figure>
```

Within a figure, text which is marked with the anchor element **<a>** can use the
shape attribute to specify a polygon by coordinates on the image to which they
refer, so that a mouse click on that portion of the image will act as a private image
map and retrieve the document pointed to. You can also use a **<credit>** element
if the image is not your own!

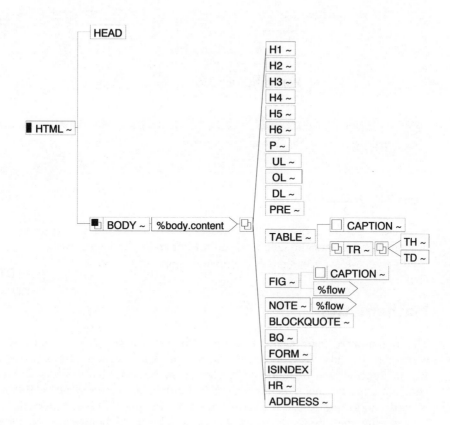

Figure B.4   Tables and figures

Tables are done with the <table> element, and can also have a caption. There is a **border** attribute to specify ruled rather than unruled tables, and several alignment options. Individual column widths and alignments can be given with the **colspec** attribute using multiple L, R, or C characters and a width for each (e.g. L40C15R10).

Each row is given using the <tr> element to hold the information, both for column headers or footers and for regular row data. Each <tr> element can then hold as many <th> (table header) or <td> (table data) elements as needed:

```
<table border>
<tr><th>Item</th><th>Quantity</th></tr><hr>
<tr><th>Population</th><td>384,000</td></tr>
<tr><th>Sample</th><td>384</td></tr>
<caption>Fig 1. Survey Frame</caption>
</table>
```

Item	Quantity
Population	384,000
Sample	384

Fig 1. Survey Frame

Figure B.5   Tables in HTML3

See Figure B.5 for a display of this using *Arena*. There are also attributes for headers to span rows and columns, and for left and right alignment.

Mathematics

The long-awaited math elements are done by using a `<math>` element *within* a paragraph (just like $T_{\!E}X$ does with the $ sign. A `model` attribute is proposed for the specification of inline or display math. Because math occurs within a paragraph, the normal paragraph markup (bold, italics, citation, etc.) is disabled in math mode, and replaced with seven elements: subscript and superscript we have already met, but there are also boxes (which act like bracketing), positional indicators for above and below, and root and array elements (Figure B.6).

The `<box>` construction provides both logical and visual bracketing (the `delim` attribute is optional and browsers should automatically size them: you specify them in pairs with the names defined in a list of HTML Math character entities, a subset of the ISO math character entities). Within the box, `<over>` and `<atop>` are used for fractions. Boxes can contain boxes, as shown in Figure B.8: to avoid the problems of editing this without a math editor, use is made of SGML's 'SHORTREF' abbreviations, which are defined in HTML3 for `<sub>` (_), `<sup>` (^) and `<box>` ({...}), based on those used by $T_{\!E}X$, so $E = mc^2$ is `E=mc^2^`, H_0 is `H_0_` and $(a + z)$ is `{(a+z)}`.

Multi-level sub- and superscripts need careful handling: $x = c^{2^3}$ is done by typing `<math>x=c^2<sup>3</sup>^m</math>` so that the superscript 3 gets applied to the 2, not as an additional superscript to the c.

Large fractions with complex formulae above and below are done with `<above>` or `<below>` elements. Each of these can contain boxes, which as the diagrams show, can themselves contain `<above>` and `<below>` elements (Figure B.9).

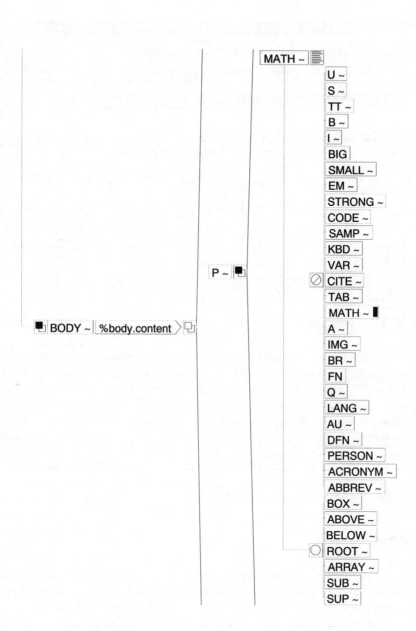

Figure B.6 Mathematics

Roots are done with the `<root>` element with an attribute also called `root` to specify the degree. The `<array>` element allows for *LATEX*-like arrays with a `coldef` attribute to supply the single letter alignment per column. Each row is contained in an `<arow>` element with each item enclosed in an `<item>` (Figure B.10).

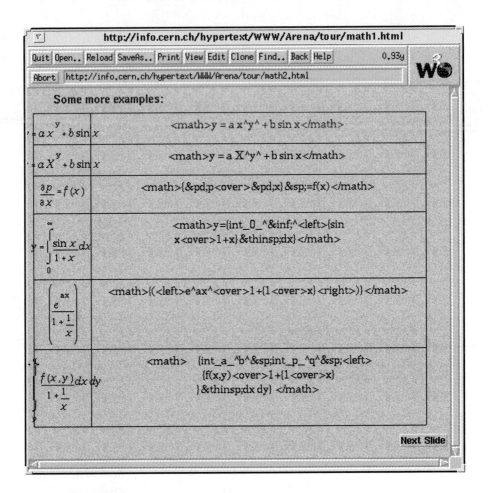

Figure B.7   Mathematics in the Arena browser

Forms

The most significant addition to forms is a proposed method of uploading files to a server. This is specified in the `<input>` element with the `file` value for the `type` attribute. You can specify what kinds of files are allowed with a new attribute, `accept`, which takes a list of media types or file patterns as its value, e.g.:

```
<input type="file" accept="image/gif, image/jpeg"
name="mypic">
```

You also need to change the `enctype` of the enclosing `<form>` element to be `multipart/form-data`.

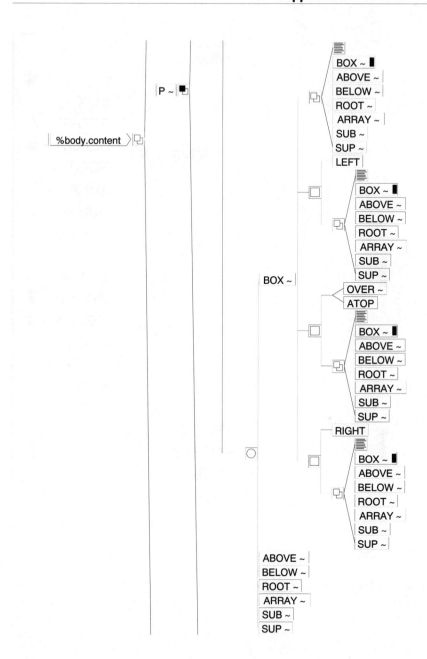

Figure B.8 Box structure logic for math

The user can then give a filename as the field value and a suitably-conformant browser will send this file to the server in a multipart MIME message. The `action`

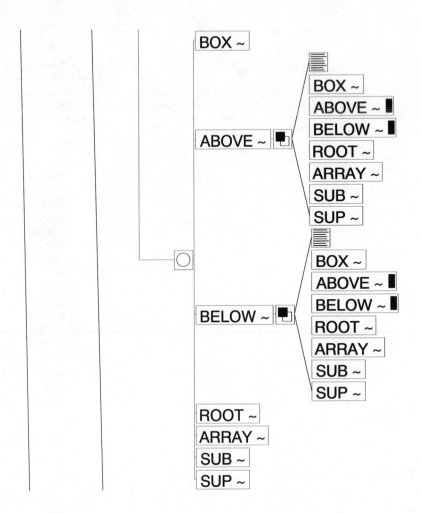

Figure B.9   Elements for larger fractions

attribute of the form may point at a program or CGI script which can handle file input. The draft specification for this can be found at `ftp://ds.internic. net/internet-drafts/draft-ietf-html-fileupload-02.txt`.

Other new `types` are `range` for allowing a pair of values separated by a comma; `scribble` for pen input from a tablet; and `audio` for sending sound to the server.

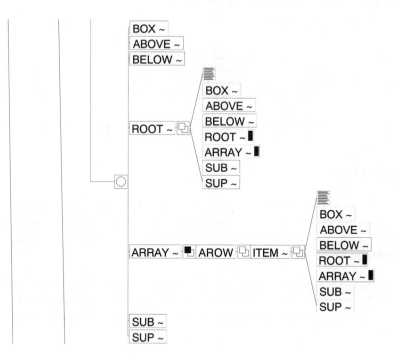

Figure B.10   HTML3 math for roots and arrays

Notes and blocks

The last few additions proposed are both block-oriented. The `<blockquote>` element is renamed `<bq>` to minimize typing for users without menu-driven editors. The `<note>` element (mentioned above for footnotes) allows the insertion of notes with a `role` attribute of `simple`, `note`, `caution`, `warning`, or `footnote`. The note can have a URL attached with the `src` attribute like an image, and a `role` attribute to specify if the note is a caution or a warning or some other quality.

There are some additional symbols added from the ISO set of character entities for publishers (Table B.1), and there is discussion of the way in which browsers might include others.

A further addition has been proposed for character entities to support bidirectional text systems (Arabic, Hebrew etc.) which are defined by ISO 10646–1:1993.

Table B.1 Additional character entities in HTML3

Name	Char	Description
		1em space in the current point size
		1en space in the current point size
—	—	em rule, used for interjections
–	–	en rule, used to separate ranges like 3–4
©	©	international copyright symbol
™	™	trademark sign
®	®	registered sign

Style sheets

Style sheets are still in the proposal stage for HTML3. Only *Emacs* **w3-mode** and the experimental *Arena* browser currently implement them. There are too many to give here, but a summary of the proposals at **http://www.w3.org/ hypertext/WWW/Style/**.

One possible solution is to let you define a class of style (say, a color), using the new **<style>**. The content of this tag is a series of statements naming a class and its style. You attach this style to any specific tag by using the **class** attribute on the tag (this example courtesy of Bill Perry):

```
<html>
<head>
<style notation="css">
p.question: text.color = red
p.answer: text.background = blue
</style>
<title>Test</title>
</head>
<body>
<p class=question>Where am I?</p>
<p class=answer>Somewhere</p>
</body>
</html>
```

However, because the style information is carried as element *content*, non-HTML3 browsers will probably display it as if it were text. An example of this is at **http://www.w3.org/hypertext/WWW/Arena/style.html**.

Pei Y. Wei's style sheet language uses inheritance to let outer element style influence inner ones unless overridden:

```
(BOLD,EMPH,STRONG            fontWeight=bold)
(I                  fontSlant=italic)
(ADDRESS
```

```
   (P              fontSlant=italic))
(OL
  (LI              numStyle=roman
    (LI            numStyle=number
      (LI          numStyle=alpha)
    )
  )
)
```

This would be referenced using a `<link>` element in the header of a file with `rel` attribute of `"style"` and give a `href` pointing to the location of the style file. The advantage of this is that it allows style files to be shared.

A proposal by Robert Raisch suggests a similar way of accessing the style file, but allows for a much finer degree of specification of the typographic elements:

```
@DEFAULT
fo(fa=ti,sp=pr,si=14,we=me,sl=ro,fo=in,bo=in,li=no,
nu=1,fn='')
ju(st=le,hy=0,ke=0) co(nu=1,wi=80) br(lo=af,ob=it)
ma(ob=it,pr=no,be=0,re=no,su=no,af=0)
ve(be=0,af=0,sp=0,of=0) in(le=0,ri=0,fi=0)
li(lo=in,ma=no,li=un,nu=1,be=no,af=no,hi=0)

# TITLE object style (font size becomes 24)
@TITLE fo(si=24)

# BODY object style (font family becomes helvetica 18pt)
@BODY fo(fa=he,si=18)
```

which specifies a default for font, justification, marking, vertical layout and linking, and then varies this for specific elements.

The metalanguage used by the Document Style Semantics and Specification Language is for specifying style sheet languages. DSSSL-Lite is an initiative to define a subset of **DSSSL** as a basis for a common style sheet language. There is considerable support for this among the SGML community where it originated.

Bert Bos bases his proposal on the format of X resource files:

```
! H1 is bold, centered, 2 sizes larger than the surrounding text,
! with lines above and below.
!
*H1.size: 2
*H1.bold: true
*H1.justify: center
```

```
*H1.rulebefore: 1.0
*H1.ruleafter: 1.0
*H1.prebreak: 2.0
*H1.postbreak: 1.0
*H1.noindent: true
```

which has the advantage that robust routines already exist for reading and parsing such syntax (from the *X Windows* software).

Appendix C

Resources

This is a short list of URLs which provide useful reference sites for ways of doing things, services offered, or examples of innovative use of the Web.

Mailing lists and Usenet newsgroups for the Web

There are a lot of mailing lists related to Web matters, and more are being created all the time. The original lists were run out of CERN, and that is still the home for the following:

- `www-talk@www0.cern.ch` (general discussion);
- `www-proxy@www0.cern.ch` (proxy servers and firewalls);
- `www-html@www0.cern.ch` (discussion of HTML);
- `web4lib@library.berkeley.edu` (delivery of library services via the Web);
- `www-announce@www0.cern.ch` (announcements of new servers and services).

Other lists relating to various aspects of Web use and management are:

- `www-speed@tipper.oit.unc.edu` (speed and performance, subscription

requests to `www-speed-request@tipper.oit.unc.edu`);
- `www-vm@sjuvm.stjohns.edu` (LISTSERV list for VM users);
- `web-support@mailbase.ac.uk` (use `join` instead of `subscribe`);
- `www-managers@lists.stanford.edu` (subscription requests should be sent to `majordomo@lists.stanford.edu`);
- `www@unicode.org` (for discussions of extending HTML to work with Unicode: send a regular `subscribe` command but set the subject to `SUBSCRIBE` as well);
- the whole issue of tighter integration of HTML and SGML (specifically, defining a MIME type for SGML) is discussed on `sgml-internet@ebt.com`.

Some browsers also have their own mailing lists: `mosaic-l@uicvm.uic.edu` and `netscape-l@irlearn.ucd.ie` (both LISTSERV). Development of some of the commercial aspects of the Web is discussed on `inet-marketing@einet.net`. Check `http://www.leeds.ac.uk/ucs/WWW/WWW_mailing_lists.html` for up-to-date details of all mailing lists.

The newsgroups for Web discussions are: `comp.infosystems.www.user` for user problems, `comp.infosystems.www.announce` (a moderated group for announcements of new servers and services, handled at `www-announce@medio.com`), `comp.infosystems.www.providers` for information providers, `comp.infosystems.www.kiosks` for discussion of unattended public clients (p. 248), `comp.infosystems.www.advocacy` for discussions for and against the Web, `comp.infosystems.www.authoring.cgi` for discussions of CGI scripts, `comp.infosystems.www.authoring.html` for discussion of writing HTML, `comp.infosystems.www.authoring.images` for graphics in the Web, `comp.infosystems.www.authoring.misc` for other aspects of information provision, and `comp.infosystems.www.misc` (pretty much everything else).

There are some platform-specific groups as well: `comp.infosystems.www.browsers.mac`, `comp.infosystems.www.browsers.ms-windows`, `comp.infosystems.www.browsers.x`, `comp.infosystems.www.browsers.misc`, `comp.infosystems.www.servers.mac`, `comp.infosystems.www.servers.ms-windows`, `comp.infosystems.www.servers.unix`, and `comp.infosystems.www.servers.misc`.

Digging for information

Various automated agents known as Robots, Spiders, or WebWanderers have been written to go out onto the network and report back on what they found. Most are harmless, but every so often, someone writes one which recursively retrieves every document on every server (if your server lasts that long!). For details of how to use them and how not to use them, see `http://web.nexor.co.uk/mak/doc/robots/robots.html`.

An example of a useful 'bot which makes its results available in searchable form is the *WorldWideWeb Worm* (a bit like *Veronica* for the Web) at `http://www.cs.colorado.edu/home/mcbryan/WWWW.html` (Figure C.1).

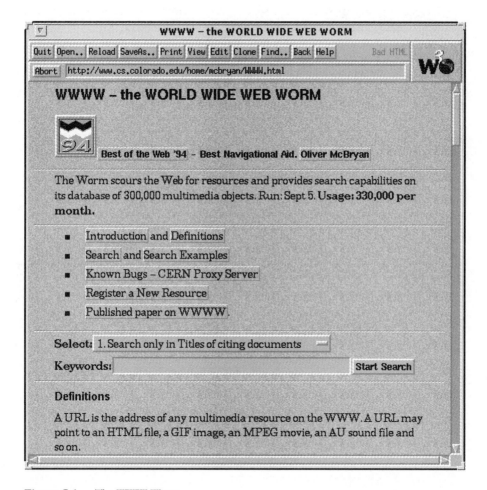

Figure C.1   The WWW Worm

Many sites now run formalized archives or catalogs of Web pages, Gopher pages, and other information resources which you can search. The *Lycos* catalog from the Carnegie Mellon University Center for Machine Translation provides probabilitistic retrieval of some 400,000 documents, with more being added every week. In addition to document pointers, it provides match score, Web links, an outline, keyword list, and excerpt for each of the top 50 documents matching your query. Details are at `http://fuzine.mt.cs.cmu.edu/mlm/lycos-home. html` and there's a mailing list for users: subscribe to `lycos-users@mail. msen.com` through `majordomo@mail.msen.com`. The server itself is at `http: //lycos.cs.cmu.edu/`.

Another popular index with both search facilities and a categorization, is the EINet Galaxy (`http://galaxy.einet.net/`): the company that makes the *WinWeb* and *MacWeb* browsers. The search facility allows separate specification of its own (Galaxy) pages, Web pages, Gopher, and Hytelnet entries.

The Yahoo catalog at Stanford University is maintained at `http://akebono. stanford.edu/yahoo` and there's a mirror at `http://www.yahoo.com`. This offers well-documented category navigation and the facility for users to submit their own suggestions for additions to the database.

Webnews is an archive of Usenet News articles about the Web in which most URLs have been 'anchorized' (that is, converted to active hypertext links): `gopher:// twinbrook.cis.uab.edu/hwebNews.80`.

Jean-Paul Chia of Drasnian Technologies maintains an index of pointers to Web information which you can subscribe to by mailing your name and email address to `www-request@drasnia.it.com.au`.

The CyberWeb is a resource center for WWW developers, organized like the usenet newsgroups in an extensive tree of Web-building and Web-using information pointers: `http://www.charm.net/~web/`.

New services like these are being added all the time: you can find their announcements on the Usenet newsgroup `comp.infosystems.www.announce`.

Appendix D

ISO and other sets of code tables

The International Standards Organization publishes many sets of codes relating to the formal International Standards. The Internet Engineering Task Force (IETF) supervises the introduction and maintenance of standards on the Internet. Some of the common and useful lists of codes and coding systems relating to the Web and published by these two bodies are included here.

In the case of SGML character entities, the ISO 8879 'Added Latin 1' codes used in HTML have already been reproduced (Table 8.1). The two-letter country codes are the ones which appear as the last part of email addresses, and the language codes are the ones which can be used in conjunction with them for the `lang` attribute of HTML3 elements. The MIME content-types are those used by servers and browsers to recognise the type of data being transmitted using HTTP.

MIME content types

The Multipurpose Internet Mail Extensions specify the valid types of message content for recognition by MIME-compliant mailing systems. HTTP browsers and servers use these for their recognition mechanism. The table given here is taken from a configuration of the NCSA server and shows the MIME content type in the lefthand column and the filetypes recognized as such in the righthand column.

Table D.1   MIME content types

This table is an example only and is not exhaustive

Content-type	Filetypes recognized
application/activemessage	
application/andrew-inset	
application/applefile	
application/atomicmail	
application/dca-rft	
application/dec-dx	
application/mac-binhex40	
application/macwriteii	
application/msword	
application/news-message-id	
application/news-transmission	
application/octet-stream	`bin`
application/oda	`oda`
application/pdf	`pdf`
application/postscript	`ai eps ps`
application/remote-printing	
application/rtf	`rtf`
application/slate	
application/x-mif	`mif`
application/wita	
application/wordperfect5.1	
application/x-csh	`csh`
application/x-dvi	`dvi`
application/x-hdf	`hdf`
application/x-latex	`latex`
application/x-netcdf	`nc cdf`
application/x-sh	`sh`
application/x-tcl	`tcl`
application/x-tex	`tex`
application/x-texinfo	`texinfo texi`
application/x-troff	`t tr roff`
application/x-troff-man	`man`
application/x-troff-me	`me`
application/x-troff-ms	`ms`
application/x-wais-source	`src`
application/zip	`zip`
application/x-bcpio	`bcpio`
application/x-cpio	`cpio`
application/x-gtar	`gtar`
application/x-shar	`shar`
application/x-sv4cpio	`sv4cpio`
application/x-sv4crc	`sv4crc`
application/x-tar	`tar`
application/x-ustar	`ustar`

Table D.1   MIME content types (continued)
This table is an example only and is not exhaustive

Content-type	Filetypes recognized
audio/basic	au snd
audio/x-aiff	aif aiff aifc
audio/x-wav	wav
image/gif	gif
image/ief	ief
image/jpeg	jpeg jpg jpe
image/tiff	tiff tif
image/x-cmu-raster	ras
image/x-portable-anymap	pnm
image/x-portable-bitmap	pbm
image/x-portable-graymap	pgm
image/x-portable-pixmap	ppm
image/x-rgb	rgb
image/x-xbitmap	xbm
image/x-xpixmap	xpm
image/x-xwindowdump	xwd
message/external-body	
message/news	
message/partial	
message/rfc822	
multipart/alternative	
multipart/appledouble	
multipart/digest	
multipart/mixed	
multipart/parallel	
text/html	html
text/plain	txt
text/richtext	rtx
text/tab-separated-values	tsv
text/x-setext	etx
video/mpeg	mpeg mpg mpe
video/quicktime	qt mov
video/x-msvideo	avi
video/x-sgi-movie	movie

Language codes

The language codes used in HTML3 are made from the relevant code of ISO 639, followed by a country code from the ISO 3166 list, separated by a period, e.g. cy.ar for Welsh as spoken in the Argentine.

Table D.2   ISO 639:1988 Language codes

This version of the table appears by courtesy of Keld Simonsen

Code	Language	Code	Language	Code	Language	Code	Language
Abkhazian	ab	French	fr	Lithuanian	lt	Sindhi	sd
Afar	aa	Frisian	fy	Macedonian	mk	Singhalese	si
Afrikaans	af	Galician	gl	Malagasy	mg	Siswati	ss
Albanian	sq	Georgian	ka	Malay	ms	Slovak	sk
Amharic	am	German	de	Malayalam	ml	Slovenian	sl
Arabic	ar	Greek	el	Maltese	mt	Somali	so
Armenian	hy	Greenlandic	kl	Maori	mi	Spanish	es
Assamese	as	Guarani	gn	Marathi	mr	Sudanese	su
Aymara	ay	Gujarati	gu	Moldavian	mo	Swahili	sw
Azerbaijani	az	Hausa	ha	Mongolian	mn	Swedish	sv
Bashkir	ba	Hebrew	iw	Nauru	na	Tagalog	tl
Basque	eu	Hindi	hi	Nepali	ne	Tajik	tg
Bengali; Bangla	bn	Hungarian	hu	Norwegian	no	Tamil	ta
Bhutani	dz	Icelandic	is	Occitan	oc	Tatar	tt
Bihari	bh	Indonesian	in	Oriya	or	Tegulu	te
Bislama	bi	Interlingua	ia	(Afan) Oromo	om	Thai	th
Breton	br	Interlingue	ie	Pashto, Pushto	ps	Tibetan	bo
Bulgarian	bg	Inupiak	ik	Persian	fa	Tigrinya	ti
Burmese	my	Irish	ga	Polish	pl	Tonga	to
Byelorussian	be	Italian	it	Portuguese	pt	Tsonga	ts
Cambodian	km	Japanese	ja	Punjabi	pa	Turkish	tr
Catalan	ca	Javanese	jw	Quechua	qu	Turkmen	tk
Chinese	zh	Kannada	kn	Rhaeto-Romance	rm	Twi	tw
Corsican	co	Kashmiri	ks	Romanian	ro	Ukrainian	uk
Croatian	hr	Kazakh	kk	Russian	ru	Urdu	ur
Czech	cs	Kinyarwanda	rw	Samoan	sm	Uzbek	uz
Danish	da	Kirghiz	ky	Sangro	sg	Vietnamese	vi
Dutch	nl	Kirundi	rn	Sanskrit	sa	Volapuk	vo
English	en	Korean	ko	Scots Gaelic	gd	Welsh	cy
Esperanto	eo	Kurdish	ku	Serbian	sr	Wolof	wo
Estonian	et	Laothian	lo	Serbo-Croatian	sh	Xhosa	xh
Faeroese	fo	Latin	la	Sesotho	st	Yiddish	ji
Fiji	fj	Latvian, Lettish	lv	Setswana	tn	Yoruba	yo
Finnish	fi	Lingala	ln	Shona	sn	Zulu	zu

Country codes

The ISO 3166 standard defines numeric, two- and three-letter codes for every country (although 'country' has become a rather flexible concept in recent years). The two-letter codes are the ones used as the final part of most email addresses and network names of servers, with the exception of the USA, where the Internet domains are used as well as the two-letter state codes followed by `.us`.

Table D.3 ISO 3166 Country codes

Entries with an asterisk (*) are provisional

Country	A2	A3	Num	Country	A2	A3	Num
Afghanistan	AF	AFG	004	Dominica	DM	DMA	212
Albania	AL	ALB	008	Dominican Republic	DO	DOM	214
Algeria	DZ	DZA	012	East Timor	TP	TMP	626
American Samoa	AS	ASM	016	Ecuador	EC	ECU	218
Andorra	AD	AND	020	Egypt	EG	EGY	818
Angola	AO	AGO	024	El Salvador	SV	SLV	222
Anguilla	AI	AIA	660	Equatorial Guinea	GQ	GNQ	226
Antarctica	AQ	ATA	010	Estonia	EE	EST	233
Antigua and Barbuda	AG	ATG	028	Ethiopia	ET	ETH	230
Argentina	AR	ARG	032	Falkland Islands (Malvinas)	FK	FLK	238
Armenia	AM	ARM	051	Faroe Islands	FO	FRO	234
Aruba	AW	ABW	533	Fiji	FJ	FJI	242
Australia	AU	AUS	036	Finland	FI	FIN	246
Austria	AT	AUT	040	France	FR	FRA	250
Azerbaijan	AZ	AZE	031	French Guiana	GF	GUF	254
Bahamas	BS	BHS	044	French Polynesia	PF	PYF	258
Bahrain	BH	BHR	048	French Southern Territories	TF	ATF	260
Bangladesh	BD	BGD	050	Gabon	GA	GAB	266
Barbados	BB	BRB	052	Gambia	GM	GMB	270
Belarus	BY*	BLR	122*	Georgia	GE	GEO	268
Belgium	BE	BEL	056	Germany	DE	DEU	276
Belize	BZ	BLZ	084	Ghana	GH	GHA	288
Benin	BJ	BEN	204	Gibraltar	GI	GIB	292
Bermuda	BM	BMU	060	Greece	GR	GRC	300
Bhutan	BT	BTN	064	Greenland	GL	GRL	304
Bolivia	BO	BOL	068	Grenada	GD	GRD	308
Bosnia and Herzegovina	BA	BIH	070	Guadeloupe	GP	GLP	312
Botswana	BW	BWA	072	Guam	GU	GUM	316
Bouvet Island	BV	BVT	074	Guatemala	GT	GTM	320
Brazil	BR	BRA	076	Guinea	GN	GIN	324
British Indian Ocean Terr	IO	IOT	086	Guinea-Bissau	GW	GNB	624
Brunei Darussalam	BN	BRN	096	Guyana	GY	GUY	328
Bulgaria	BG	BGR	100	Haiti	HT	HTI	332
Burkina Faso	BF	BFA	854	Heard and McDonald Is	M	HMD	334
Burundi	BI	BDI	108	Honduras	HN	HND	340
Byelorussia	BY	BYS	112	Hong Kong	HK	HKG	344
Cambodia	KH	KHM	116	Hungary	HU	HUN	348
Cameroon	CM	CMR	120	Iceland	IS	ISL	352
Canada	CA	CAN	124	India	IN	IND	356
Cape Verde	CV	CPV	132	Indonesia	ID	IDN	360
Cayman Islands	KY	CYM	136	Iran (Islamic Republic of)	IR	IRN	364
Central African Republic	CF	CAF	140	Iraq	IQ	IRQ	368
Chad	TD	TCD	148	Ireland	IE	IRL	372
Chile	CL	CHL	152	Israel	IL	ISR	376
China	CN	CHN	156	Italy	IT	ITA	380
Christmas Island	CX	CXR	162	Jamaica	JM	JAM	388
Cocos (Keeling) Islands	CC	CCK	166	Japan	JP	JPN	392
Colombia	CO	COL	170	Jordan	JO	JOR	400
Comoros	KM	COM	174	Kazakhstan	KZ	KAZ	398
Congo	CG	COG	178	Kenya	KE	KEN	404
Cook Islands	CK	COK	184	Kiribati	KI	KIR	296
Costa Rica	CR	CRI	188	Korea, Dem People's Rep	KP	PRK	408
Côte D'Ivoire	CI	CIV	384	Korea, Republic of	KR	KOR	410
Croatia	HR	HRV	191	Kuwait	KW	KWT	414
Cuba	CU	CUB	192	Kyrgyzstan	KG	KGZ	417
Cyprus	CY	CYP	196	Lao People's Dem Rep	LA	LAO	418
Czechoslovakia	CS	CSK	200	Latvia	LV	LVA	428
Denmark	DK	DNK	208	Lebanon	LB	LBN	422
Djibouti	DJ	DJI	262	Lesotho	LS	LSO	426

Table D.3   ISO 3166 Country codes (continued)

Entries with an asterisk (*) are provisional

Country	A2	A3	Num	Country	A2	A3	Num
Liberia	LR	LBR	430	Saint Lucia	LC	LCA	662
Libyan Arab Jamahiriya	LY	LBY	434	Saint Vincent & Grenadines	VC	VCT	670
Liechtenstein	LI	LIE	438	Samoa	WS	WSM	882
Lithuania	LT	LTU	440	San Marino	SM	SMR	674
Luxembourg	LU	LUX	442	Saudi Arabia	SA	SAU	682
Macau	MO	MAC	446	Senegal	SN	SEN	686
Madagascar	MG	MDG	450	Seychelles	SC	SYC	690
Malawi	MW	MWI	454	Sierra Leone	SL	SLE	694
Malaysia	MY	MYS	458	Singapore	SG	SGP	702
Maldives	MV	MDV	462	Slovenia	SI	SVN	705
Mali	ML	MLI	466	Solomon Islands	SB	SLB	090
Malta	MT	MLT	470	Somalia	SO	SOM	706
Marshall Islands	MH	MHL	584	South Africa	ZA	ZAF	710
Martinique	MQ	MTQ	474	Spain	ES	ESP	724
Mauritania	MR	MRT	478	Sri Lanka	LK	LKA	144
Mauritius	MU	MUS	480	St. Helena	SH	SHN	654
Mexico	MX	MEX	484	St. Pierre and Miquelon	PM	SPM	666
Micronesia	FM	FSM	583	Sudan	SD	SDN	736
Moldova, Republic of	MD	MDA	498	Suriname	SR	SUR	740
Monaco	MC	MCO	492	Svalbard and Jan Mayen Is	SJ	SJM	744
Mongolia	MN	MNG	496	Swaziland	SZ	SWZ	748
Montserrat	MS	MSR	500	Sweden	SE	SWE	752
Morocco	MA	MAR	504	Switzerland	CH	CHE	756
Mozambique	MZ	MOZ	508	Syrian Arab Republic	SY	SYR	760
Myanmar	MM	MMR	104	Taiwan, Province of China	TW	TWN	158
Namibia	NA	NAM	516	Tajikistan	TJ	TJK	762
Nauru	NR	NRU	520	Tanzania, United Rep of	TZ	TZA	834
Nepal	NP	NPL	524	Thailand	TH	THA	764
Netherlands	NL	NLD	528	Togo	TG	TGO	768
Netherlands Antilles	AN	ANT	532	Tokelau	TK	TKL	772
Neutral Zone	NT	NTZ	536	Tonga	TO	TON	776
New Caledonia	NC	NCL	540	Trinidad and Tobago	TT	TTO	780
New Zealand	NZ	NZL	554	Tunisia	TN	TUN	788
Nicaragua	NI	NIC	558	Turkey	TR	TUR	792
Niger	NE	NER	562	Turkmenistan	TM	TKM	795
Nigeria	NG	NGA	566	Turks and Caicos Islands	TC	TCA	796
Niue	NU	NIU	570	Tuvalu	TV	TUV	798
Norfolk Island	NF	NFK	574	Uganda	UG	UGA	800
Northern Mariana Islands	MP	MNP	580	Ukraine	UA*	UKR	804*
Norway	NO	NOR	578	Ukrainian	UA	UKR	804
Oman	OM	OMN	512	United Arab Emirates	AE	ARE	784
Pakistan	PK	PAK	586	United Kingdom	GB	GBR	826
Palau	PW	PLW	585	United States	US	USA	840
Panama	PA	PAN	590	United States (islands)	UM	UMI	581
Papua New Guinea	PG	PNG	598	Uruguay	UY	URY	858
Paraguay	PY	PRY	600	Uzbekistan	UZ	UZB	860
Peru	PE	PER	604	Vanuatu	VU	VUT	548
Philippines	PH	PHL	608	Vatican City State (Holy See)	VA	VAT	336
Pitcairn	PN	PCN	612	Venezuela	VE	VEN	862
Poland	PL	POL	616	Viet Nam	VN	VNM	704
Portugal	PT	PRT	620	Virgin Islands (British)	VG	VGB	092
Puerto RICO	PR	PRI	630	Virgin Islands (U.S.)	VI	VIR	850
Qatar	QA	QAT	634	Wallis and Futuna Islands	WF	WLF	876
Reunion	RE	REU	638	Western Sahara	EH	ESH	732
Romania	RO	ROM	642	Yemen, Republic of	YE	YEM	887
Russian Federation	RU	RUS	643	Yugoslavia	YU	YUG	890
Rwanda	RW	RWA	646	Zaïre	ZR	ZAR	180
Sâo Tome and Principe	ST	STP	678	Zambia	ZM	ZMB	894
Saint Kitts and Nevis	KN	KNA	659	Zimbabwe	ZW	ZWE	716

Table D.4   North American top-level domains

Domain	Members
.edu	educational organizations
.com	commercial companies
.mil	military establishments
.gov	government offices
.org	non-governmental organizations
.net	Internet Service Providers

HTTP status codes

The HTTP specification gives the following codes as responses to various situations. You only see them if there is an error (such as a file not found), but they are transmitted as part of the response from the server to the client. You can read more about these codes at `http://www.w3.org/hypertext/WWW/ Protocols/HTTP/HTRESP.html`

Success

- `OK 200` — The request was fulfilled.
- `Created 201` — POST of form data OK. New URI for document supplied.
- `Accepted 202` — Request accepted but not yet processed.
- `Partial Information 203` — Information returned is not definitive.
- `No Response 204` — Request accepted but no action needed by browser.

Error

- `Bad request 400` — Bad syntax in URL.
- `Unauthorized 401` — User not permitted access to this document by this method.
- `PaymentRequired 402` — Charging required.
- `Forbidden 403` — Server is not permitted to do whatever was asked.
- `Not found 404` — File or directory does not exist.
- `Internal Error 500` — Server cannot operate.
- `Not implemented 501` — This server cannot do the requested operation.
- `Service temporarily overloaded 502` — (to be discussed).
- `Gateway timeout 503` — (to be discussed).

Redirection

- `Moved 301` — The URL has moved.
- `Found 302` — The URL is in a different location but redirection has been used.

- Method 303 — (discussion).
- Not Modified 304 — URL is unchanged since last access.

Suggested values for link relationships

The `rel` and `rev` attributes to the `<link>` and `<a>` elements are intended to indicate the relationship between the current document and the one pointed to by the link (or the reverse relationship in the case of `rev`).

The following keywords are suggestions for these link classes, and the list is under revision by Murray Maloney of SCO for the IETF Working Group on HTML. They include items raised in discussion as well as those from the list originally proposed by Tim Berners-Lee at `http://info.cern.ch/hypertext/WWW/MarkUp/Relationships.html` and some already in use by (and on the wish-list for) the in-house help browser used by SCO. It has also been proposed that there should be a registration authority, and that unregistered values might be used for experimental purposes if they are start with `X-`. Values marked with an asterisk are reserved for internal definition by browsers.

Table D.5   Values for `rel` and `rev` under consideration

Keyword	Usage
made	Link describes the author of the current document.
home*	Link is the current document's 'home page'.
back*	Linked document is earlier in a series.
forward*	Linked document is next in a series.
bibliography	Linked document contains a bibliography.
bookmark	Link is a pointer into a longer document.
contents	Linked document is a related table of contents.
glossary	A glossary associated with the current document.
hotlist	Links to useful related URLs.
index	An index for use with the current document.
navigate	Linked document contains navigational aids.
top or origin	Linked document is the top-level of this one.
parent	Linked document is the parent in this hierarchy.
child	Current document is the parent in this hierarchy.
sibling	Linked document is a sibling of the current one.
begin and end	Identify a user-defined sequence of documents.
previous and next	Identify preceding and following documents in a sequence.
artwork	Identifies a document containing artwork.
book	Identifies a document containing a book.
journal	Identifies a document containing a journal.
magazine	Identifies a document containing a magazine.
manual	Identifies a document containing a manual.
map	Identifies a document containing a map.
newspaper	Identifies a document containing a newspaper.

proceedings	Identifies a document containing proceedings.
program	Identifies a document containing a program.
report	Identifies a document containing a report.
thesis	Identifies a document containing a thesis.
abstract	Linked document is an abstract of this one.
biblioentry	Linked document is a bibliographic entry.
citation	Linked document is a bibliographic citation.
definition	Identifies definition of a term.
footnote	Footnotes relating to the current document.
include	Linked document is to be included in current document.
copyright	Linked document contains a statement of copyright.
disclaimer	Linked document is a disclaimer for the current one.
trademark	Linked document contains a trademark notice.
author	Linked document identifies the author.
editor	Linked document identifies the editor.
publisher	Linked document identifies the publisher.
urc	Link to a Uniform Resource Citation.
banner	Identifies link to non-scrolling information.
stylesheet	Identifies link to a stylesheet.

Appendix E

Authors and Suppliers

This is a list of the companies and individuals mentioned in the book. The information given was correct at the time of writing, but in the case of large or multinational corporations, it may be faster to contact your local office rather than the head office address given.

Abelbeck Software *VersaTerm*
2457 Perkiomen Avenue, Reading PA 19606, USA.

Adobe Systems, Inc. *PostScript Acrobat*
1585 Charleston Road, Mountain View CA 94039, USA.
http://www.adobe.com/

Carles Bellver *BBEdit*
Universitat Jaume I, Castelló, Spain.

Booklink Technologies Inc. *InternetWorks*
Northland Building, 2150 Washington Street, Newton MA 02162, USA.
http://www.booklink.com

John Bradley *xv*
1053 Floyd Terrace, Bryn Mawr PA 19010, USA. +1 215 898 8813
bradley@cis.upenn.edu

Carnegie Mellon University Center for Machine Translation   *Lycos*
Center for Machine Translation Pittsburgh PA 15213, USA. `fuzzy@cmu.edu`

CookWare   *Virtual Contractor and home page authoring*
+1 317 769 5049 (Fax: +1 317 769 6513) `iceman@netcom.com`

Brooks Cutter   *W3new*
AT&T Paradyne Corporation PO Box 2826, Largo FL 34649–2826, USA. +1
813 530 8152

Cyberspace Development Inc.   *The Internet Adapter*
3700 Cloverleaf Drive, Boulder CO 80304, USA. +1 303 938 8684
`http://marketplace.com`

Datastorm Technologies   *ProComm*
2401 Lemone, Columbia MO 65205, USA.+1 314 449 9401

Drasnian Technologies   *WWW Index*
Perth, Western Australia. +61 9447 6261 (Fax: +61 9 447 4098)
`jean-paul@drasnia.it.com.au`

Electronic Book Technologies   *Rainbow DTD*, *DynaWeb*, *DynaBook*
1 Richmond Square, Providence RI 02906, USA. +1 401 421 9550
`http://www.ebt.com`

Exoterica Corporation   *OmniMark*
1545 Carling Avenue, Suite 404, Ottawa K1Z 8P9, Ontario, Canada. +1 613
722 1700 (Fax: +1 613 722 5706) `info@exoterica.com`

Finesse Liveware   *List of Internet Service Providers*
1032 Golf Court, Mountain View CA 94040, USA. +1 415 967 6338

Forté, Inc.   *Free Agent*
`http://www.forteinc.com/forte`

FTP Software, Inc.   *PC/TCP*
2 High Street, N Andover MA 01845–2620, USA. +1 508 655 4000

Matthew Gray   *Comprehensive list of WWW sites*
`http://www.mit.edu:8001/people/mkgray/mkgray.html`

GRIF S.A.   *GriF Symposia*
Immeuble «Le Florestan» 2, Boulevard Vauban 66, 78053 St Quentin en
Yvelines CEDEX, France.+33 1 30 12 14 30 `http://www.grif.fr`

Hyperion   *uncgi*
173 Sherland Avenue, Mountain View CA 94043, USA. +1 415 691 9755
`koreth@hyperion.com`

Impactron Ltd *Adapta-Kit*
72–78 Brighton Road, Surbiton KT6 5PP, Surrey, England. +44 181 390 8522
(Fax: +44 181 943 3153)

Information Dimensions Ltd *BASIS Webserver*
Centre Point, 103 New Oxford Street, London WC1A 1QT, England. +44 71
497 1403 (Fax: +44 71 497 3453) `burns@idl.idi.oclc.org`

Institut für Informatik und angewandte Mathematik *Htgrep*
Universität Bern, Neubrückstrasse 10, CH–3012 Bern, Switzerland. +41 31
631 8681 (Fax: +41 31 631 3965) `http://iamwww.unibe.ch/~oscar/`

Intercon Systems Corporation *TCP/Connect II*
950 Herndon Parkway, Herndon VA 22070, USA. +1 703 709 5500 (Fax: +1
703 709 5555)
`http://www.intercon.com/pi/tcp-connect-mac.html`

Intermind Corporation *EnCompass*
1101 N Northlake Way, Suite 106, Seattle WA 98103–9714, USA.

Legal Information Institute *Cello*
Cornell Law School +1 607 255 9093 `shelden@fatty.law.cornell.edu`

Andreas Ley *giftrans*
`ftp://julian.uwo.ca/pub/unix/utilities/giftrans/`

Leonardo Loureiro *LView*
1501 East Hallandale Beach Boulevard #254, Hallandale FL 33009, USA.
`mmedia@world.std.com`

Microelectronics and Computer Technology Corporation *MacWeb*
3500 West Balcones Center Drive, Austin TX 78759–6509, USA. +1 512 338
3430 `hardin@mcc.com`

Micromind, Inc. *SlipKnot*
417 West 120 Street, Suite 6B, New York NY 10027, USA.
`http://www.interport.net/slipknot/slipknot.html`

Microsoft Corporation *MS-Windows, SGML Author for Word*
3635 157th Avenue, Building 11, Redmond WA 98052, USA.
`http://www.microsoft.com/`

Microstar Software Ltd *Near&Far*
34 Colonnade Road North, Nepean K2E 7J6, Ontario, Canada.

Heiko Münkel *hm–html-menus*
`muenkel@tnt.uni-hannover.de`

National Center for Supercomputing Applications   *Mosaic, NCSA HTTPD*
University of Illinois at Urbana-Champaign, Computing Applications Building, 605 E. Springfield Avenue, Champaign IL 61820, USA.
http://www.ncsa.uiuc.edu/

NEC Systems Laboratory CST   *Mosaic for Socks*
1525 Walnut Hill Lane, Irving TX 75038, USA. +1 214 518 3490
ylee@syl.dl.nec.com

NetManage   *Chameleon*
10725 North De Anza Boulevard, Cupertino CA 95014, USA. +1 408 973 7171 (Fax: +1 408 257 6405)
http://www.netmanage.com/netmanage/nm6.html

Netscape Communications Corporation   *Netscape*
650 Castro Street, Suite 500, Mountain View CA 94041, USA. +1 415 254 1900   (Fax: +1 415 254 0239) http://www.netscape.com

NetUSA   *List of Web Service Providers*
Network-USA. http://www.nwusa.com

News and Observer Publishing Company   *NandoX*
127 W Hargett Street, Raleigh NC 27601, USA. +1 919 8362834   (Fax: +1 919 836 2814) zonker@nando.net

Nice Technologies   *HTML for Word 2.0*
Chemin des Hutins, Veraz, 01170 Gex, France. +33 50 42 49 40

Omni Development Inc.   *OmniWeb*
312 Belmont Ave E, Seattle WA 98102–5304, USA. +1 206 720 2955
http://www.omnigroup.com/

Mark Podlipec   *Xanim*
podlipec@wellfleet.com

Process Software Corporation   *Purveyor*
959 Concord Street, Framingham MA 01701, USA. +1 508 879 6994
http://www.process.com

PKware, Inc.   *PKzip, PKunzip*
9025 N Deerwood Drive, Brown Deer WI 53223, USA.
http://www.pkware.com/

P-Stat, Inc.   *P-Stat*
PO Box AH, , Princeton NJ 08542, USA. sebbie@pstat.com

QPC Software *WinQVT/Net*
109 Willow Pond Way, Penfield NY 14526, USA.

Qualcomm, Inc. *Eudora*
6455 Lusk Boulevard, San Diego CA 92121, USA.
http://www.qualcomm.com

Quarterdeck Corporation *WebAuthor*
150 Pico Boulevard, Crow's Nest 1918, Santa Monica CA 90405, USA.
http://www.qdeck.com/webauthor/fact.html

Chuck Shotton *MacHTTP*
http://www.uth.tmc.edu/mac_info/machttp_info.html

Silicon Graphics *WebFORCE*, *WebMagic*
2011 N Shoreline Boulevard, Mountain View CA 94043, USA. +1 415 960
1980 http://www.sgi.com

SoftQuad *Author/Editor*, *HoTMetaL*, *Panorama*
56 Aberfoyle Crescent, Suite 810, Toronto, Canada. sales@sq.com

Spry, Inc. *Mosaic*, *Secure HTTP*, *Internet-in-a-Box*
316 Occidental Avenue South, Suite 200, Seattle WA 98104, USA.
http://www.spry.com

Spyglass Inc. *Enhanced Mosaic*
1800 Woodfield Drive, Savoy IL 61874, USA. +1 217 355 6000
http://www.spry.com

SRI International *List of Lists*
333 Ravenswood Avenue, Menlo Park CA 94025, USA. +1 415 859 6073
mail-server@sri.com

Lennart Staflin *psgml*
ftp://anubis.ac.hmc.edu/pub/emacs/packages/psgml/

Starlight Software *PC-Write*
11900 Grand Place, St Louis MO 63131, USA. +1 314 965 5630

TEX Users Group
1850 Union Street, #1637, San Francisco CA 94123, USA. +1 415 982 8449
(Fax: +1 415 982 8559) tug@tug.org
http://www.ucc.ie/info/tex/tug/tug.html

Trumpet Software International *Trumpet Winsock*
PO Box 1649, Hobart, Tasmania 7001, Australia. +61 002 487 049
ftp://ftp.utas.edu.au/pc/trumpet

ViaCrypt, Inc.   *PGP*
2104 West Peoria Avenue, Phoenix AZ 85029, USA. +1 602 944 0773 (Fax:
+1 602 943 2601) `70304.41@compuserve.com`

Nick Williams   *HTMLtext*
Systems Architecture Research Centre, City University, London EC1V 0HB,
England. +44 71 477 8551 (Fax: +44 71 477 8587)
`njw@cs.city.ac.uk`}

David Woakes   *WSArchie*
`david@maxwell.demon.co.uk`

WordPerfect Corporation   *WordPerfect SGML Edition*
1555 North Technology Way, Orem UT 84057, USA.
`http://www.wordperfect.com`

Bibliography

Akass, C. (Dec 1994), 'The whole world in his hands', *Personal Computer World* pp. 380–383.

Anon. (1994), 'So much for the cashless society', *The Economist* **333**(7891).

Berners-Lee, T. (1990), Worldwideweb: Proposal for a hypertext project, Technical report, CERN. `http://info.cern.ch/hypertext/WWW/Proposal.html`.

Berners-Lee, T. (1994), Universal Resource Identifiers in WWW, Internet Draft, CERN, `draft-bernerslee-www-uri-00.txt.ps`.

Berners-Lee, T., Fielding, R. and Frystyk, H. (1994), Http/1.0 internet draft, Technical Report 2nd ed., IETF. `ftp://ds.internic.net/internet-drafts/draft-fielding-http-spec-01.ps`.

Borenstein, N. and Freed, N. (1993), Mime (multipurpose internet mail extensions, Technical report, Bellcore, Innosoft. RFC1521, `http://ds.internic.net/rfc/rfc1521.ps`.

Burnard, L. and Sperberg-McQueen, M. (1994), Proposals of the Text Encoding Initiative, Technical report, Oxford University Computing Centre.

Copinger, W. A. and James, E. P. S. (n.d.), *Copyright*, 13th edn, . 0–421–39200–2.

Cornish, W. R. (1989), *Intellectual Property: patents, copyright, trade marks and allied rights*, 2nd edn, Sweet & Maxwell. 0–421–34980–4.

Crocker, L. (July 1995), 'PNG: The Portable Network Graphic Format', *Dr Dobbs Journal*, **232**, 36–44.

Dern, D. P. (1994), *The Internet Guide for New Users*, McGraw-Hill, `ig4nu@world.std.com`. 0–07–016511–4.

Dietz, A. (1987), *Copyright Law in the European Community*, Sijthoff & Noordhoff, Alphen aan den Rijn.

Fielding, R. (1994), 'The meta element', `html-wg@oclc.org` .

Flynn, P. (1994), 'A network acronym server', *J. Info. Networking* **2**(1), 74–76.

Gaffin, A. (1993), Guide to the Internet, Technical report, Electronic Frontier Foundation, `ftp://ftp.eff.org/pub/Net_info/EFF_Net_Guide/`.

Gass, J. E. (1994), 'Making the most of the worldwideweb for your organization', `http://www.gsfc.nasa.gov/documents/making_most_www.html` .

Goldfarb, C. F. (1990), *The SGML Handbook*, Clarendon Press.

Gray, M. (1995), Comprehensive list of www sites, Technical report, net.Genesis Corp., `http://www.netgen.com/cgi/comprehensive`.

Guy, D. and Leigh, G. (1981), *The EEC and Intellectual Property*, Sweet & Maxwell. 0–421–23420–2.

Krol, E. (1994), *The Whole Internet User's Guide and Catalog*, Nutshell Handbooks, O'Reilly. 1–56592–025–2.

Kruse, V. (1939), *The Right of Property*, OUP.

Laddie, H., Prescott, P. and Vitoria, M. (1980), *The Modern Law of Copyright*, Butterworths. 0–406–61694–9.

Lamport, L. (1988), 'Document production: visual or logical?', *TUGboat* **9**(1), 8–10.

Liang, F. M. (1983), [Hyphenation], PhD thesis, Stanford University. ISBN: 0–201–13447–0.

Lottor, M. (1995), 'Internet domain survey'. Network Wizards, PO Box 343, Menlo Park, CA 94026–0343, USA.

McEvilly, C. (n.d.), 'How to make great www pages', http://www.c3.lanl.gov/~cim/webgreat/first.html.

Peltu, M. (1994), 'Hold the front screen', *Computing* p. 42.

Pepper, S. (n.d.), 'The whirlwind guide to sgml tools'.

Raggett, D. (1995), *Electronic Publishing on the WorldWideWeb: The Definitive Guide to HTML 3.0*, Addison-Wesley, Reading, Mass.

Smith, A. P. (1994), 'Hyper$T_{\!E\!}X$: a working standard', *Baskerville* 4(5), 6–9.

Smith, C. M. (1857), *A Working Man's Way in the World*, Printing Historical Society reprint (1967), 3rd issue edn, William and Frederick G Cash.

Stallman, R. (1986), The GNU Manifesto, Technical report, Free Software Foundation.

Treese, W. (1995), 'The internet index', http://www.openmarket.com/info/internet-index/current.html.

Treloar, A. (1994), 'Architectures for networked information: a comparative study of gopher and the world-wide web', *J. Info. Networking* 2(1), 23–46.

Index

Page numbers appearing in **bold type** refer to the pages on which technical terms are first defined. References in *italics* are to products mentioned in the text. References in ***bold italics*** are to the functions of browser and server software. References to HTML elements and attributes are printed in `typewriter type`.

A

`<a>` 182–185, 193–195, 197, 201, 202, 205, 302, 324

`<abbrev>` 301

Abelbeck Software 28

Abort transfer 100

`<above>` 304

accents 40, **168**

`accept` 306

Acrobat 231, 327

`<acronym>` 301

`action` 213, 223, 224, 307

Adapta-Kit 329

`<address>` 172, 174

Adobe 195–197, 231

Agora 39, 40

AIR Mosaic Express 20, 248

`align` 188, 220, 299, 301

`alt` 188, 195, 209, 211

Alverson Software 28

AMosaic 91, 242

`&amp;` 162

method   186, 213, 223
methods   186, 205
Microcom Networking Protocol
  See MNP
MicroMind   30, 90
Microsoft   27, 28, 80, 294
Microstar   135
minimization   **133**
MNP   25
model   304
modem   **5**, 23, **23**
  cable   23
  port   15
Morris, Mary   5, 22
Mosaic   xii, 9, 21, 79–81, 85, 88, 89,
  91, 93, 99, 100, 105, 106, 124,
  143, 180, 207, 211, 248, 263, 265,
  297, 330, 331
Mosaic for Socks   330
Motif   87
Mozilla   *See* Netscape
mpack   67
MS-Windows   9, 20, 28, 30, 37, 61,
  66, 74, 80, 82–85, 89, 90, 93,
  120, 121, 124, 180, 187, 196, 201,
  242, 250, 262, 329
MS-Word   226, 252
multiple   221
munpack   67
Murray, James   187

N

n   204
name   183, 184, 215, 217, 219,
  299, 300
namespace   **27**
NandoX   330
National Centre for
  Supercomputing Applications
  see also NCSA, 80
  166, 229
NCSA   6, 91

NCSA HTTPD   330
Near&Far   xiii, 135, 329
NEC Systems Lab   265
Neou, Vivian   49
nested lists   153
NetManage   20
NETNORTH   57
netpbm   88
Netscape   20, 50, 79, 85, 93, 97,
  100, 105, 106, 123, 168, 187, 193,
  194, 228, 229, 242, 297, 330
Netscape Communications
  Corporation   76, 79, 85, 242,
  243
NETSERV   57, 58
Netsite   242, 243, 283
Netware   27
network   **16**
  addresses   27, 30
  card   15, 28
  costs   19
  information services   4
  Internet   15
  local-area   27
  names   29, 30
  software   27
  traffic   4
Network-USA   6
news   *See* Usenet News
NeXT   83, 84
<nextid>   204, 205
NICE Technologies   119
Nierstrasz, Oscar   252
nn   50
NNTP   33
notation   299
<note>   300, 309
Novell Corporation   27
nowrap   299
NSFnet   4
number sign   170

O

O'Reilly & Associates   91, 241
`<ol>`   146, 148
Omni Development Inc   84
OmniImageFilter   84
OmniMark   295, 328
OmniWeb   330
Open Local   99, 105, 130, 142
Open Text Corporation   256
Open URL   50, 99, 100, 102,
   196
OpenMarket, Inc.   72
`<option>`   220, 221
Options   4
OS/2   20
`<over>`   304

P

`<p>`   81, 140, 141, 173, 229
P-Stat   330
packets   **28**
PageMaker   226
Paint   196
Panorama   81, 231, 290, 331
Panorama Pro   81
parity check   32
password   **23**, 97, 180, 283
   form field type   217
PAT   256
`<pb>`   230
Pbmplus   88, 196
PC-Write   124, 331
PC/TCP   328
Pepper, Steve   117
Perl   78, 211, 241, 246, 247, 250,
   252, 263, 295
permanent connection   5
Perry, Bill   78, 310
`<person>`   301
personal page   139, 244
PGP   70, 286, 332

Phoenix   120
phone number   31
phone port   15
photographs   196
PhotoShop   195–197
Pitkow, James   4, 262
PKunzip   66, 330
PKzip   66, 330
PMosaic   80
PNG   187
Point-to-Point Protocol   *See* PPP
port   **98**, 181
   HTTP   236
   modem, RS-232C, phone, serial
      15
   number   178, 181, 236
Portable Network Graphic Format
   See PNG
`post`   257
PostScript   xix, 5, 55, 87, 103, 104,
   111, 113, 115, 193, 194, 196, 197,
   228, 231, 295, 327
pound   170
   N. American #   *See* hash
      mark
   sterling etc. £   171
PPP   29, 37, 283
`<pre>`   134, 159, 161, 174, 208,
   229, 251
Preferences   4
preformatted text   134, 159, 188
Pretty Good Privacy   *See* PGP
Print   103
privacy   10, 268, 283
Process Software Corporation
   241
ProComm   28, 38, 76, 328
Prodigy   23
protocols   **16**, 96
proxy   87, 240, **265**
psgml   331
Purveyor   241, 330

Q

\<q\> 301
qt2www 295
QuarkXPress 226
Quarterdeck Corporation 119
" 162

R

Raggett, Dave 130
Rainbow DTD 290, 328
Raisch, Robert 311
\<range\> 298
RARE xi
Refresh 101
rel 185, 186, 205, 311, 324
Reload 101, 142, 192
Reply 46
Reply/Include 46
rev 185, 186, 205, 324
rn 50
role 300, 309
root 305
\<root\> 305
rows 215
RS-232C port 15
RTFtoHTML 294
RUNOFF 113, 114

S

\<s\> 164, 301
Safe-Tcl **257**
\<samp\> 160
Save 47
Save As... 103, 119, 197
scheme **178**
SCO 324
scripts
  login 37
  server 250
Sculptor 117
search term **178**

Secure HTTP 331
SecureWeb 283
security 10
\<select\> 215, 220, 221
selected 221
semicolon 134, 162, 168, 170
Send 44
seqnum 299
serial cable **25**
Serial Line Internetworking
  Protocol *See* SLIP
serial port 15
server 21, 27, **178**, **236**
  Archie 58
  client–server 110
  definition 110
  Domain Name 32
  gateway 32
  image mapping 198
  mailing lists 48
  registry 72
  software 236
  terminal 35
  Usenet News 50
  Web 71, 235
  Web mail 40
SerWeb 286
Setup 33
SGI 122, 243
SGML **114**, 115, 119, 311
  database search 256
SGML Author for Word 329
SGML2TEX xix, 295
sgmls 117
shape 302
shareware 68
shell script *See* scripts
Shotton, Chuck 240
­ 167
Silicon Graphics, Inc. *See* SGI
size 217, 221
SLIP 29, 37, 283

Notes

Notes

Notes

Practical UNIX Security

By Simson Garfinkel & Gene Spafford
1st Edition June 1991, 512 pages, ISBN 0-937175-72-2

Practical UNIX Security tells system administrators how to make their UNIX system either - System V or BSD - as secure as it possibly can be without going to trusted system technology. The book describes UNIX concepts and how they enforce security, tells how to defend against and handle security breaches, and explains network security (including UUCP, NFS, Kerberos, and firewall machines) in detail. If you are a UNIX system administrator or user who deals with security, you need this book.

"Timely, accurate, written by recognized experts... covers every imaginable topic relating to Unix security. An excellent book and I recommend it as a valuable addition to any system administrator's or computer site manager's collection."
– Jon Wright, *Informatics (Australia)*

Where to purchase these books?

Please contact your local bookshop, in case of difficulties contact us at one of the addresses below -

ORDERS
International Thomson Publishing Services Ltd
Cheriton House, North Way, Andover, Hants SP10 5BE, UK
Telephone: 01264 332424/Giro Account No: 2096919/
Fax: 01264 364418
Email: UK orders - ITPUK@ITPS.CO.UK
       Outside UK orders - ITPINT@ITPS.CO.UK

SALES AND MARKETING ENQUIRIES
International Thomson Publishing
Berkshire House, 168/173 High Holborn, London WClV 7AA, UK
Tel: 0171-497 1422 Fax: 0171-497 1426
e-mail: Info@ITPUK.CO.UK

MAILING LIST
To receive further information on our Networks books, please send the following information to the London address -
Full name and address (including Postcode)
Telephone, Fax Numbers and e-mail address

sendmail

By Bryan Costales, with Eric Allman & Neil Rickert
1st Edition November 1993, 830 pages, ISBN 1-56592-056-2

Although sendmail is used on almost every UNIX system, it's one of the last great uncharted territories – and most difficult utilities to learn – in UNIX system administration. This book provides a complete sendmail tutorial, plus extensive reference material. It covers the BSD, UIUC IDA, and VR versions of sendmail.

"The program and its rule description file, sendmail.cf, have long been regarded as the pit of coals that separated the mild Unix system administrators from the real fire walkers. Now, sendmail syntax, testing, hidden rules, and other mysteries are revealed. Costales, Allman, and Rickert are the indisputable authorities to do the text."
– Ben Smith, *Byte*

DNS and BIND

By Cricket Liu & Paul Albitz
Ist Edition October 1992, 418 pages ISBN 1-56592-010-4

DNS and BIND contains all you need to know about the Internet's Domain Name System (DNS) and the Berkeley Internet Name Domain (BIND), its UNIX implementation. The Domain Name System is the Internet's "phone book"; it's a database that tracks important information (in particular, names and addresses) for every computer on the Internet. If you're a system administrator, this book will show you how to set up and maintain the DNS software on your network.

"At 380 pages it blows away easily any vendor supplied information, and because it has an extensive troubleshooting section (using nslookup) it should never be far from your desk – especially when things on your network start to go awry :-)"
– Ian Hoyle, BHP Research, Melbourne Laboratories

MH & xmh: E-mail for Users & Programmers

By Jerry Peek
2nd Edition Septetnber 1992, 728 pages, ISBN 1-56592-027-9

Customizing your email environment can save time and make communicating more enjoyable. *MH & xmh: E-Mail for Users & Programmers* explains how to use, customize, and program with the MH electronic mail commands available on virtually any UNIX system. The handbook also covers *xmh*, an X Window System client that runs MH programs. The second edition added a chapter on mhook, sections explaining under-appreciated small commands and features, and more examples showing how to use MH to handle common situations.

Smileys

By David W Sanderson
1st Edition March 1993, 93 pages, ISBN 1-56592-041-4

"For a quick grin at an odd moment, this is a nice pocket book to carry around
:-) If you keep this book near your terminal, you could express many heretofore
hidden feelings your email ;-) Then again, such things may be frowned upon at
your company :-(No matter, this is a fun book to have around."
– Gregory M. Amov, *News & Review*

TCP/IP Network Administration

By Craig Hunt
1st Edition August 1992, 502 pages ISBN 0-937175-82-X

TCP/IP Network Administration is a complete guide to setting
up and running a TCP/IP network for administrators of
networks of systems or lone home systems that access the
Internet. It starts with the fundamentals: what the protocols do
and how they work, how to request a network address and a
name (the forms needed are included in an appendix), and
how to set up your network. Beyond basic setup, the book
discusses how to configure important network applications,
including sendmail, the r* commands, and some simple setups
for NIS and NFS. There are also chapters on troubleshooting and security. In
addition, this book covers several important packages that are available from the
Net (such as *gated*). Covers BSD and System V TCP/IP implementations.

Managing Internet Information Services

By Cricket Liu, Jerry Peek, Russ Jones, Bryan Buus & Adrian Nye
1st Edition Winter 1994/95 (est), 400 pages, ISBN 1-56592-062-7

This comprehensive guide describes how to set up information services to
make them available over the Internet. Providing complete coverage of all
popular services, it discusses why a company would want to offer Internet
services and how to select which ones to provide. Most of the book describes
how to set up email services and FTP, Gopher, and World Wide Web servers.

"*Managing Internet Information Services* has long been needed in the Internet
community, as well as in many organizations with IP-based networks.
Although many on the Internet are quite savvy when it comes to administering
these types of tools, MIIS will allow a much larger community to join in and
perhaps provide more diverse information. This book will be a welcome
addition to my Internet shelf."
– Robert H'obbes' Zakon, MITRE Corporation

Connecting to the Internet
By Susan Estrada
1st Edition, August 1993
188 pages, ISBN 1-56592-061-9

This book provides practical advice on how to get an Internet connection. It describes how to assess your needs to determine the kind of Internet service that is best for you and how to find a local access provider and evaluate the services they offer.

Knowing how to purchase the right kind of Internet access can help you save money and avoid a lot of frustration. This book is the fastest way for you to learn how to get on the Internet. Then you can begin exploring one of the world's most valuable resources.

"A much needed 'how to do it' for anyone interested in getting Internet connectivity and using it as part of their organization or enterprise. The sections are simple and straightforward. If you want to know how to connect your organization, get this book."
– Book Review, *ISOC News*

Learning the UNIX Operating System
By Grace Todino, John Strang & Jerry Peek
3rd Edition, August 1993
108 pages, ISBN 1-56592-060-0

If you are new to UNIX, this concise introduction will tell you just what you need to get started and no more. Why wade through a 600-page book when you can begin working productively in a matter of minutes? It's an ideal primer for Mac and PC users of the Internet who need to know a little bit about UNIX on the systems they visit. This book is the most effective introduction to UNIX in print. The third edition has been updated and expanded to provide increased coverage of window systems and networking. It's a handy book for someone just starting with UNIX, as well as someone who encounters a UNIX system as a "visitor" via remote login over the Internet.

If you have someone on your site who has never worked on a UNIX system and who needs a quick how-to, Nutshell has the right booklet. *Learning the UNIX Operating System* can get a newcomer rolling in a single session. It covers logging in and out; files and directories; mail; pipes; filters; background-ing; and a large number of other topics. It's clear, cheap, and can render a newcomer productive in a few hours." – *;login*

!%@:: A Directory of Electronic Mail Addressing & Networks
By Donnalyn Frey & Rick Adams
4th Edition June 1994, 662 pages. ISBN 1-56592-046-5

This is the only up-to-date directory that charts the networks that make up the Internet, provides contact names and addresses, and describes the services each network provides. It includes all of the major Internet-based networks, as well as various commercial networks such as CompuServe, Delphi, and America Online that are "gatewayed" to the Internet for transfer of electronic mail and other services. If you are someone who wants to connect to the Internet, or someone who already is connected but wants concise, up-to-date information on many of the world's networks, check out this book.

"The book remains the bible of electronic messaging today. One could easily borrow the American Express slogan with the quip 'don't do messaging without it.' The book introduces you to electronic mail in all its many forms and flavors, tells you about the networks throughout the world… with an up-to-date summary of information on each, plus handy references such as all the world's subdomains. The husband-wife team authors are among the most knowledgeable people in the Internet world. This is one of those publications for which you just enter a lifetime subscription." – Book Review, *ISOC News*

The Mosaic Handbooks

Mosaic is an important application that is becoming instrumental in the growth of the Internet. These books, one for Microsoft Windows, one for the X Window System, and one for the Macintosh, introduce you to Mosaic and its use in navigating and finding information on the World Wide Web. They show you how to use Mosaic to replace some of the traditional Internet functions like FTP, Gopher, Archie, Veronica, and WAIS. For more advanced users, the books describe how to add external viewers to Mosaic (allowing it to display many additional file types) and how to customize the Mosaic interface, such as screen elements, colors, and fonts. The Microsoft and Macintosh versions come with a copy of Mosaic on a floppy disk; the X Window version comes with a CD-ROM.

The Mosaic Handbook for Microsoft Windows
By Dale Dougherty and Richard Koman
Ist Edition October 1994, 234 pages. ISBN 1-56592-094-5 (Floppy disk included)

The Mosaic Handbook for the X Window System
By Dale Dougherty, Richard Koman and Paula Ferguson
Ist Edition, October 1994, 220 pages, ISBN 1-56592-095-3 (CD-ROM included)

The Mosaic Handbook for the Macintosh
By Dale Dougherty & Richard Koman
Ist Edition October 1994 , 220 pages, ISBN 1-56592-096-1 (Floppy disk included)

INTERNET

Books from O Reilly & Associates

The Whole Internet User's Guide & Catalog
By Ed Krol
2nd Edition, April 1994
574pages, ISBN 1- 56592-063-5

The best book about the Internet just got better! This is the second edition of our comprehensive – and bestselling – introduction to the Internet, the international network that includes virtually every major computer site in the world. In addition to email, file transfer, remote login, and network news, this book pays special attention to some new tools for helping you find information. Useful to beginners and veterans alike, this book will help you explore what's possible on the Net. Also includes a pull-out quick-reference card.

"An ongoing classic."
– *Rochester Business Journal*

"The book against which all subsequent Internet guides are measured, Krol's work has emerged as an indispensable reference to beginners and seasoned travelers alike as they venture out on the data highway."
— *Microtimes*

"The Whole Internet User's Guide Catalog will probably become the Internet user's bible because it provides comprehensive, easy instructions for those who want to get the most from this valuable electronic tool."
— David J. Buerger, Editor, *Communications Week*

"Krol's work is comprehensive and lucid, an overview which presents network basics in clear and understandable language. I consider it essential."
— Paul Gilster, *Triad Business News*

On CompuServe

COMPUSERVE FOR EUROPE
Roelf Sluman

CompuServe, the world's largest personal on-line service, allows access to a world of information and services – plus a gateway to the Internet, the information super highway. News, financial reports, hobbies, travel, entertainment, interest groups, forums and electronic mail are just a few of the range of services available on-line via CompuServe. Written with the European user in mind, this is the ideal guide to this on-line service. Whether an existing member or a first-time user, it provides help and advice in a readable, accessible way. It also provides a WinCIM disk free, a key program for CompuServe access – plus $15* credit for new and existing users.
CompuServe is an international service and is priced in $US. Billing is in local currency at the prevailing rate.
December 1994/448pp/1-850-32121-3/paper

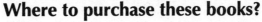

Where to purchase these books?
Please contact your local bookshop, in case of difficulties, contact us at one of the addresses below -

ORDERS
International Thomson Publishing Services Ltd
Cheriton House, North Way, Andover, Hants SP10 5BE, UK
Telephone: 0264 332424/Giro Account No: 2096919/
Fax: 0264 364418

SALES AND MARKETING ENQUIRIES
International Thomson Publishing
Berkshire House, 168/173 High Holborn, London WCIV 7AA,UK
Tel: 071-497 1422 Fax: 071-497 1426
e–mail: Info@ITPUK.CO.UK

MAILING LIST
To receive further information on our Networks books, please send the following information to the London address –
Full name and address (including Postcode)
Telephone, Fax Numbers and e-mail address

Books from

International Thomson Publishing

On The Internet

PIECING TOGETHER MOSAIC
Navigating the Internet and the World Wide Web
Steve Bowbrick, 3W Magazine

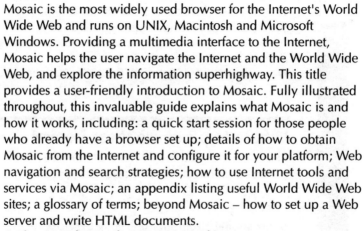

Mosaic is the most widely used browser for the Internet's World
Wide Web and runs on UNIX, Macintosh and Microsoft
Windows. Providing a multimedia interface to the Internet,
Mosaic helps the user navigate the Internet and the World Wide
Web, and explore the information superhighway. This title
provides a user-friendly introduction to Mosaic. Fully illustrated
throughout, this invaluable guide explains what Mosaic is and
how it works, including: a quick start session for those people
who already have a browser set up; details of how to obtain
Mosaic from the Internet and configure it for your platform; Web
navigation and search strategies; how to use Internet tools and
services via Mosaic; an appendix listing useful World Wide Web
sites; a glossary of terms; beyond Mosaic – how to set up a Web
server and write HTML documents.
Spring 1995/300pp/1-850-32142-6/paper

SPINNING THE WEB
How to Provide Information on the Internet
Andrew Ford

An indispensable guide for all those who provide or intend to
provide information on the World Wide Web, or want to make
the most of their existing services, this book for the first time
draws together all of the most up to date information and details
of contemporary resources into one essential volume. Providing
exclusive coverage of Web features, the book includes an
overview of Web facilities, how to create hypertext documents,
security issues, how to set up a server and the selection and
evaluation of software. A variety of examples from current Web
sources are included.
December 1994/250pp/1-850-32141-8/paper